JOHANN SEBASTIAN BACH
CHRISTMAS ORATORIO (BWV 248)

ANCORAE

Steunpunten voor studie en onderwijs

Volume 19

JOHANN SEBASTIAN BACH
CHRISTMAS ORATORIO (BWV 248)

Ignace Bossuyt
translated by Stratton Bull

Leuven University Press
2004

© 2004 Leuven University Press / Universitaire Pers Leuven / Presses Universitaires de Louvain
Blijde-Inkomststraat 5, B-3000 Leuven (Belgium)

All rights reserved. Except in those cases expressly determined by law, no part of this publication may be multiplied, saved in an automated data file or made public in any way whatsoever without the express prior written consent of the publishers.

ISBN 90 5867 421 5

D / 2004 / 1869 / 73

NUR: 664

Cover: Lejon Tits

TABLE OF CONTENTS

Author's note for the English translation   9

Foreword (by Philippe Herreweghe)   11

To the reader   13

Introduction   15

General context   19

The setting: Leipzig, 1734/1735	19
The Christmas Oratorio: an oratorio?	22
The liturgical function of the Christmas Oratorio	26
The themes and the 'libretto': Lutheran orthodoxy and Pietism	28
The overall structure	32
The parody 'problem'	34

The textual and musical components   37

The Gospel text: the story	37
The Gospel text: direct speech	40
The chorale	42
The poetic interpolations	44
Chorus	44
Recitativo accompagnato	47
Aria	49
The instrumentation	53

The six cantatas in detail   57

I   *Jauchzet, frohlocket, auf, preiset die Tage*   57

	Introduction	57
1	Jauchzet, frohlocket, auf, preiset die Tage	59
2	Es begab sich aber zu der Zeit	64

3	Nun wird mein liebster Bräutigam	67
4	Bereite dich, Zion	69
5	Wie soll ich dich empfangen	75
6	Und sie gebar ihren ersten Sohn	77
7	Er ist auf Erden kommen arm	78
8	Großer Herr, o starker König	81
9	Ach mein Herzliebes Jesulein	84

II *Sinfonia - Und es waren Hirten in derselben Gegend* 85

	Introduction	85
10	Sinfonia	87
11	Und es waren Hirten	90
12	Brich an, o schönes Morgenlicht	91
13	Und der Engel sprach zu Ihnen	92
14	Was Gott dem Abraham verheißen	93
15	Frohe Hirten, eilt, ach eilet	94
16	Und das habt zum Zeichen	96
17	Schaut hin, dort liegt im finstern Stall	97
18	So geht denn hin, ihr Hirten	97
19	Schlafe, mein Liebster	99
20	Und alsobald war da bei dem Engel	101
21	Ehre sei Gott in der Höhe	102
22	So recht, Ihr Engel	105
23	Wir singen dir in deinem Heer	106

III *Herrscher des Himmels* 108

	Introduction	108
24	Herrscher des Himmels	109
25	Und da die Engel von ihnen gen Himmel fuhren	111
26	Lasset uns nun gehen gen Bethlehem	111
27	Er hat sein Volk getröst'	112
28	Dies hat er alles uns getan	113
29	Herr, dein Mitleid, dein Erbarmen	113
30	Und sie kamen eilend	116

31	Schließe, mein Herze, dies selige Wunder	118
32	Ja, ja, mein Herz soll es bewahren	120
33	Ich will dich mit Fleiß bewahren	120
34	Und die Hirten kehrten wieder um	121
35	Seid froh dieweil	122

IV Fallt mit Danken, fallt mit Loben   124

	Introduction	124
36	Fallt mit Danken, fallt mit Loben	125
37	Und da acht Tage um waren	127
38	Immanuel, o süßes Wort!	127
39	Flößt, mein Heiland	131
40	Wohlan, dein Name soll allein	134
41	Ich will nur dir zur Ehren leben	135
42	Jesus richte mein Beginnen	137

V Ehre sei dir, Gott, gesungen   139

	Introduction	139
43	Ehre sei dir, Gott, gesungen	141
44	Da Jesus geboren war	143
45	Wo ist der neugeborne König	144
46	Dein Glanz all Finsternis verzehrt	146
47	Erleucht auch meine finstre Sinnen	147
48	Da das der König Herodes hörte	149
49	Warum wollt ihr erschrecken	150
50	Und ließ versammlen alle Hohepriester	151
51	Ach, wenn wird die Zeit erscheinen?	152
52	Mein Liebster herrschet schon	154
53	Zwar ist solche Herzensstube	154

VI Herr, wenn die stolzen Feinde schnauben   156

	Introduction	156
54	Herr, wenn die stolzen Feinde schnauben	158
55	Da berief Herodes die Weisen	160

56	Du Falscher, suche nur den Herrn	161
57	Nur ein Wink von seinen Händen	161
58	Als sie nun den König gehöret hatten	163
59	Ich steh an deiner Krippen hier	164
60	Und Gott befahl ihnen im Traum	165
61	So geht! Genug, mein Schatz	165
62	Nun mögt ihr stolzen Feinde schrecken	166
63	Was will der Höllen Schrecken nun	168
64	Nun seid ihr wohl gerochen	169

Bibliography   171

Indices   179

Index of names	179
Index of works	182

SUPPLEMENT

Music examples

AUTHOR'S NOTE FOR THE ENGLISH TRANSLATION

This monograph originally appeared in Dutch in 2002. As I have noted in the introduction, the book was the result of a realization that no study of Bach's *Christmas Oratorio* existed in Dutch. Since this is equally the case for English, a number of positive reactions led to the decision to provide a translation of the book, in the hope that it might make one of Bach's masterpieces more accessible for many English speakers as well.

For this English edition, I would like to supplement my words of thanks in the introduction with an expression of sincere gratitude to the following people:

Hilde Lens-Gielis of the Leuven University Press, who took the decision to have my work translated and made the necessary funds available;

Stratton Bull, who, as native speaker, musician and long-time resident of Flanders, is equally at home in Dutch and English, making him the ideal person for the job of translating this book;

My colleague Prof. John Irving of the University of Bristol (UK), who kindly agreed to cast a critical eye on the final version of the English text;

Richard Stokes (Westminster School, London, UK) for permission to use his exemplary English translation of the text of the *Christmas Oratorio* and other fragments from Bach cantatas (cf. Bibliography Stokes 1999);

The music publisher Bärenreiter (Kassel), for granting permission to make use of their published scores of compositions by Johann Sebastian Bach for the music examples in this English edition as well.

Ignace Bossuyt
Department of Musicology
Catholic University of Leuven
Belgium

FOREWORD

I was most pleased to accept Professor Bossuyt's invitation to write a foreword to this book. I myself read the manuscript with great interest, and although I have been fortunate enough to conduct the complete cycle of the *Christmas Oratorio* many times, and have recorded the work, I gained new insights. I am sure this will be to my benefit in future performances, for which I am truly grateful.

Performing Bach remains a difficult task. Just when you seem to have come up with a solution to one problem, another one seems to crop up.

The generation of Harnoncourt and Leonhardt laid down a firm foundation, making possible a more authentic Bach than previously. By now, most people are convinced that the cantatas are definitely at their best with fewer forces, with Baroque instruments, with the appropriate singers – in short, an approach to style that is now cautiously termed 'historically informed'.

In recent years, Baroque ensembles have produced singing and playing of increasing quality, sometimes all but perfect. And yet the stylistic framework appears to be extremely flexible. This is clearly audible in the sometimes spectacular differences in the sounding result of this one approach. Despite similar ideas concerning timbre, tuning, articulation, phrasing, ornamentation and the like, recordings can ending up sounding diametrically opposed.

This likely has partly to do with the performers' personalities and backgrounds – for which we may be thankful, for complete uniformity would be very dull. At the same time, we should never stop reconsidering a number of essential points.

In the first place, there is the specific religious content and its rhetorical form, the cornerstone of every Bach cantata. For any full-blooded musician, these gloriously conceived arias and choruses represent a permanent temptation to revel in pure music-making, and that with the blessing of an enthusiastic audience all too easily indulged with surprising tempos, swinging rhythms, nifty effects and anything that sounds 'unusual', and hence 'authentic'. Johann Sebastian Bach, however, wrote "Ad Majorem Dei Gloriam". Even though everyone knows this in theory, it can never be emphasized enough in performance. Whether this is always the case is open to some doubt; likewise it may be asked whether the modern concert world even encourages such an approach.

The second point complicates matters. No matter how important the identifiable content (and rhetoric) may be, the essential substance of Bach's music lies elsewhere. This substance is heard in its purest form in *The Art of Fugue*: no one can escape the unfathomable and at the same time crystal-clear poetry of this fascinating play of lines. Here it is as if the structure of thought itself were made audible, before this thought had knowledge of reality.

The most difficult task is to find the right balance between the rhetorical eloquence, the power of the affects, and the sound, which only comes into being by being directed in time and space.

Above one of the canons in the *Musical Offering* Bach wrote: QUAERENDO INVENIETIS ('seek and ye shall find'). The more one deepens one's knowledge, the less chance there is of losing one's way in this quest. In this spirit I heartily recommend the present book to all.

Chiusure, August 2002

Philippe Herreweghe

TO THE READER

This publication is in fact only one panel of a triptych, to be completed by the reader-listener with a score and a CD recording of Bach's *Christmas Oratorio*.

The score, edited by W. Blankenburg and A. Dürr, is published by Bärenreiter (Kassel-Basel-London-New York-Prague), 6th ed., 1998.
There are a number of possibilities:
1. The so-called 'study score', based on the *Urtext* from the *Neue Bach Ausgabe* (reference: TP 85).
2. The piano reduction, in which all the instrumental parts have been reduced to two staves (reference: BA 5014 90).
3. As part of the monumental *Neue Bach Ausgabe*, in larger format (reference BA 5014 01).
4. For the Bach year of 2000, Bärenreiter published a number of Bach's vocal works, originally as part of the *Neue Bach Ausgabe*, in three volumes in a handy paperback format (*Bach. Die großen Vokalwerke. The Great Vocal Works*). The *Christmas Oratorio* is included in volume 3.

The facsimile edition of Bach's autograph, an extremely informative and fascinating document, was published by Bärenreiter in 1960. Edited by A. Dürr, the score includes a commentary. A second edition was published in 1984: *Johann Sebastian Bach. Weihnachts-Oratorium BWV 248 (Documenta Musicologica. Zweite Reihe: Handschriften-Faksimiles, XIII)*, ed. by A. Dürr, Kassel-Basel-London, 1984.

An abundance of CD recordings is available. A virtually complete overview is found at www.jpc.de. See also www.bach-cantatas.com/IndexVocal.htm.
The following are my personal recommendations:
- conducted by John Eliot Gardiner (Archiv Produktion 449-217-2, recorded 1987), with Nancy Argenta (soprano), Ann-Sophie von Otter (mezzo-soprano), Anthony Rolfe-Johnson and Hans Peter Blochwitz (tenors), Olaf Bär (bass), Monteverdi Choir, English Baroque Soloists
- conducted by Philippe Herreweghe (Virgin VCD 7 90781-2, recorded 1989), with Barbara Schlick (soprano), Michael Chance (alto), Howard Crook (tenor),

Peter Kooij (bass), Choir and Orchestra of Collegium Vocale Gent

- conducted by Ton Koopman (Erato 0630-14635-2, recorded 1996), with Lisa Larsson (soprano), Elisabeth von Magnus (alto), Christoph Prégardien (tenor), Klaus Mertens (bass), Amsterdam Baroque Orchestra & Choir

- conducted by René Jacobs (Harmonia Mundi France HMC 901630.31, recorded 1997), with Dorothea Röschmann (soprano), Andreas Scholl (alto), Werner Güra (tenor), Klaus Hager (bass), Rias-Kammerchor, Akademie für Alte Musik Berlin

- conducted by Masaki Suzuki (BIS CD 941/2, recorded 1998), with Monica Frimmer (soprano), Yoshikazu Mera (countertenor), Gerd Türk (tenor), Peter Kooij (bass), Bach Collegium Japan.

INTRODUCTION

Every year during the Christmas period, the six-part *Christmas Oratorio* by Johann Sebastian Bach is performed either in part or in whole at concert venues the world over. Over recent decades, this composition has enjoyed increasing popularity, approaching or even equaling the appeal of the same composer's *St. Matthew* and *St. John Passions*. However, despite this increase in familiarity listeners have yet to become acquainted with the work in detail. The Bible story found in Luke and Matthew, telling of the birth of Christ, the adoration of the shepherds, the wrath of King Herod and the arrival of the Wise Men from the East may be well known, but how many listeners have considered carefully the added texts of the chorales, the recitatives and the arias, or taken the time to ponder the connection between the reflective interpolations and the original story? Some depth of knowledge of the religious thought forming the background to this liturgical composition and of the link between the biblical text and the commentary on it is essential to the full enjoyment of a musical masterwork that is not only overwhelming with its powerful, emotionally-charged musical structure, but is also the 'product' of a period and a world now more than three centuries behind us and is thus rooted in a time and a Zeitgeist far removed from our own.

The present text is intended to provide the inquisitive listener with a guide to exploring the many layers of meaning found in Bach's *Christmas Oratorio*. The first section offers a general sketch of the specific context in which this composition was created, during Bach's time as cantor at the Thomaskirche in Leipzig at the end of 1734, shedding light on the work's liturgical function and taking a closer look at the biblical and broader religious themes; this is supplemented by an introduction to its general musical structure and the use of musical material from earlier cantatas (the technique of 'parody'). As preparation for the subsequent discussion of the six parts of the oratorio in turn, this first section will also focus on the contemporary textual and musical components of the oratorio genre, of which Bach's composition is a prime example.

The second section is a detailed discussion of the 64 movements making up the work, with a focus on three aspects: the text, the music and the relation between the two. The nature of the musical setting and its structure, whether recitative (secco or accompagnato), aria, chorus or chorale, depends on the nature of the text, be it prose (the Bible story) or poetry (the chorales and the inserted commentary), narrative or dramatic (indirect or direct speech). Moreover, the music was governed by the particular musical canons of the day, which largely determined and regulated the structure of each section and the coherence between successive sections or those at a greater remove from one another: such considerations include tonality and tonal relations, consonance and dissonance, as well as structuring patterns like the da capo form and the ritornello.

In his vocal music Bach clearly aimed for the best possible setting of the text's content, which naturally led him to draw on all the means then at his disposal, including certain melodic turns of phrase, harmonic progressions and rhythmic figures which made his intentions clear and intelligible. In order to get to the essence of Bach's oeuvre, the reader-listener must be prepared to become immersed in the literary and musical idiom, the specific terminology and 'grammar' of the day. It goes without saying that an ideal reading and 'listening' is only possible with the aid of the score, or at least a piano reduction, of the *Christmas Oratorio*. The musical examples found here are merely an initial and necessary form of orientation that can help the listener up to a point, but they are in fact only a supplement, a point of departure. They can in no way replace a full score.

The immediate reason for writing this book was the lack of a Dutch-language 'study and listening guide' for this composition, a work that is mainly known in German-speaking countries - although even there the number of monographs is limited. Of the existing books in German, two in particular deserve mention: the 1967 'Werkmonographie' by Alfred Dürr, the leading expert on the Bach cantatas, *Johann Sebastian Bach. Weihnachtsoratorium BWV 248*, in which the author directs his attention chiefly to musical analyses; and *Das Weihnachtsoratorium von Johann Sebastian Bach* (1982) by theologian and musicologist Walter Blankenburg, a work that has been frequently reprinted (most recently in 1999) and which focuses more on the religious and ideological background to the composition (besides musical analyses). Also worth reading is Günter Jena's introduction, geared to a wider audience, *Brich an, o schönes Morgenlicht. Das Weihnachtsoratorium von Johann Sebastian Bach* (1997, reprinted 1999), which couples brief analyses with more personally-tinted reflections that are the fruit of his experience as a conductor in Hamburg. An indispensable resource is the extensive volume on Bach's vocal music in the highly respectable *Bach Handbuch* of 1999, edited by Konrad Küster, professor of musicology at the university of Freiburg and among other things the author of the book *Der junge Bach* (1996). Besides Alfred Dürr's standard work on Bach's cantatas (*Johann Sebastian Bach. Die Kantaten*, 7th edition in 1999) and the three-volume study of the cantatas, *Die Welt der Bach Kantaten* (which appeared between 1995 and 1998) under the editorship of Christoph Wolff, several excellent basic monographs written in the 'Bach year' of 2000 are worth mention: Martin Geck, *Bach. Leben und Werk* (translation in English: Martin Geck, *Bach*), Arno Forchert, *Johann Sebastian Bach und seine Zeit*, Christoph Wolff, *Johann Sebastian Bach. The Learned Musician*, and Malcolm Boyd, *Bach* (3rd revised edition in the series *The Master Musicians*). Especially instructive are, in addition, two encyclopedic, alphabetical works: *J.S. Bach*, edited by Malcolm Boyd (in the *Oxford Composer Companions* series, 1999) and *Das Bach-Lexikon*, edited by Michael Heinemann (volume 6 of the *Bach-Handbuch*, 2000, an ongoing series); to these may be added various chapters in *The Cambridge Companion to Bach*, published in 1997 by John Butt. For further literature, such as studies of particular topics related to this work, I refer the reader to the bibliography. A brilliant, inexhaustible and above all user-friendly work instrument for hunting down practically any publication on Bach (now at more than 19,000 titles and counting) is the website set up by Yo Tomita of Queen's University, Belfast: www.music.qub.ac.uk/~tomita/bachbib.html.

Finally, I owe a word of thanks to all those who have helped me in the preparation, writing and completion of this monograph.

To my wife, Rolande Wallays, who continues to share my enthusiasm for Bach, a shared joy which remains, as always, a double joy.

To Philippe Herreweghe for accepting my invitation to write the foreword to this monograph. I asked him because I know that Bach has gained a place deep in his heart and soul: each of his performances of one of Bach's works is, even in repeat performances, a refreshing and inspiring experience for him, his musicians and his audience.

To Bart Demuyt, Katelijne Schiltz and Fons de Haas, critical readers of my initial and subsequent versions of this text, who provided corrections and remarks.

To Leentje De Buysser, specialist in Germanic languages, who carefully sifted through the text for spelling and other linguistic problems.

To the Leuven University Press, and in particular Hilde Lens-Gielis, for agreeing once again to include one of my books in the university catalogue.

To the music publisher Bärenreiter (Kassel), who granted permission to take musical examples from its published scores of Bach compositions (*Christmas Oratorio, St. Matthew Passion, B minor Mass* and several cantatas).

And finally, to all potential reader-listeners, without whom this book would have no reason to exist...

GENERAL CONTEXT

The setting: Leipzig, 1734/1735

By the time Bach composed his *Christmas Oratorio* in the Fall of 1734, he had been active as the cantor at the Thomasschule for more than ten years. In May of 1723, he had been appointed as successor to Johann Kuhnau, after a great deal of discussion in the city council, where two parties held differing views concerning this position. The heart of the debate was that one group expected the Thomascantor above all to possess qualities as a teacher, next to his qualities as a musician, while the other group showed a preference for a multitalented musician. The choice of Bach, who was able to count on the support of the second group, was ultimately reached after a compromise between the two parties. However, this did not signal the end of the often intense debates concerning the cantor's precise job.[1]

The Thomascantor was recognized in Leipzig as the most important musician in the city. He was responsible for the music in four churches: the two main churches, the Thomaskirche and the Nikolaikirche, together with the Neue Kirche (the former Franciscan Barfüsser Kirche) and the smaller Peterskirche. He also carried out various musical duties in the city. For these duties he had at his disposal the students of the Thomas- schule, who consisted of four groups (*Cantoreien*), as well as the professional city musicians who performed the often virtuoso instrumental parts. For the more modest musical performances in the Neue Kirche and at the Peterskirche, he could call on assistants. The Thomascantor himself was the director of the musical performances at the Thomaskirche and the Nikolaikirche, churches in which highly demanding musical works, especially cantatas with soloists, choir and instruments were essential weekly components of the liturgical services. Normally, such works were performed every Sunday alternately in one of the churches, but not infrequently a given work was performed in the two churches on the same day (in the morning

---

1 In this connection see especially U. Siegele, *Bachs politisches Profil oder Wo bleibt die Musik?* in Bach H, pp. 14-18 and A. Beyer, *Thomaskantorat*, in Bach L 2000, pp. 520-521. Such debates had also raged in Kuhnau's time.

and afternoon), as was the case for the first performance of the *Christmas Oratorio* (see below).[2]

Bach, however, also laid claim to other functions besides the office of cantor, leading to conflicts and making life miserable for himself (and his opponents!). The position of music director at the Neue Kirche entailed responsibility for a Collegium Musicum, a grouping of non-professional but talented instrumentalists, mainly university students. This ensemble had been established in 1702 by Georg Philipp Telemann, then a student in Leipzig. The Collegium Musicum gave well-attended weekly concerts in Gottfried Zimmermann's coffee house. Bach gained control over this group only in March 1729, after the death of the Neue Kirche organist, who had claimed the position for himself. Bach carried out this time-consuming but musically rewarding function until 1737, continuing thereafter sporadically until around 1744. Another conflict that also dragged on for many years involved the responsibility for the music in the university church of St. Paul.[3]

Although Bach more than once considered seeking his fortune elsewhere – for example, in 1730[4] - he remained Thomascantor in Leipzig until his death in 1750. The years around 1730 were, however, crucial for Bach. Until then, his main task had been the composition of cantatas for each Sunday of the church year and the special feast days (such as Christmas). The first version of his monumental *St. Matthew Passion* likely dates from 1727. By 1729, Bach had built up a substantial body of compositions for the liturgy on which he could freely draw in subsequent years. This left him freer to turn his attention to other genres, such as secular cantatas and instrumental works (concerti, orchestral suites and sonatas), including works intended for performance by the Collegium Musicum. It was also at this time that he pursued the idea of publishing a number of extensive cycles of keyboard works, a project which would become the *Clavier-Übung*, appearing in four parts between 1731 and 1741/42 and representing an unrivalled encyclopedic compendium of the genres of the day for harpsichord and organ (partita, Italian concerto, French overture, variations, prelude, fugue and chorale arrangements).[5]

---

2   For an overview of the liturgical services with music in the four churches, see Wolff 2000, pp. 250-253.
3   Wolff 2000, pp. 311-315.
4   Referred to in the oft-cited letter to his former school friend Georg Erdmann (see Wolff 2000, pp. 342-343).
5   *Clavier-Übung* I, BWV 825-830 (six partitas or suites for harpsichord, 1731; individual pieces had

Bach very clearly broadened his horizons as a composer starting in 1729, attempting to break out of the exclusivity of his function as Thomascantor. He began increasingly to look beyond the boundaries of the city of Leipzig, establishing closer contacts with secular courts, liaisons that enabled him to improve his standing. In the Spring of 1729, he stayed for a number of days at the court of the duke of Weissenfels, where he had been a regular guest for many years. There he was honored with the title of court Kapellmeister. In addition, he intensified his existing relations with the court (and the musicians[6]) of Elector Friedrich August I of Dresden, who had converted to Catholicism in order to become king of Poland. The royal family was regularly invited to Leipzig as guests, for such occasions as the celebration of a name day or the birthday of the ruler or a member of his family. Between 1727 and 1742, Bach organized a number of 'Extra-ordinaire Concerten' in their honor. These concerts were made up of movements by Bach himself, celebratory compositions that usually took the form of secular cantatas with the feel of little operas, usually featuring characters from classical mythology (and termed *dramma per musica*). Two of the works written in 1733 became a mine of material for 're-use' in the *Christmas Oratorio*: September 5 saw a performance of the cantata *Lasst uns sorgen, lasst uns wachen* (BWV 213, known under the title *Hercules auf dem Scheidewege*), written for the birthday of Friedrich Christian, the elector's eleven-year-old son; while on December 8, the birthday of the boy's mother, Electress Maria Josepha of Saxony, was honored with the cantata *Tönet, ihr Pauken! Erschallet, Trompeten!* (BWV 214). In July of that year, Bach had traveled to Dresden to present Elector Friedrich August II with the Kyrie and Gloria from what would eventually become the *B minor Mass*. Bach hoped this gift would aid him in his quest for the prestigious title of *Hofcompositeur* (a title he was granted in 1736). His eldest son, Wilhelm Friedemann Bach, had recently been appointed organist at the Sophienkirche in Dresden, where his father had previously given a number of astonishing organ recitals. Father and son also went to the opera house, where the Italian operas by Johann Adolf Hasse were all the rage.[7]

---

    already appeared from 1726), II, BWV 971 and 831 (an Italian concerto and a French overture for harpsichord, 1735), III, BWV 552, 669-689 and 802-805 (prelude and fugue, organ chorales, four duets, 1739) and IV, BWV 988 ('Aria mit verschiedenen Veränderungen', better known as the 'Goldberg Variations', 1741 or 1742). For an overview of the contents of the four volumes, see Wolff 2000, pp. 380-381.

6   Including Sylvius Leopold Weiss, Johann Georg Pisendel, Johann David Heinichen and Jan Dismas Zelenka.

7   On 13 September 1731, he probably attended the premiere of Hasse's opera *Cleofide*. A celebratory

It was in this varied context of the years around 1730, as Bach's musical world widened considerably, that the *Christmas Oratorio* came into being, seeing the light of day in the final months of 1734.

The Christmas Oratorio: an oratorio?

The six-part cantata cycle known in German as the *Weihnachts-Oratorium* was given the Latin title *Oratorium tempore nativitatis Christi* ('Oratorio for the season of the birth of Christ') by the composer on the autograph score.[8] The text booklet, which appeared in print in 1734 shortly before the work's first performance, bore the following German title: *Oratorium, welches Die heilige Weyhnacht über in beyden Haupt Kirchen zu Leipzig musiciret wurde* ('Oratorio, which during the Holy Christmastime was performed in both main churches in Leipzig').

These authentic documents clearly show that Bach himself considered this work to be an oratorio, even if it did not strictly fit the genre as it was generally understood at the time. As in Italy, where the oratorio was born, the term in Germany referred to a multi-sectioned dramatic composition with vocal and instrumental parts and based on a religious subject presented in poetic form, similar to the libretto of an opera. Themes were drawn from the Bible, including the central events from the life of Christ – especially the Passion, as well as the Nativity and the Resurrection – and stories from the Old Testament. Themes from the history of the church were also treated; for instance, the events leading up to the institution of the Reformation (celebrated October 31), as well as the Christian virtues. Since oratorios differed from opera in being performed without staging and in churches, a 'narrator' (the *testo*) held the story together, providing continuity.

The most important center of the oratorio in Germany was Hamburg, where a tradition of biblical operas already existed. The first large-scale oratorio was heard there in 1704: *Der blutige und sterbende Jesu*, on a text by Christian Friedrich Hunold (known as Menantes) and set to music by Reinhard Keiser, the leading composer of German operas in the city. The work can be described as a 'Passion oratorio'. In it the story of Christ's Passion, as found in the four Gospels, is presented in a poetic

---

poem was published in the Dresden newspaper in honor of the concert that Bach played on the famous Silbermann organ in the Sophienkirche the following day.

8   The German word 'Weihnachten' means literally 'blessed night'.

and highly emotional form in order to move the hearts of the faithful. The absence of the original Bible texts, together with the dramatic, opera-inspired presentation were, however, not to the liking of the city council and the clergy, whose protests were nonetheless unable to hinder the success of a genre that met with the increasing approval of audiences. A libretto written by the leading Hamburg poet, Barthold Heinrich Brockes, *Der für die Sünde der Welt gemarterte und sterbende Jesu*, became very popular. It was set to music for the first time in 1712, again by Reinhard Keiser, and shortly thereafter was heard in versions by three other famous composers, Georg Philipp Telemann (1716), Georg Friedrich Handel (1715 or 1716) and Johann Mattheson (1718).

A broadening of the term 'oratorio' led to its use for compositions on texts of alternating prose and poetry, with fragments from the Bible and sometimes Protestant chorales. The best known type of such compositions was the 'oratorio Passion', the greatest examples of which are the two preserved Passions by J.S. Bach (the *St. John Passion*, BWV 245, first version 1724; and the *St. Matthew Passion*, BWV 244, first version 1727). The point of departure here is the original Bible text of the Passion story taken from one of the four Gospels and supplemented by chorales (representing the reactions of the congregation of the faithful) and newly written, reflective poetic interpolations (representing the contemplations of the individual believer). In a nod to the strict oratorio form with its completely new libretto, these reflective interventions were sometimes spoken by allegorical figures, such as the Daughter of Zion in the *St. Matthew Passion*, which Bach borrowed from Hunold's *Der blutige und sterbende Jesu* (and which also appears in Brockes text). Equally, in the more than forty oratorio Passions composed by Telemann in Hamburg, fictitious, allegorical figures appear to provide commentary and interpretation for the action.[9]

Bach's *Christmas Oratorio* continues in the line of the oratorio Passion since in its narrative sections the Gospel text describing the events of Christmas are taken over unchanged. Bach undoubtedly found the term oratorio to be warranted because of the central theme of Christ's birth, which creates a coherent whole of the six cantatas. The many added texts point to the oratorio composed on a libretto, especially those set to music as recitativo accompagnato and sung by unnamed characters. A number of interventions for alto solo could, for instance, symbolize

---

9 On the oratorio in Germany, see especially Smither 1977, pp. 105-171. See also Bossuyt, 1995.

the Virgin Mary as a personification of faith and by extension represent the whole Church.[10]

Bach was, of course, not the first composer to find inspiration in the Christmas story, even though it never had the same attraction for composers as did the Passion. From his immediate area he would undoubtedly have been familiar with the *Actus Musicus auf Weih-Nachten* ('Musical drama on Christmas'), a composition of 1683 by Johann Schelle, Johann Kuhnau's predecessor as Thomascantor in Leipzig.[11] In this work, the Evangelist's text from Luke (2:1-20) are interrupted by verses from *Vom Himmel hoch da komm ich her*, a chorale which Bach would also use (three times) in the *Christmas Oratorio* as well as in the first version of his *Magnificat* (BWV 243a); these interpolations clearly suggest that the *Magnificat* was intended for Christmas (of 1723, his first year in Leipzig).[12]

The title *actus musicus*, which was mainly in use in Saxony and Thuringia, was applicable to compositions in which a biblical story was supplemented with other texts, such as chorales. This genre, with its rather limited dimensions, thus formed in important intermediary step between the historia and the oratorio. The *historia* is completely based on the original Bible text, with the exception of an introduction and a conclusion in which the theme of the story is respectively announced and concluded by, for example, a hymn of thanks or a prayer. The most common subject for the *historia* in Lutheran Germany was the Passion, followed by the Resurrection (the Easter story) and, to a somewhat lesser degree, the Christmas story. Of the composers who produced *historiae*, Heinrich Schütz was without a doubt the greatest master.[13] The *Historia der Auferstehung* (on the Resurrection) dates from

---

10 See Blankenburg 1999, p. 31.

11 A 1729 inventory of the Thomasschule mentions "Musicalische Sachen" ('musical items') by Schelle, with the note: "These items were in the possession of Herr Johann Sebastian Bach" ("Diese Sachen hat der Cantor Herr Johann Sebastian Bach in seiner Verwahrung") (Blankenburg 1999, p. 26 and p. 28).

12 The *Magnificat* most often heard today is a later version (BWV 243, 1732-1735), which does not include the Christmas interpolations. Without the chorales, the Magnificat could be used in liturgical situations not associated with Christmas. The second version may have been created in 1733 when Bach wrote the Mass with Kyrie and Gloria (BWV 232; see Wolff 2000, p. 367) for the court of Saxony. Among Bach's other known treatments of this chorale are the *Canonische Veränderungen über das Weihnachtslied: Vom Himmel hoch da komm ich her* (BWV 769), one of Bach's last compositions (1747). Both Schelle's actus musicus and Bach's Christmas Oratorio also include the chorale *Gelobest seist du, Jesu Christ*, as well as an instrumental 'pastorale' (Blankenburg 1999, p. 30).

13 For more on the historia and the actus musicus in Lutheran Germany, see Smither 1977, pp. 3-37.

1623. More than forty years later came the *Historia der Geburt* (1664) and shortly thereafter three *historiae* on the Passion story as found in Luke, John and Matthew respectively (ca. 1665-1666). In these works, Schütz succeeded masterfully in combining the older polyphonic tradition, which he continued to defend fervently, with the new compositional practices from Italy (the recitative and concerted styles).[14] A line can be drawn from the Schütz *historia* via the *actus musicus* (by Schelle, one of Schütz's pupils) through to the oratorio of Bach's time. The latter composer's *Christmas Oratorio* is the final chapter in a tradition that went back to the early 17th century and which was especially strong in Bach's native region.[15] This is not to suggest that Bach primarily looked to the past, but on the contrary made use of the contemporary stylistic trends that drew on genres such as the Italian opera and the concerto.[16] It is, however, a fact that the musical interest in the Christmas story was strongly rooted in Bach's area, so that tradition naturally formed an important source of inspiration.

In the years following the composition of the *Christmas Oratorio*, Bach continued to show an interest in the oratorio genre. He wrote two similar compositions, probably between 1735 and 1738, which like most of his cantatas, have only one part and are thus much more restricted in scope than the *Christmas Oratorio*. One of these works, the *Easter Oratorio* (*Oratorium festo paschali* or *Oster-Oratorium*, BWV 249), may be considered a true oratorio, with a completely original, poetic text presenting four 'characters': Maria (the mother of James), Maria Magdalene, Peter and John; these parts are distributed over the four vocal parts of, respectively, soprano, alto, tenor and bass. The dramatic development is very limited: Peter and John, followed by the two women, go the tomb on Easter morning, to discover that Christ has risen. They express their joy and their desire to see their Lord again.[17] The other oratorio has at its subject the Ascension of Christ (*Oratorium festo ascensionis Christi* or *Himmelfahrts-Oratorium*, BWV 11). As in the *Christmas Oratorio*, Bach here takes the biblical text as his point of departure, setting to music descriptions of Christ's leave-taking and ascension as found in the Gospels of Luke and Mark and in the

---

14 See Bossuyt 1991.
15 Bach's predecessor, Kuhnau, wrote a Christmas cantata, *Vom Himmel hoch da komm ich her*, which has been lost (Blankenburg 1999, pp. 30-31).
16 Küster 1999, pp. 467-470.
17 Smither 1977, p. 156 and Dürr 1999, pp. 311-315.

Acts of the Apostles.[18] The first performance of this work probably took place on 19 May 1735.[19]

What distinguishes Bach's oratorios from others written around the same time, especially in Hamburg, is their specifically liturgical function. Like his church cantatas, they formed part of the service of worship.[20] The title page of the text booklet of the *Christmas Oratorio* clearly indicates that the performance took place in the two main churches in Leipzig, the Thomaskirche and the Nikolaikirche.

The liturgical function of the Christmas Oratorio

No cantatas were performed in church services held during the three weeks before Christmas. As in Lent, the period before Easter, this was a time for penance and preparation for a central church festival, a time when large-scale musical performances were not permitted. At the end of 1734, Bach concentrated on the composition of the *Christmas Oratorio*, a cycle of six cantatas intended for six specific days between Christmas (December 25) and Epiphany (January 6).

In Bach's time, the cantata was seen as a musical extension of the Bible reading, especially the Gospel, a tradition that went back to Luther's time. In the 16th century, this musical 'commentary' consisted of a polyphonic *motet*, a vocal composition on one or more verses from the Bible reading for the day, embodying the basic theme of the liturgical feast. With the increasing influence of Italian music in 17th-century Germany, this genre developed into a more extended and varied composition, with the addition of instruments (the 'concerted motet') and the use of non-biblical texts, such as chorales and newly written poetry commenting on the readings from the Old or New Testament. Such works became a form of 'musical sermon', in which exegetical-theological explanations were united with practical, moral advice for a Christian way of life.[21] This evolution led to the creation of a composition in several sections, the *cantata*, where each section was clearly distinct, not only in terms of

---

18 Smither 1977, p. 168 and Dürr 1999, pp. 382-386.
19 There is no absolute certainty concerning the date of this first performance. It is also not known precisely when the *Easter Oratorio* was performed for the first time (likely around 1738). The version then performed was a reworking of a cantata for the Easter liturgy on 2 April 1725. The work was later reprised (ca. 1743/46 and on Easter, 6 April 1749). See BWV 1998, p. 279 and p. 282. See also K. Küster 1999, pp. 355-356 and pp. 471-472.
20 S. Heighes, 'Oratorio', in *Bach OCC* 1999, p. 334.
21 Wolff 2000, p. 255.

text but also scoring and style. These sections included

(1) choral settings of one or more verses from the Bible, written in imitative counterpoint, the style which had reached its highpoint in the work of the 16th-century polyphonists from the Low Countries, as well as that of the Roman composer Palestrina (the *stile antico*),

(2) solo recitatives and arias in the Italian style (the *stile moderno*), often settings of newly written texts,

(3) appropriate chorales in the traditional German style (the so-called Cantionalstil), and (sometimes)

(4) independent instrumental sections (*sinfonia, sonata*), usually functioning as introductions.

Besides the cantata, which was seen as *Haupt-Music* ('main music') and was performed by professional singers and instrumentalists under the direction of the cantor, the service included organ music and chorales sung by the congregation. In Leipzig the Sunday-morning service lasted three to four hours, beginning at seven o'clock in the morning. The sermon, which followed the cantata and the Creed, took approximately one hour. The services of both main churches, the Thomaskirche and the Nikolaikirche, were attended by some 2000 people. As noted, the performance of the cantata alternated between the two churches on a weekly basis, except on major feast days, when the music was performed in both churches, one in the morning and the other in the afternoon. The printed text booklet of the *Christmas Oratorio* provides an overview of the performances of the six cantatas:

I	Christmas	morning: Nikolaikirche
		afternoon: Thomaskirche
II	Second Christmas Day	morning: Thomaskirche
		afternoon: Nikolaikirche
III	Third Christmas Day	Nikolaikirche
IV	New Year's Day	morning: Thomaskirche
		afternoon: Nikolaikirche
V	Sunday after New Year's Day	Nikolaikirche
VI	Epiphany	morning: Thomaskirche
		afternoon: Nikolaikirche.[22]

---

22   Wolff 2000, p. 254. For a facsimile of the libretto, see Neumann 1974, pp. 448-455.

Cantatas III and V were performed only in the Nikolaikirche. The morning service was the celebration of the Eucharist, the afternoon was Vespers.[23]

A concept of such magnitude, in which the performance of one work was spread over a number of days, was not new. Schelle's actus musicus may also have been performed in this way.[24] Bach's oft-cited visit to Dietrich Buxtehude in Lübeck in the Fall of 1705 may have inspired him to compose such a multi-part oratorio. As it happens, when Bach was in the northern city the extended oratorios by Buxtehude, *Castrum Doloris* and *Templum Honoris*, were performed as *extra-ordinaire Abend-Music* in the Marienkirche on two consecutive days (December 2 and 3), on the occasion of the death of Emperor Leopold I and his succession by his son Joseph I. The renowned Lübeck *Abendmusiken* were well attended concerts performed on Sundays in Advent. Buxtehude organized these concerts from 1673 until his death in 1707.[25]

The themes and the 'libretto': Lutheran orthodoxy and Pietism

In each of the six cantatas, one specific aspect of the Incarnation of Christ takes a central place:

I	The birth of Christ,
II	The annunciation to the shepherds,
III	The shepherds at the manger,
IV	The Naming of Jesus
V	The Wise Men and Herod,
VI	The Adoration of the Wise Men.

---

23 Cantatas III and V were not repeated in the afternoon at the Thomaskirche because concerted music was not performed on the Third Christmas Day and on the Sunday after New Year's (Leaver 1997b, p. 93). Vespers (*Betstunde*, *Vesperpredigt* or *Vespergottesdienst*) was the evening service (the word 'Vespers' comes from the Latin *ad vesperas*, 'in the evening'), which had been taken over from the Pre-Reformation order of services (the so-called 'offices') held outside the context of mass celebrations. On Sundays and feast days, extra music was performed in Vespers as well (Leaver 1997a, p. 44).

24 Blankenburg 1999, p. 36.

25 Smither 1977, pp. 81-102. Most of the compositions for the *Abendmusiken* have been lost, including *Castrum Doloris* and *Templum Honoris*. The printed text booklet for both works has, however, been preserved, revealing the ambitious scale of the compositions, which make use of an extended group of voices and instruments. See also Wolff 1993, pp. 41-55 (chapter 5: *Buxtehude, Bach, and Seventeenth-Century Music in Retrospect*).

In order to create a continuous narrative, Bach does not always keep to the content of the Gospel for the day. On the Third Christmas Day (III), the reading is taken from the prologue to the Gospel of John ("In the beginning was the word..."), a text heavy on theology but in which the narrative element is lacking. The flight to Egypt, which is the subject of the Gospel reading for the Sunday after New Year's Day (V), is completely absent in Bach's version, since it fits chronologically only after the Adoration of the Magi. This episode forms the heart of the Epiphany story, and thus of cantata VI.

The following overview represents a comparison between the texts of the official Gospel readings and the cantata texts of the *Christmas Oratorio*.

Feast Day:		Gospel:	*Christmas Oratorio*:
I	Christmas	Luke 2:1-14	Luke 2:1 and 3-7
II	Second Christmas Day	Luke 2:15-20	Luke 2:8-14
III	Third Christmas Day	John 1:1-14	Luke 2:15-20
IV	New Year's Day	Luke 2:21	Luke 2:21
V	Sunday after New Year's Day	Matthew 2:13-23	Matthew 2:1-6
VI	Epiphany	Matthew 2:1-12	Matthew 2:7-12.[26]

Because Bach made no use of the unsuitable first chapter of John (III), he spread the story of the birth and of the shepherds (Gospels I and II) over cantatas I to III. The procedure was similar in cantatas V and VI: in V the flight to Egypt is left out and the story of the Wise Men from the east (Gospel VI) is spread out over cantatas V and VI. Bach planned the performance of the work on these particular six days for the Christmas season of 1734-1735, when a Sunday fell between New Year's and Epiphany, but not between Christmas and New Year's.[27]

The Bible provides the raw material for the Christmas story which, as we have seen, is then commented upon and worked out in further detail in added texts. These additions are of two sorts: chorales and freely written poetic contemplations.[28] The

---

[26] Dürr 1967, p. 7 and Blankenburg 1999, p. 34.

[27] Dürr 1967, p. 8 and, in detail, Küster 1999, pp. 474-476. In 1735 the Sunday after New Year's fell on January 2. There is no record of later performances of the *Christmas Oratorio*. As a six-part cycle, it could have fit the years 1739/40, 1744/45 and 1745/46, when there was a Sunday between New Year's and Epiphany. Performances of separate cantatas cannot, however, be ruled out (Blankenburg 1999, p. 34).

[28] In his 1745 *St. John Passion*, Telemann referred to the added texts as *poetische Betrachtungen* ('poetic contemplations'). See Bossuyt 1995, p. 34 ff.

identity of the author of the contemplative texts in Bach's *Christmas Oratorio* is not known. A plausible candidate is the prolific occasional poet, Christian Friedrich Henrici, better known as Picander, who from 1725 worked regularly with Bach, supplying texts for the *St. Matthew Passion* and a number of cantatas.[29] For the chorale texts with their accompanying melodies, Bach drew on the rich treasury of congregational music that had become the common repertoire in the vernacular since Luther's time. In our discussion of the separate cantatas, we shall look in greater detail at these contemplative interpolations, which fit ideologically with two divergent movements within the Reformation: on the one hand orthodox-Lutheran doctrine, the objective teaching of the truth as revealed by the Bible and interpreted by theologians; and on the other, Pietistic devoutness, a subjective form of religious practice, based more on personal devotion. Both movements had their fervent defenders, with robust argumentation from both sides.

In the *Christmas Oratorio* texts, as well as those of other compositions, both religious conceptions found a place, although Bach's own education together with his personal faith and his milieu made of him a confirmed adherent of orthodox Lutheranism. The basic doctrine of Luther's theology rests on the key phrase, *sola scriptura, sola gratia, sola fide* ('only through the Bible, through grace and through faith'). The first and foremost authority is not the institution of the Church, but the Bible, which contains the truth as revealed by God. The redemption of the sinner depends not on that person himself or herself, but on God's grace (this is the so-called 'Doctrine of Justification') – and only those who believe can count on God's compassion.[30] These ideas are regularly expressed in the texts of Bach's cantatas. The concepts of grace and belief are also raised in the *Christmas Oratorio*.[31]

---

29 The attribution of the texts of the *Christmas Oratorio* to Picander remains hypothetical, since they do not appear in his collected poetry, which was published in Leipzig in five volumes between 1727 and 1751 under the title *Ernst-schertzhaffte und satyrische Gedichte* ('Serious-humorous and satirical poems').

30 Leaver 1997a, pp. 37-38. Leaver (pp. 41-42) discusses a number of marginal comments written by Bach in his personal copy of the so-called 'Calov Bible', which only resurfaced in the 1960s. This version of the Lutheran Bible, annotated by the theologian Abraham Calov appeared in Wittenberg in 1681-82 (*Die deutsche Bibel*). One of Bach's notes states that "in devotional music, God is always present with his grace" ("bey einer andächtigen Musique ist allezeit Gott mit seiner Gnaden Gegenwart"; cited by Geck 2000b, p. 718). See in this connection especially Leaver 1983 and Leaver 1985.

31 Grace in nos. 41 (*Ich will nur dir zu leben ehren*) and 53 (*Zwar ist solche Herzensstube*), belief in de nos. 31 (*Schließe, mein Herze*) and 54 (*Herr, wenn die stolzen Feinde schnauben*).

Leipzig was, however, not only a bulwark of 'strict Lutherans' but also the city where in 1686 the theologian August Hermann Francke became co-founder of the so-called *Collegium Philobiblicum*, an association which was a driving force behind the Pietistic movement in the city.[32] Francke's writings were known to Bach, whose library contained a number of them.[33] Several years after composing the *Christmas Oratorio*, Bach wrote a number of pieces for the songbook (*Musikalisches Gesangbuch*) of Georg Christian Schemelli, an edition with a strong Pietistic slant which appeared in 1736 in Leipzig. In the foreword, the melodies by Bach included in the edition (BWV 439-507) are described as "partly newly composed, partly improved in the continuo by him [Bach]" ("theil ganz neu componirt, theils auch von Ihm in General-Bass verbessert"), so that it is difficult to make out which songs he himself wrote and which ones he simply provided with a new basso continuo line.[34] As a composer, Bach can clearly not have been a confirmed adherent of Pietism, since the followers of this movement were against the kind of 'learned', complex liturgical music, with its links to opera, which the Thomascantor produced on a weekly basis.[35] This did not, however, prevent the occasional appearance of Pietistic concepts in some texts, as, for instance, in the symbolism of the bride and bridegroom (representing the soul and Christ),[36] with their fervent longing to be united, and the intimate, loving and emotionally-charged relationship with Jesus (found particularly in some of the chorales of Paul Gerhardt, the so-called "Ich-Lieder", texts written in the first person, – see below – and other free texts[37]). In the discussion of the separate cantatas in detail, Pietistic elements will be considered.

---

32 In this connection see especially the chapter *Bach und der Pietismus* in Geck 2000a, pp. 88-108.
33 Geck 2000b, p. 717.
34 NBR 1998, p. 170 and Geck 2000b, pp. 207-208. Geck notes the "intimate, moderate Pietistic tone" of Schemelli's collection.
35 The controversy surrounding *Theatralische Kirchen-Music* led to heated and often long debates between proponents and detractors. One example was the clash between the respected music theoretician, Johann Mattheson, and Joachim Meyer, professor in law from Göttingen, who unleashed a paper war in 1727 with his treatise *Unvorgreiffichen Gedancken über die neulich eingerissene Theatralische Kirchen-Music* ('Modest thoughts on the newly fashionable theatrical church music"; see Forchert 2000, pp. 163-164).
36 See, for example, nos. 3 (*Nun wird mein liebster Bräutigam*), 4 (*Bereite dich, Zion*: "... Eile, den Bräutigam sehnlichst zu lieben") and 61 (*So geht! Genug* : "... Er soll mein Bräutigam verbleiben").
37 See especially the recitative with chorale, no. 38: *Immanuel, o süßes Wort*.

The overall structure

The choice of the scoring and basic key of each cantata indicates a well thought-out overarching concept. In each cantata, the vocal scoring consists of a choir of soprano(s), alto(s), tenor(s) and bass(es), and a four-voice ensemble of soloists (there are no solos for the alto in IV and VI).[38] The fixed instrumental ensemble is made up of strings (first and second violins, violas) and basso continuo (organ, harpsichord, cello, violone, optional bassoon), supplemented by various wind instruments. The following table indicates the supplementary instruments in each cantata (with the number of instruments in brackets) as well as the keys:

	Key:	Scoring:
I	D major	traverso (2), oboe (2), trumpet (3) and timpani (2), in solo movements also oboe d'amore (2)
II	G major	traverso (2), oboe d'amore (2), oboe da caccia (2)
III	D major	traverso (2), oboe (2), trumpet (3) and timpani (2), in solo movements also oboe d'amore (2)
IV	F major	corno da caccia (2), oboe (2)
V	A major	oboe d'amore (2)
VI	D major	oboe (2), trumpet (3) and timpani (2), in solo movements also oboe d'amore (2).

Both in terms of keys and scoring, Bach clearly aimed for a cyclical structure. D major is the key of the first and last cantatas, which also share the same scoring; especially noteworthy is the use in these two cantatas of trumpets and timpani, instruments that symbolize kingship (a reference to Christ as descendent of King David).[39]

Within the six-part cycle, Bach designed the first three works as a separate, distinct group:

(1) They are intended for performance on three successive days (the first, second and third days of Christmas) and tell the story of Christ's birth and the visit of the

---

38 Without here entering into the discussion concerning the merits of a one-on-a-part versus a full-choir scoring for Bach's 'choir', a debate initiated by the opposing arguments of Joshua Rifkin and Ton Koopman, I refer the reader to the most recent literature on this matter: Parrott 2001 (with an extensive bibliography on the whole subject), Rifkin 2002, Geck 2003 and Rifkin 2003.

39 Leaver 1997b, p. 96.

shepherds, as found in the second chapter of Luke.

(2) The traverso (transverse flute) is called for only in these first three cantatas.

(3) For the third cantata, Bach opts both for D major and for the use of trumpets and timpani, thus creating a direct link with the first cantata.

(4) In all three cantatas, the concluding movements are linked with the opening in some way. The third cantata ends with a repetition of the work's concerted opening chorus (*Herrscher des Himmels*, no. 36 = no. 24). This rather unusual, grandiose finale rounds off the first cycle of three cantatas on a festive note. The scoring of trumpets and timpani is also called for in the closing chorale of the first cantata (*Ach mein Herzliebes Kindelein*, no. 9), so that it, too, ends with a reference to its opening movement (*Jauchzet, frohlocket*, no. 1). In the final movement of the second cantata, the chorale *Wir singen dir in deinem Heer* (no. 23), Bach again establishes a connection with the opening movement, in this case with an instrumental sinfonia (no. 10): in the instruments – the strings and the woodwinds – he quotes the themes from the sinfonia.[40]

The coherence between the first three cantatas is also strengthened through the three appearances of the chorale melody *Vom Himmel hoch da komm ich her*, at the end of the first and second cantatas (on, respectively, the texts *Ach mein herzliebes Jesulein*, no. 9 and *Wir singen dir in deinem Heer*, no. 23), as well as half way through the second cantata on the words *Schaut hin, dort liegt im finstern Stall* (no. 17). At this last place, the exact center of the first three cantatas taken together, Bach chooses a low setting of the chorale melody in C major: the low range and the relatively great distance from the opening key of D major 'downwards' (the subdominant of the subdominant) may represent God's 'descent' into the 'dark stable' (of this sinful world).[41]

The second 'triptych' (cantatas IV to VI) is related to the first group by the fact that again only the first and last cantatas (IV and VI) include brass instruments (horns in IV, trumpets in VI). At the very end, Bach accentuates the cyclical conception of the *Christmas Oratorio* by returning to the melody of the first chorale from the first cantata (*Wie soll ich dich empfangen*, no. 5) for use as the last chorale (*Nun seid ihr wohl gerochen*, no. 64). Bach's use of this melody, known best from its use in the *St. Matthew Passion* with the text *O Haupt voll Blut und Wunden*, is said by some to be a foreshadowing of Christ's suffering (see below).[42]

---

40   Leaver 1997b, p. 96.
41   Dürr 1967, pp. 40-41.
42   Dürr 1967, p. 42 (negative interpretation) and Leaver 1997b, p. 98 (positive interpretation).

In terms of keys, most of the cantatas are linked to the central key of D major or one of its neighboring keys, with the second cantata in the key of the subdominant G major and the fifth in the dominant A major. Only cantata IV falls outside this pattern: its main key is F major, the tonality built on the mediant of the cycle's tonic key, D major.

All these elements reveal the extent to which Bach designed the *Christmas Oratorio* as a cyclical structure and a coherent whole in terms of its narrative and its music, a fact reflected both in the text and in a number of musical factors.[43]

The parody 'problem'

Like the *B minor Mass* (BWV 232), and the four *Missae Breves* (BWV 233-236), Bach 'recycled' previously composed music from sacred and (especially) secular cantatas in the *Christmas Oratorio*. He apparently felt that significant works which would otherwise be performed only once a year (church cantatas) or even on one single occasion (celebratory secular cantatas) should be given the chance to be performed more often. Settings of the ordinary of the mass (*Kyrie*, *Gloria*, *Credo*, *Sanctus* and *Agnus Dei*) could in principle be performed at any mass celebration. Since Bach in his Christmas Oratorio mainly borrowed from his secular cantatas, he no doubt aimed to break from the exclusive character of an occasional work. As noted, he drew chiefly on two cantatas that he had written the previous year, in 1733, for birthday celebrations of members of the elector's family in Dresden (BWV 213 and BWV 214). He took another movement from a third secular cantata, *Preise dein Glücke, gesegnetes Sachsen* (BWV 215), which he had written for the visit of the elector Friedrich August II to Leipzig. That visit coincided with the first anniversary of the ruler's election as king of Poland, on 5 October 1734. A contemporary chronicle notes that the university students presented a performance in honor of the king, who had arrived rather unexpectedly on October 2, giving Bach only a few days to write a cantata of more than half an hour and rehearse it with his Collegium Musicum![44] It cannot be completely ruled out that in such situations Bach sometimes reused material, but this was likely seldom the true reason for placing an earlier work in a new context. Time pressure may, however, have indeed played a

---

43   For more on this aspect, see especially Steiger 1981/1982.
44   Dürr 1999, pp. 911-912.

role in the preparation of the final part of the *Christmas Oratorio*, which is an almost complete borrowing of a cantata composed shortly before (in 1733 or 1734).[45]

It is also possible, but not certain, that he reworked further fragments (nos. 45 and 51) from other, now lost compositions (the *St. Mark Passion*, BWV 247, and another cantata, see below). This was indeed a case of 'reworking', since Bach seldom simply 'quoted' the music whole, simply giving it a new text. A comparison between the *Missae breves* and their model cantatas offers valuable insight into the techniques used by Bach for such reworking.[46] The choice of a model was in the first place inspired by a relationship suggested by the musical expression. The borrowing was warranted because in an independent section of a composition Bach usually aimed for a unity of expression (one 'basic emotion') and likewise made highly concentrated use of the musical material (often the reworking of one motif or several related motifs). This tightly-knit unity of expression and style facilitated the 'transplantation' of musical material to another, similar context, although Bach then often adapted the original to certain affective nuances. The changes made to the original were often radical and more than just a matter of transposition (in order to fit a movement into the tonality of its new cantata) or changes in scoring; complete sections or fragments were regularly reworked or rewritten according to the new context, so that producing a parody of an existing composition may sometimes have been more demanding than simply composing a new piece![47]

This widely used and accepted compositional technique of the time, a standard procedure that entailed recycling, arranging, reworking or transplantation, is known as 'parody'. The Romantic, 19th-century aesthetics of originality long promoted a tendency to look on such practices as evidence of a lamentable 'lack of inspiration', but in the 20th century, such negative judgments have, happily, been tempered. There is indeed no reason – especially when it comes to a master craftsman such as

---

45   Except for several instrumental parts, this cantata (BWV 248/VIa) has been lost. The text is also not known. Geck 2000b, p. 469, writes: "Apparently towards the end of his labors on the *Christmas Oratorio*, exhaustion or time pressure forced Bach to find a way to round off his major project without expending too much energy." For more on BWV 248a, see especially Häfner 1977: Häfner formulates the hypothesis that BWV 248a was likely another cantata in honor of a member of the Saxon royal family, namely the festive welcoming to Leipzig of the elector on 21 April 1733.

46   Bossuyt 2000, pp. 22-26 and passim.

47   Küster 1999, p. 474: "Parodying (probably sometimes more complicated than simply producing a new composition!) is thus an integral part of Bach's approach to his own music, and is not a question of basically giving one version preference over another." Mann 1989, p. 115: "Bach's wondrous craftsmanship is so concentrated that ever new creative impulses arise in the process of composition", and p. 124: "Existing works generate new works."

Bach – to suggest that music of the highest quality should suddenly be reduced in some way by its use in another work or adapted to another situation, usually identical or at least related.[48] The context can in the case of the *Christmas Oratorio* certainly be considered to be related, as the two most important model cantatas (BWV 213 and 214) were written for the celebration of the birthdays of secular rulers and were now transferred to the celebration of the birth of Christ, the divine ruler. During the *ancien régime*, the royal majesty of earthly kings was interpreted as a reflection of God's kingship, even if the royal person in question did not always act in an exemplary fashion in his or her politics or lifestyle. In any case, the honor was directed not so much to the actual person but rather to the dignity that he or she represented on earth.[49]

The parodied movements are especially arias and choruses on freely written poetry (a total of eleven movements in cantatas I to V), and seldom recitatives, which are usually too strongly linked to specific texts (such as the Bible story). Only in cantata VI, which is virtually a carbon copy of a model now almost completely lost, are a few recitative fragments taken over and provided with newly written texts, as is the concluding chorale (a total of seven movements). This brings to eighteen the number of borrowed movements in the *Christmas Oratorio* out of a total of 64. One aria (*Schließe, mein Herze*, no. 31) and one chorus (*Ehre sei dir, Gott, gesungen*, no. 43, the opening chorus of cantata V) were originally intended by Bach to be parodies, but he subsequently opted for an 'original' concept. All the secco recitatives on Bible texts are newly composed (16 movements), as are the accompagnato recitatives commenting on the action in cantatas I-IV (ten movements), the chorales (except for the concluding chorale of VI, making a total of thirteen movements) and the introductory instrumental sinfonia of cantata II. Concerning the possible use of parody for the trio *Ach, wenn wird die Zeit erscheinen* (no. 51) and the chorus *Wo ist der neugeborne König der Jüden* (no. 45), the jury is still out.[50] Bach's parody technique will be considered further in the discussion of the separate cantatas.

---

48 In this connection see especially the following publications: Dürr 1956, Neumann 1965, Häfner 1987, Mann 1989, Schulze 1989, Schulze 1997, Bossuyt 1999, pp. 45-48, Bossuyt 2000, passim and Steiger 2002, pp. 249-268.
49 Leaver 1997b, p. 96.
50 Dürr 1967, p. 5 and Blankenburg 1992, p. 13. See also in particular Küster 1999, p. 482 (in connection with no. 45). The hypothesis that this chorus may have come from the *St. Mark Passion* is held by von Holst 1968.

THE TEXTUAL AND MUSICAL COMPONENTS

Each of the six cantatas is made up of a number of textually and stylistically varying components. Before looking at each of the cantatas separately in greater detail, we shall first consider the different types of text and the way in which they are given musical form.

The Gospel text: the story

The narrative structure of the *Christmas Oratorio* is based on the Gospel texts of Luke and Matthew, which are spread over the six cantatas so that the events of Christmas from the birth to the visit of the Wise Men from the East are presented as one continuous and coherent whole. As we have seen, in order to realize this continuity Bach sometimes deviates from the reading of the day, which would normally determine the theme of the cantata. In particular, he does not make use of the first chapter of John for cantata III.

The Gospel narrative is sung by the tenor soloist in recitative style, as in the Italian chamber cantata or the opera. The type of recitative employed is the *recitativo secco* ('dry recitative') or *recitativo semplice* ('simple recitative'), in which the basso continuo, accompanying the voice, plays sustained chords, often sparsely placed. On this foundation, the singer declaims his text, aiming for the best possible presentation of each word, since the primary goal of the composer and the performer is the intelligibility of the text. Melody (rising or falling, comprising smaller or larger intervals or repeated tones) and rhythm (short or long notes, repeated notes of equal length or a varied succession of lengths) are perfectly synchronized. The progress of a recitative is determined by word-accent and syntax (as indicated by the punctuation), together with the emotional or illustrative content of the text.[51]

---

[51] In his *Musicalisches Lexikon oder Musicalische Bibliotec* (1732), Johann Gottfried Walther describes the recitative as a "manner of singing drawn as much from declamation as from singing, as if one declaimed while singing or sang while declaiming: thus one aims more for the expression of affects than keeping the prescribed beat" ("Sing-Art, welche eben so viel von der Declamation als von dem Gesange hat, gleich ob declamirte man singend, oder sänge declamirend: da man denn folglich mehr befließen ist die Affectus zu exprimiren, als nach dem vorgeschriebene Tacte zu singen"). See Walther 1732, p. 464 (entry on 'Recitativo').

Because of the crucial importance of the element of declamation, the recitativo secco is generally strictly syllabic (one note per syllable) and there are no repetitions of text. Bach's contemporary Georg Philipp Telemann wrote of the requirements of a good recitative. In the foreword to his cycle of cantatas, *Harmonischer Gottesdienst* (1725), he emphasizes as one of the basic conditions for a good recitative the "optimum maintenance of the natural accentuation of our German language" ("die Natürliche Accentuation unserer Teutscher Mund-Art möglichst beybehalten"). In a second series of *Harmonischer Gottesdienst* cantatas (1731/1732), he adds that "the composer should speak [in the recitative], and do so intelligibly" ("Der Componist soll in der selbigen reden, und zwar verständlich")[52] The composer was thus required to be a (good) orator, who clearly and intelligibly and with the appropriate rhetorical means (such as ostentatious questions or pauses, or strong accents) aimed not only to inform the listeners, but to move them, so that, as Telemann writes (in the same passage), "the emotions found in the text are aroused" ("die in der Poesie befindlichen Regungen erwecket werden mögen").[53]

A brief example from the first cantata of the *Christmas Oratorio* (no. 6) can serve as an illustration:
(1) Und sie *gebar* ihren ersten *Sohn*,
(2) und *wikkelte* ihn in *Windeln*
(3) und *legte* ihn in eine *Krippen*,
(4) denn sie *hatten* sonst keinen *Raum* in der Herberge (Luke 2:7) (music example 1).

Translation:
(1) And she brought forth her first-born Son,
(2) And wrapped him in swaddling clothes,
(3) And laid him in a manger,
(4) Because there was no room for them in the inn.

---

52 Johann Adolf Scheibe, whose fame rested mainly on his attacks on Bach's art (in *Der Critisher Musicus*, 1737), also wrote an *Abhandlung vom Recitativ* ('Discourse on recitative') in which he remarks that the basis of recitative is the "most emphatic and precise imitation of the speech of men" ("nachdrücklichste und genaueste Nachahmung der Rede des Menschen"; quoted in Dürr 1994, p. 152).
53 Bossuyt 1995, p. 26 ff.

The sentence may be divided into four fragments. The first three begin with the conjunction "und" ("and"), which link the ensuing three phases of one event with one another:
(1) the birth of the baby,
(2) the baby wrapped in swaddling clothes, and
(3) the baby laid in a manger –
followed by (4) an explanatory sentence, giving the reason for this somewhat strange turn of events ("denn": "for").

This syntactical structure is reflected in the recitative by a short pause between the fragments. The most important word accents fall precisely on the first or third beats – the 'strong beats' – of the four-beat measure (accents are here indicated in italics).[54] The accents other than those highlighted (in italics) all fall squarely on the beat, and never on the second half of a beat (e.g., "*ihr*-en" and "*er*-sten" fall respectively on the third and fourth beats of the bar). The distribution of these accents and the syllables lying between them allows the rhythm to progress in an easy, flowing alternation of quarter notes, eighth notes and sixteenth notes. However, the word "Herberge" breaks the pattern: the note g on the accented syllable "*Her-*" already begins on the second beat of the bar, a syncopation which is held into the third beat. The word then suddenly concludes on two sixteenth notes. This 'illogical' way of finishing a phrase is found nowhere else in the whole work, revealing Bach as a dynamic orator, as he strives to follow Telemann's admonition to "stir emotions" ("Regungen zu erwecken"), drawing an 'illogical' turn of events to the attention of the (believing) listener: the fact that Mary, Joseph and the baby are not welcome at the inn is both astonishing and dumbfounding.

The melodic line rhetorically interprets the content of the text: the birth of a first son is a major event, illustrated by a rising, 'positive' line with its highest note on a' on the accented syllable of "ersten." From that moment, the melody proceeds downwards in a 'negative' direction: this child, with his divine origins, humbles himself by being born in a manger. The text is also brought to life through its

---

54 Practical instructions for the composition of recitatives may be found in a very informative text by Gottfried Heinrich Stölzel, a contemporary of Bach and court Kapellmeister in Gotha. His *Abhandlung vom Recitativ*, the first specialized treatise on the recitative, was never actually published. The name Stölzel (himself an interesting composer and respected by Bach) is linked to the aria *Bist du bei mir*, one of the best known pieces from the 1725 *Klavierbüchlein* of Anna Magdalena Bach: the aria is likely not by Bach, but Stölzel (see BWV 1998, p. 308). A number of basic principles from Stölzel's treatise on the recitative are discussed by Küster 1999, pp. 121-123.

harmonic treatment. The 'positive' note of *f-sharp* (the note *f*, 'raised' a semitone) in measure 1 is canceled out by being lowered to an *f* in bars 3 and 4, thus changing the expected major tonality (built on the note *d*) to minor and suggesting the movement from 'positive' to 'negative'. Each fragment ends on a progressively lower note: "Windeln" on *a'*, "Krippen" on *f* and "Herberge" on the lowest note *d'*.[55] In the midst of this process, Bach also highlights two words through two wide, ascending intervals: (1) on the 'causal' word "denn" ("for", followed by the explanation) and (2) on the word "Raum" (there was – shame! – no "room" at the inn for these people, with the word meant both in a physical and affective sense). Bach strongly accentuates "Raum": the rising major sixth is immediately followed by a descending octave.

The vocal line is supported by chords which accelerate rhythmically throughout the course of the recitative: the climax on the word "Herberge" is thus created by the gradual shortening of the chords, from whole notes (mm. 1-3) to half notes (m. 4) to quarter notes (m. 6). In barely thirty seconds, a text is musically presented in a highly concentrated form and at the same time interpreted in a completely convincing way.

The Gospel text: direct speech

Compared to the Passion story, the number of fragments in direct speech in the Christmas Oratorio is relatively limited. These are usually rather short utterances spoken by individual characters (the angel to the shepherds, nos. 13 and 16; Herod to the Wise Men, no. 55) or groups (the angels' song of praise on the birth of Christ, no. 21; the shepherds urging one another to go to Bethlehem, no. 26; the Wise Men seeking the new-born king, no. 45; and the high priests and scribes telling Herod of the predictions of Christ's birth, no. 50).

The soloists' interventions, or so-called *soliloquentes*, take the form of recitativo secco, as in the Passions, although the characters in question do not always speak themselves, sometimes being represented by the voice of the Evangelist (tenor). The annunciation of the angels to the shepherds is, as might be expected, sung by a soprano (no. 13); the continuation of this message is, however, given to the

---

55 Blankenburg 1999, p. 47, interprets this descending D-minor triad (*a'* – *f* – *d'*) as a "symbolic reference to God's incarnation" (and compares the passage to the descending B-minor triad used in the *Et incarnatus est* from the *B minor Mass*). See also Dürr 1967, p. 18.

Evangelist (no. 16). This can be explained by the interruption of the angel's speech by a recitative (no. 14) and an aria (no. 15): a recitativo secco for soprano would be highly unusual immediately following an aria. The words of Herod (no. 55) are, appropriately, given to a bass voice as recitativo secco.

The texts spoken by groups (*turbae*) are conceived as choruses with added instruments, in the style of the motet (the choir of the angels, no. 21; of the shepherds, no. 26; and of the Wise Men, no. 45). Characteristic of the motet style *in stile antico* is the through-composed structure, where each new text fragment is developed on a new musical subject, resulting in a succession of different fragments (A, B, C, D...). The style is generally contrapuntal, and usually imitative. The instruments often only double the vocal parts (a practice known as *colla parte*), with generally no independent role of their own.[56]

The setting of the words of the shepherds (no. 26) offers an example of a chorus in direct speech:
(1) Lasset uns nun gehen gen Bethlehem
(2) und die Geschichte sehen die da geschehen ist (music example 2).

Translation:
(1) Let us now go even unto Bethlehem,
(2) and see this thing which is come to pass.

The two fragments are stylistically related by the contrapuntal style of writing. The first is more strictly imitative, on a subject that is presented in both 'rectus' and 'inversus' (ascending and descending) forms. According to some scholars, this is a reference to a change on a personal level: the road to Bethlehem implies a complete 'about-face'.[57] The presentation of the subject in the opposite direction could also represent the amazement and confusion of the shepherds; on the other hand, this could simply be seen as an interesting compositional technique, in use since the 16th century, without any specific symbolic intention. Typical for the stile antico is the

---

[56] Dürr 1967, pp. 18-22. On the stile antico in Bach, see especially Wolff 1968 and, in connection with the *Missae breves*, Bossuyt 2000, p. 18 and pp. 27-33.

[57] Dürr 1967, p. 46, with reference to Smend 1966, pp. 36-37: "The voices answer one another in the opposite direction, a form of reversal symbolic of the 'conversion' inherent in penance, without which there is no way to Christ." This interpretation is, however, questioned by Blankenburg 1999, p. 78.

colla parte in the instruments, as the oboes d'amore I and II, the second violin and viola double the vocal parts of the soprano, alto and tenor. A feature not usually found in the stile antico is the addition of the independent instrumental part (in rapid sixteenth notes) played by two flutes and the first violin; this is evidently a musical rendering of the shepherds' haste and excitement.

The chorale

Among those movements which comment on the action are the chorales, with their traditional texts and melodies. The earliest chorales, such as *Ein feste Burg is unser Gott*, go back to Luther, who diligently promoted a repertoire of simple melodies with texts in the vernacular, singable by the congregation in the liturgy. With this ideal in mind, the often long chorale texts are arranged in strophic form (the melody of the first verse applying to all the rest), the setting of the text is almost completely syllabic and there are usually only two different lengths of notes (one half the length of the other). The structure of the melody is usually in a a b form, a repetitive structure in which the music of the first two lines (a) is repeated for the next two, followed by new material (b). With their tuneful melodies, without large or unusual leaps, chorales were easy to learn and remember. Bach usually drew on melodies from the 16th and 17th centuries, the period in which most of this repertoire was produced.

As early as the beginning of the 16th century, chorale melodies were set polyphonically, both in the contrapuntal-imitative style and in more homophonic (chordal) versions. From the end of the 16th century, the so-called *Cantionalstil* was widely practiced. In this style the melody was put in the upper voice (soprano) and harmonically supported in the three lower voices (alto, tenor and bass). Bach followed in this tradition for the chorale settings that conclude his cantatas or those inserted into his Passions (such as *O Haupt voll Blut und Wunden* in the *St. Matthew Passion*, expressing the reaction of the faithful to Christ's flagellation and crowning with thorns). The chorale settings in the *Christmas Oratorio* reveal Bach's delight in rich and expressive harmony, with no hint of routine in the settings of these well-known melodies.

The first chorale, *Wie soll ich dich empfangen* (no. 5), a reaction of the pious Christian to Christ's Incarnation, shows clearly the amount of care that Bach takes in working out musical details (music example 3). The added parts are much more richly worked out than in a normal four-voice harmonization in the Cantionalstil: Bach sets up an almost constant and complementary eighth-note movement, the result of a chain of flowing passing notes in stepwise motion and dissonant suspensions which spice up the harmony.[58] With this manner of harmonization, Bach was making a statement against the increasingly prevalent, simple choral settings, in which the harmony and the lower voices were completely subordinate to the melodic line in the upper voice. As in his more complex compositions – large-scale choruses, arias, fugues... – in his chorale settings Bach aimed for a "musikalische Vollkommenheit", a musical perfection, for which he was praised by Meister Johann Birnbaum, his Leipzig friend and ally against the attacks of the avant garde.[59]

In these chorale settings, the instruments (some or all) usually play colla parte. However, Bach sometimes composed chorales with independent instrumental intermezzos, such as the concluding chorales of cantata I, *Ach mein herzliebes Jesulein*, no. 9, cantata II, *Wir singen dir in deinem Heer*, no. 23, cantata IV, *Jesus richte mein Beginnen*, no. 42, and cantata VI, *Nun seid ihr wohl gerochen*, no. 64. Elsewhere, Bach combines recitatives with chorales, as in cantata IV (*Immanuel, o süßes Wort*, no. 38, and *Wohlan, dein Name soll allein*, no. 40).[60]

In his choice of chorales for use in this work, Bach showed a preference for later, 17th-century pieces and not, as in many of the cantatas, for the repertoire of early Protestantism (by Luther and his successors). With five chorale texts, Paul Gerhardt takes first place, followed by Johann Rist and Luther himself, with three each. Of four other authors, also from the 17th century, each has one poem (Christoph Runge, Georg Weissel, Johann Franck and Georg Werner).[61] Chorale texts by 17th-century poets, partly under the influence of the Thirty Years War (1618-1648), were increasingly expressions of personal devotion and subjective emotions; this led to a preponderance of the so-called 'Ich-Lieder' in the *Christmas Oratorio* (e.g., *Wie soll*

---

58 In connection with chorale settings in Cantionalstil by his father, Carl Philipp Emmanuel Bach spoke of the "very exceptional harmonic setting and the natural flow of the inner voices and the bass" ("ganz besondere Einrichtung der Harmonie und das natürlich fließende der Mittelstimmen und des Basses"; quoted by Walter 1999, p. 59).

59 Geck 2000a, pp. VI-VII. In lieu of a foreword to his book ('Statt eines Vorwortes') Geck examines the chorale *Dein Glanz all Finster uns verzehrt* (no. 46 from the *Christmas Oratorio*), providing commentary under the title 'Bachs Vollkommenheiten' ('Bach's perfections').

60 Dürr 1967, pp. 22-25. On p. 45 Dürr provides an overview of all the chorale texts from the *Christmas Oratorio*, with their accompanying melodies.

61 Dürr 1967, p. 8.

ich dich empfangen by Paul Gerhardt, the first chorale in the oratorio).[62] Gerhardt's texts came to be widely known in the Leipzig area only from the beginning of the 18th century.[63] Bach occasionally cited a verse from one of Gerhardt's poems in his cantatas, but only one cantata out of his whole cycle of chorale cantatas is based on a text by the poet, again a typical 'Ich-Lied' (*Ich hab in Gottes Herz und Sinn*, BWV 92, composed for Sunday, 28 January 1725).[64]

Since most of the chorale texts follow a fixed poetic scheme, they could be sung both on an older melody or a newly composed one. This explains why the same melody often turns up with different texts. The texts themselves could run to any number of verses, from which the composer could select as desired. Thus, for example, the chorale *Wie soll ich dich empfangen* (no. 5) was sung on the same melody as the well-known Passion chorale *O Haupt voll Blut und Wunden* (also by Gerhardt). This melody actually derived from a secular love-song, *Mein Gmüt ist mir verwirret*, composed in 1601 by Hans Leo Hassler.[65] A possible, but disputed, connection intended by Bach – that between Christ's birth and his subsequent suffering – will be considered later.

The poetic interpolations

Newly written texts – whether commentaries, meditations or morals – are set to music in the *Christmas Oratorio* in the form of choruses, recitatives or arias.

Chorus

Bach employs choral settings on free texts as the opening movement in five of the six cantatas (I, *Jauchzet, frohlocket*, no. 1; III, *Herrscher des Himmels, erhöre das Lallen*, no. 24; IV, *Fallt mit Danken*, no. 36; V. *Ehre sei dir, Gott, gesungen*, no. 43; VI. *Herr, wenn die stolzen Feinde schnauben*, no. 54). The exception is the second cantata, which begins with an instrumental sinfonia. In contrast to the choruses on Bible

---

62 Marshall/Leaver 2001, p. 742.
63 Blankenburg 1999, p. 46.
64 Dürr 1999, pp. 259-265. The second cycle composed by Bach in Leipzig (1724-1725) includes most of his 'chorale cantatas', in which the first and last verses of the chorale text are imported intact, while the other verses are rewritten and set as recitatives and arias (Dürr 1999, pp. 49-52 and Wolff 2000, pp. 275-281 and, in more detail, Küster 1999, pp. 242-291).
65 This melody was soon united with the funeral text, *Herzlich tut mich verlangen* (Blankenburg 1999, p. 46).

texts, which are stylistically inspired by the motet *in stile antico*, these opening choruses are extended works *in stile concertato*, the concerted style, characterized by the interplay of voices and instruments. Unlike the choruses *in stile antico*, the concerted movements for choir feature instruments with an independent function (so-called *obbligato* instruments): besides accompanying the vocal parts, they enter into dialogue with them and also present their own musical material in ritornellos. A *ritornello* is an instrumental introduction that returns refrain-like throughout a movement to provide a bridge between solo passages in a concerto (as in the violin concertos of Antonio Vivaldi) or an aria (Italian operas). The ritornello generally includes thematic material that is further developed in the instrumental or vocal solos. Bach transplants this ritornello structure, characteristic of the concerto and the aria, into the choruses of his oratorios, Passions and cantatas. One particular feature of his approach is the overlapping of instrumental ritornellos and vocal fragments, as he often allows the voices to begin before the ritornello has ended, or has the ritornello play simultaneously with a sung section. This 'transplantation' of a vocal fragment into the ritornello is referred to in German as *Choreinbau*, or more generally, *Vokaleinbau*, which might be translated 'choral in-building' or 'vocal in-building'.[66] The structure of these concerted choruses often takes the A-B-A or da capo form chiefly associated with the solo aria (see below), where the first section (A) is repeated whole after the second section (B) which has a different text and sometimes contrasting music. Since the repetition is identical, the second A is not written out, and the words *da capo* ('from the beginning') are placed at the end of the B section. The A section ends with the indication *fine* ('end'), with a *fermata* over the final note (a half circle with a dot, indicating a note to be held longer).

The opening chorus of the *Christmas Oratorio* provides an excellent illustration of (1) the ritornello structure, (2) de A-B-A form and (3) the *concertato* principle. The text is as follows:

A

Jauchzet, frohlocket, auf, preiset die Tage,
Rühmet, was heute der Höchste getan!
Lasset das Zagen, verbannet die Klage,
Stimmet voll Jauchzen und Fröhlichkeit an!

---

66 Bossuyt 2000, pp. 34-35, followed by a in-depth discussion of the concerted choruses in the *Missae breves* by Bach (pp. 36-59). See also Dürr 1967, pp. 35-38.

B
Dienet dem Höchsten mit herrlichen Chören,
Lasst uns den Namen des Herrschers verehren!

Translation:
A
Rejoice, be glad! Come, praise the days!
Glorify what the Lord has done this day!
Set fear aside, banish lamentation!
Strike up a song of rejoicing and merriment!
B
Serve the All Highest with glorious choirs!
Let us worship the name of the Lord!

The text is split into 4 + 2 lines divided between the A and B sections of the da capo form. After B, the A is repeated in its entirety.

The following scheme elucidates the structure of this chorus on the basis of its ritornello structure:

A
1 Ritornello: instrumental (mm. 1-33)
2 Ritornello with Choreinbau on the text of A ("Jauchzet, frohlocket," mm. 33-81)
3 Fragment from the ritornello: instrumental (mm. 81-89)
4 Ritornello with Choreinbau on the text of A (mm. 89-137).
B
1 Chorus section on the first line of B ("Dienet dem Höchsten"), with supporting, less independent instrumental parts (mm. 137-170)
2 Fragment from the ritornello of A: instrumental (mm. 170-185)
3 Continuation of the ritornello in the instruments with Choreinbau on the second line of B ("Lasst uns den Namen," m. 186-201).
A: repeat.

As was customary, the vocal fragments are linked by short but clearly recognizable echoes of material from the ritornellos (A3 and B2). The return of the ritornello in B creates a thematic connection to the A section; since the text of B is indeed something of a continuation of A, there is little reason to create a complete musical break. The B section does contrast in that during the first phrase (B1), the instruments do not take on a concerted role (and also do not refer to the ritornello) and the trumpets and the timpani fall silent (except for a minor appearance of the first trumpet in B2, a simple repetition of an f-sharp). The limitation of the instrumentation in the middle section is a frequent feature of the da capo form. This chorus will be examined in greater detail in the discussion of the separate cantatas.

Recitativo accompagnato

One of the most striking characteristics of the *Christmas Oratorio* is the relatively large number of reflective, commenting texts presented in the form of *recitativo accompagnato* or accompanied recitative. Nine movements are recitatives of this sort (nos. 3, 14, 18, 27, 32, 49, 52, 56 and 61), while in four other parts, chorales are combined with an accompagnato (nos. 7, 38, 40 and 45). One of the recitatives on an added text is the short recitativo secco (no. 22, *So recht, Ihr Engel*). Another is rather unusual: a recitativo secco for four soloists and basso continuo (no. 63, *Was will der Höllen Schrecken nun*); Bach places this movement strategically before the concluding chorale, creating an emotionally-charged penultimate moment.

In the accompagnato recitatives, Bach complements the basso continuo with instrumental parts (strings and/or winds), which fill out the chords indicated in the bass, or develop their own independent motifs. In the *Christmas Oratorio*, the motivic use of the instruments is fairly limited: they tend to double the long-held chords played by the basso continuo (nos. 27, 32, 52, 56) or accentuate notes in the chord (no. 14). Sometimes their role is more substantial (for example in nos. 3, 18, 49 and 61), but not on the same level of comprehensive motivic development as in several of the accompagnato recitatives in the *St. Matthew Passion*.[67]

Two examples can serve as illustrations. In the recitative, *Ja, ja, mein Herz soll es bewahren* (no. 32), two flutes hold notes from the chords indicated by the figures in the basso continuo (music example 4). At the beginning of *So geht! Genug, mein Schatz* (no. 61), the two oboes (oboe d'amore) likewise follow the harmony of the basso continuo, but starting from m. 4 they begin to take on more individual roles,

---

67   Dürr 1967, pp. 25-26. Küster 1999, pp. 120-121 employs the term *ausinstrumentiertes Secco* ("secco with instrumentation") for an accompagnato recitative in which the instruments play the continuo chords and *motivgeprägtes Accompagnato* ("motivic accompagnato") for recitatives in which the instruments take on a more independent role, with their own motifs. In Bach's time, the term *Accompagnato-Rezitativ* was customary for the first type and *Arioso* for the second.

with changes in tempo and dynamics (allegro – adagio [an acceleration followed by a slowing down] and forte – piano), making this recitative more dramatic (music example 5). By way of comparison, consider the beginning of the intense recitativo accompagnato, *Ach Golgotha, unselges Golgotha*, from the *St. Matthew Passion*, in which the two oboes (oboe da caccia) play their own separate motifs from the outset (music example 6).

In contrast with the prose of the Bible narrative, these added recitative texts are written in rhyming verse, on a basic meter with regular accents. As a rule, poets showed a preference for iambic verse (short-long), sometimes with varying numbers of stressed syllables in the different lines (3, 4, 5…).[68] An excellent example of such poetry is the first recitativo accompagnato from the *Christmas Oratorio* (music example 7): *Nun wird mein liebster Bräutigam* (no. 3). The numeral next to the text refers to the number of stressed syllables and the letter m or f to either a masculine or feminine ending.[69]

Nun wird mein liebster Bräutigam,	4 - m
Nun wird der Held aus Davids Stamm,	4 - m
Zum Trost, zum Heil der Erden,	3 - f
Einmal geboren werden.	3 - f
Nun wird der Stern aus Jakob scheinen,	4 - f
Sein Strahl bricht schon hervor.	3 - m
Auf, Zion, und verlasse nun das Weinen,	5 - f
Dein Wohl steigt hoch empor!	3 - m

Translation:
Now shall my most beloved bridegroom,
Now shall the hero of David's line,

---

68   Erdmann Neumeister, writing in the foreword to his 1704 *Geistlicher Cantaten statt einer Kirchen-Music* ("Sacred cantatas instead of church music", a collection of texts in which he imported modern forms from the Italian chamber cantata – such as the recitative and aria – into the Protestant church cantata), states that "iambic verse is best for recitative: the shorter the more pleasing, and the easier to set to music" ("So nimmt man zum Recitativ Jambische Verse. Je kürtzer aber, je angenehmer, und je bequemer sie zu componiren sind") (Dürr 1994, p. 153).

69   An accented syllable is also known as the 'arsis', while an unaccented syllable is referred to as the 'thesis'. The term 'masculine ending' indicates a line concluding with an arsis, and a 'feminine ending' with a thesis.

For the solace and salvation of all the earth,
At last be born.
Now shall the star of Jacob shine,
Already its light is breaking forth.
Arise, Zion, and leave weeping now,
Thy salvation rises up on high.

The poet has alternated the number of feet per line (three or four, and one time five) and the endings (masculine or feminine), creating a total of five combinations (three or four accented syllables per line with a masculine or a feminine ending, and one time five accented syllables with a feminine ending). The notes on the accented syllables are never shorter than on the preceding unaccented ones, with one exception, the sixteenth note on "und" in the line "Auf, Zion, und verlasse nun das Weinen," a conjunction that clearly calls for more emphasis. Bach also places an eighth-note rest before "und," functioning as a musical comma after "Auf, Zion" (note also the sixteenth-note rest after "zum Trost"). He respects – and clarifies – the poetic structure by placing an eighth-note rest after every line. The basic unit of the syllabic declamation is the eighth note. Each accented syllable falls on one of the four beats in the measure (compare with the Bible recitative no. 5, above). The eighth note is sometimes lengthened to a dotted eighth note on an accented syllable within the line ("*Bräu*tigam" and "hoch") or to a quarter note on a masculine (accented) ending ("Braü*tigam*," "Stamm," "herv*or*"; on "em*por*" the quarter note is split into two eighths). As a result of their irregular lengths, the lines do not always end on the same beat within the measure (line 1 ending at the end of the measure, lines 2, 3, 4, 7 and 8 on a first beat, line 5 on a third beat).[70] For other salient features connected with typical melodic turns of phrase and elements of text expression in recitatives, the reader is referred to the detailed discussions of the separate cantatas.

Aria

The most lyrical and virtuoso parts of the oratorio are the arias, numbering twelve in total (nos. 4, 8, 15, 19, 29, 31, 39, 41, 47, 51, 57 and 62). The scoring is highly varied, usually for one vocal soloist (soprano, alto, tenor or bass) with one or more

---

70 For an example of a similar analysis, in this case a recitative from Bach's cantata *Jesu, der du meine Seele* (BWV 78), see Dürr 1994, pp. 154-157 (the recitative *Ach! ich bin ein Kind der Sünden*).

obbligato instruments and basso continuo. One of the arias is a duet for soprano and bass (no. 29, *Herr, dein Mitglied, dein Erbarmen*), and another a trio for soprano, alto and tenor (no. 51, *Ach, wenn wird die Zeit erscheinen*). The most unusual and commented upon aria is *Flößt, mein Heiland, flößt dein Namen* (no. 39), for soprano solo and a second soprano as 'echo'.[71]

The instrumental parts – generally for one or two soloists, especially winds (trumpet, flute, oboe and oboe d'amore), as well as violin – are predominantly conceived in the concerted style. This means that the instruments introduce the aria with a ritornello and then continue in dialogue with the voice. The form preferred by Bach is the da capo aria then prevalent. The scoring and the choice of the voice, as well as the tempo and tonality are generally determined by the text. In contrast with ongoing, narrative or reflective recitative, the musical development of the aria text aims to expand on a central idea or one central emotion; this accounts for the text repetition and the often virtuoso melodic development, sometimes rich with melismas.[72]

It is no accident, for instance, that Bach calls for a trumpet, the 'royal' instrument, for the bass aria *Großer Herr, o starker König* (no. 8), a movement in the 'radiant' key of D major. In the lullaby *Schlafe, mein Liebster* for alto solo (no. 19), which follows a recitative in which the shepherds are exhorted to go in search of the child and sing him a "Lied zur Ruhe" ("Song of peace"; in no.18, *So geht nun hin, ihr Hirten geht*), the violins are joined by a flute and no fewer than four oboes, instruments traditionally linked to pastoral scenes. The movement is a typical example of a da capo aria with its normal A-B-A structure:

A
Schlafe, mein Liebster, genieße der Ruh,
Wache nach diesem vor aller Gedeihen.
B
Labe die Brust,
empfinde die Lust,
Wo wir unser Herz erfreuen!

---

71 Dürr 1967, pp. 28-35.

72 Mattheson writes that "an aria should always be a well-conceived, reflective basic dictum and axiom, with a clear affect" ("eine Arie soll eigentlich nichts anders seyn, als ein wohlgefaßter, mit einem gewissen Affect versehener, nachdencklicher Haupt-Spruch, und Axioma") (*Critica Musica*, I/1, 1722, cited by Dürr, 1994, p. 153).

Translation:
A
Sleep, my darling, enjoy Thy rest,
Henceforth watch over the well-being of all!
B
Refresh the heart,
Taste the joys
That gladden our hearts!

The aria is constructed as follows:
A
1 Instrumental ritornello: strings, oboe d'amore (I and II), oboe da caccia (I and II), solo traverso and basso continuo (mm. 1-28)
2 Vocal fragment I: Vokaleinbau with the ritornello on the text of A (mm. 28-56)
3 Instrumental ritornello (second part of the ritornello, mm. 56-69)
4 Vocal fragment II: Vokaleinbau with the ritornello on the text of A (mm. 69-96)
5 Instrumental ritornello (first part of the ritornello, mm. 96-112)
B
One vocal + instrumental fragment on the text of B (mm. 113-152). Initially new thematic material, subsequently reprising the second part of the ritornello. The scoring is reduced: only strings and solo flute (without the four oboes). The traverso doubles the alto voice at the octave.

Characteristic are the text repetitions and the extensive melismas, expressing the joy in the word "erfreuen" with exuberance, especially at the end.

The metrical structure of the arias varies considerably. While the preference in the recitative is for iambic verse, trochees (long-short) and dactyls (long-short-short) are also used in the aria form. The text of *Schlafe, mein Liebster* is written in dactyls (with alternating endings), except for the last sentence ("wo wir unser Herz erfreuen"), which is trochaic. The opening chorus, *Jauchzet, frohlocket* (see above) is written completely in dactyls. Each line has four accented syllables, with either masculine or feminine endings. The aria *Großer Herr* consists of lines with six trochees and four accents, again with either masculine or feminine endings. An example of a combination of iambs, trochees and dactyls is the aria *Erleucht auch meine finstre Sinnen* (no. 47).

In the arias, which include many text repetitions, the correct accentuation is not followed as strictly as in the recitative. The melody unfolds more independently, often in melismatic lines, and is less linked to the rules of spoken language. The accented syllables in the aria are generally respected, but the way in which they are emphasized can vary greatly. Johann Mattheson distinguishes three possibilities: metrical accents (*Glieder der Zeit*), accents of duration (*der Noten Dauer*) and melodic accents (*die Erhebung oder Erniedrigung der Stimme*).[73] In the A part of the aria *Schlafe, mein Liebster*, the accented syllable usually corresponds to the metrical accent (the first beat of the 2/4 measure: "*Schla*fe mein *lieb*ster, ge*nie*ße der *Ruh*, *wa*che nach *die*sem vor *al*ler Ge*dei*hen"), sometimes coupled with durational and/or melodic accents – see for example the very long notes at the beginning of this aria: "*Schla*fe, mein *lieb*ster, ge*nie*ße" and the melismas on "*wa*che" and "*al*ler" (music example 8). The accented syllable -*dei*- in "Gedeihen" is sometimes placed on the second beat (a non-accented beat) but does receive a durational accent (a quarter note, preceded by an eighth note on "Ge-"). On the final words, "schlafe" and "wache nach diesem vor aller Gedeihen" (mm. 84-96), Bach changes the metrical accents on "*schla*fe," "*wa*che" and "*die*sem" into durational and/or melodic accents (music example 9). "Schlafe" (mm. 84-87) begins on the second half of the second beat, but is tied into the next measure (quarter note) and is lengthened by an eighth note (durational accent). The first note is also the highest (melodic accent): $g'-e'-f\text{-sharp}'$ and $c''-a'-b'$. The word "wache" (m. 88) is accented melodically: the word begins on the second half of the first beat of the measure, but the first syllable is accentuated by a rising melisma of four sixteenth notes. "Diesem" in m. 90 is comparable with "schlafe." The placing of the accents becomes more problematic in the last, trochaic line "wo wir unser Herz erfreuen." Here the accents usually (but not always) fall on the first or the second beat, sometimes leading to conflict situations (e.g., in mm. 128-129: metrical accent on "wir"). However, this is not disturbing here, as Bach in this line concentrates mainly on the melismatic, expressive setting of the word "erfreuet," so that the event directly preceding it escapes our attention! Mattheson puts it this way: "Melody, like oratory, has its own accents" ("Melodica hat eben so wohl, als die Sprach-Kunst, ihre eignen Accente").[74] Pure melody must sometimes be allowed to run its own course. The aria, unlike the recitative, is not completely

---

73   Dürr 1994, p. 158.
74   Dürr 1994, p. 158.

geared towards the text, but is concerted music as well, with the essential participation of instruments.[75]

The instrumentation

The only purely instrumental section in the *Christmas Oratorio* is the 'sinfonia' introducing the second cantata (no. 10). The central theme of this cantata is the angel's message to the shepherds, announcing Christ's birth. The instrumental prelude takes an appropriately 'pastoral' form, a practice that had come to be a commonplace in the Baroque period, with such typical characteristics as the use of oboes (in reference to the shepherds' pipes), organ points (prolonged notes in the bass, in imitation of the drone of the bagpipe) and the so-called *siciliano* meter of 6/8 or 12/8.[76] This is the only cantata from the *Christmas Oratorio* in which Bach calls for a group of four oboes: two oboes d'amore and two oboes da caccia; these complement the strings, two flutes and basso continuo.

As we have seen, the instrumentation changes in each cantata. In the concerted choruses on newly written texts and in several chorale settings, the contribution of the instruments is essential; this is doubly so in the arias, in which one or more instrumental soloists join in as equal partners with the solo voice. In the choruses on Bible texts and in the chorale in Cantionalstil, the instruments generally double the vocal parts. In the secco recitatives, the basso continuo (organ, harpsichord, cello, violone, and possibly bassoon) supports the singer's line.[77] Occasionally, instruments are accorded more substantial roles in accompanied recitatives (see above).

As with the singers, Bach makes heavy demands on the instrumentalists. Professional musicians, such as the city musicians in Leipzig, both string and wind players, were expected to master a number of instruments. Special techniques were developed on some instruments in order to render the technically demanding and virtuoso parts playable; one example is the technique of *Clarinblasen* on the trumpet and horn, which made it possible to play chromatically in the instrument's highest register.[78] While the trumpet was associated with kingship, the horn had long been

---

75 "The aria has a sort of double face, it is both a song and a concert-piece at the same time" (Dürr 1994, p. 161).
76 Jung 1980, pp. 198-200.
77 In connection with the instrumentation of the continuo for Bach, see especially: Dreyfus 1987 and Williams 1994.

linked to hunting, one of the favorite pastimes of the aristocracy in Saxony, as elsewhere. Bach likely composed his 'Hunt Cantata', *Was mir behagt ist nur die muntre Jagd* (BWV 208), in 1713 for Duke Christian of Saxe-Weissenfels, an avid hunter, who celebrated his birthday on February 23. The horn was here the obvious choice as solo instrument.[79] Bach calls for two *corno da caccia* ('hunting horns') in cantata IV of the *Christmas Oratorio*, a festive work for New Year's Day, the day of Jesus' Naming; and yet this work has a less triumphant sound than cantatas I, II, and IV, in which a group of three trumpets and timpani symbolizes Christ's kingship. In the 'royal aria', *Großer Herr, o starker König* in the first cantata (no. 8), a solo trumpet enters into dialogue with the bass soloist. Bach added an ensemble of three trumpets and timpani in the later version of the third and fourth orchestral suites (BWV 1068 and 1069, Leipzig 1725 and later), which were originally scored without brass and percussion (the first versions seem to date from around 1716-1718).[80] In the concerts given by the Collegium Musicum in Leipzig – and for the performance of the *Christmas Oratorio* – Bach could probably call on the services of the city's professional wind players. Until 1734, the year in which the oratorio was written, the senior member of the 'Stadtpfeifer', Johann Gottfried Reiche, played the demanding first trumpet parts in Bach's works. He died on 6 October 1734, just a few months before the performance of the *Christmas Oratorio*.[81]

Bach's preferred solo wind instrument was clearly the oboe. For orchestral parts he opted for a 'normal' oboe, while in arias he tended towards variants of this instrument, the oboe d'amore and the oboe da caccia. The oboe found its way into German ensembles in the second half of the 17th century, following its use by Jean-Baptiste Lully in his French *tragédies lyriques*. The instrument had a leading role in the orchestra, on a par with the violin; indeed, the two instruments often shared the same part. In Bach's vocal music, there are more than 200 obbligato oboe parts. Many of these were especially written for Johann Caspar Gleditsch, a city musician in Leipzig and Bach's favored soloist. He was one of the advocates of the oboe d'amore, an instrument with a bulb bell and slightly longer than the oboe,

---

78   For more on the instruments in Bach's time, see especially Rampe 2000, pp. 278-310.
79   For more on this cantata, see Dürr 1999, pp. 875-881.
80   Rampe 2000, pp. 266-276.
81   Reich is pictured with his instrument on an engraving (1727) by C.F. Rosbach, after E.G. Haussmann. He died after being overcome by the smoke from a torch, combined with extreme exertion during the performance of one of Bach's celebratory cantatas for the Saxon court (*Preise dein Glücke, gesegnetes Sachsen*, BWV 215). See Smithers 1987.

allowing it to extend its register a few notes downwards. This instrument, for which Bach wrote about half of his oboe parts, was probably invented in Leipzig around 1715. The repertoire for oboe d'amore, written almost exclusively between 1717 and 1760, has a typically German flavor.[82] In the *Christmas Oratorio* the oboe d'amore plays a solo part (with either one or two instruments) in no fewer than sixteen movements: one chorale (no. 7), three choruses (nos. 21, 43, 45), five accompanied recitatives (nos. 3, 14, 18, 52, 61) and six arias (nos. 4, 19, 29, 47, 57, 62). In the sinfonia (no. 10) of the second cantata (and in other parts of this 'pastoral cantata') the oboe d'amore is joined by the oboe da caccia, a type of oboe which could also reach lower notes. The normal oboe is used as an orchestral instrument in four of the five opening choruses (nos. 1, 24, 36, 54), in the concluding chorale of cantata IV (no. 42) and as a solo instrument in the echo aria for soprano *Flößt, mein Heiland* (no. 39). The bassoon, the bass instrument of the woodwind family, usually functions as a continuo instrument. In instrumental works, the bassoon sometimes has an obbligato part together with the oboes, forming a 'woodwind choir' (e.g., the Brandenburg Concerto No. 1, BWV 1046, and the second Bourrée from the Orchestral Suite No. 1, BWV 1066, a trio for two oboes and bassoon).[83]

Other wind instruments used at the time included the recorder and the flute. Two flutes, but no recorders, are called for in the *Christmas Oratorio*. The transverse flute or *traverso* enjoyed great popularity in Bach's time (and later), partly thanks to the composer and virtuoso Johann Joachim Quantz, who wrote an authoritative treatise on playing the instrument (*Versuch einer Anweisung die Flöte traversiere zu spielen* ['On playing the transverse flute'], 1752). Bach maintained personal contacts with Quantz, who for a time was employed at the court in Dresden. Quantz later became the personal flute teacher to Friedrich the Great in Berlin. Bach visited the ruler in 1747, shortly thereafter composing the *Musical Offering* (BWV 1079) for him, a group of movements that includes a trio sonata for traverso, violin and basso continuo. In the *Christmas Oratorio*, flutes appear only in the first three cantatas, the actual 'Christmas cycle'. Their function is comparable with that of the oboes, often appearing as orchestral instruments (in the choruses nos. 1, 21, 24, and in the chorale no. 23). In the shepherd's chorus *in stile antico*, on the Bible text *Lasset uns nun gehen* (no. 26), the two flutes double the virtuoso violin part. The same role, doubling the violin, is played by the flute in the bass aria with trumpet (*Großer Herr*,

---

82   Rampe 2000, pp. 282-285.
83   Rampe 2000, pp. 286-287.

no. 8). In the 'lullaby' aria for alto *Schlafe, mein Liebster* (no. 19), the flute part is again limited to shadowing the vocal part (an octave higher), creating a beautiful color effect. In two accompanied recitatives, the flutes fill out the continuo chords (nos. 27 and 32). The only truly independent solo for flute is found in the aria *Frohe Hirten, eilt, ach eilet* (no. 15), in which the traverso performs a virtuoso duet with the tenor.

The string group is made up of the regular members of the violin family, the violin, viola and cello. In the *Christmas Oratorio* only the violin takes the spotlight as a solo instrument. A cello or violone plays the melody line of the basso continuo. The viola generally plays notes that fill out the chords (although in Bach's music the instrument regularly takes a more independent role). Besides its function as an ensemble instrument in the choruses, the violins play the continuo chords in several accompanied recitatives: for the words of the angel to the shepherds, *Fürchtet euch nicht* (no. 13), in the recitative with chorale *Immanuel* (no. 38), in the recitative-like interruption in the chorus of the Wise Men, *Wo ist der neugeborne König* (no. 45) and in the recitative *Du falscher, suche nur den Herrn* (no. 56). The violin is also frequently called on as soloist, either alone or in tandem, including movements in which it doubles a wind instrument (the oboe d'amore in the aria *Bereite dich Zion*, no. 4, and the flute in the shepherds' chorus, *Lasset uns nun gehen*, no. 26, see above). Truly independent violin solos are found in three arias: the alto aria *Schleiße, mein Herze* (no. 31), the aria for tenor *Ich will nur dir zu Ehren leben* (no. 41, with two solo violins) and the trio for soprano, alto and tenor, *Ach, wenn wird die Zeit erscheinen* (no. 51).

This overview reveals the rich variation of the vocal and instrumental scoring in the *Christmas Oratorio*. Such richness is also found in Bach's other major vocal works, such as the *St. John Passion*, the *St. Matthew Passion* and the *B minor Mass*. It should also be clear from this survey that Bach also strived for an ever-changing texture of styles (stile antico and stile moderno; contrapuntal and homophonic) and genres (recitative, aria, chorale…), often opting for original combinations (e.g., recitative with chorale, nos. 7, 38 and 40) or for less common scorings (such as a four-voice recitative, no. 63, or accompagnato recitatives with four oboes, nos. 14 and 18).

THE SIX CANTATAS IN DETAIL

I Jauchzet, frohlocket, auf, preiset die Tage

Introduction

The first cantata, for Christmas Day, consists of nine movements. The introductory chorus, *Jauchzet, frohlocket, auf, preiset die Tage* (no. 1), is followed by eight movements, ordered symmetrically and divided into two related groups of four:

Group I:
no. 2 Recitativo secco (narrative): *Es begab sich aber zu der Zeit*
no. 3 Recitativo accompagnato: *Nun wird mein liebster Bräutigam*
no. 4 Aria: *Bereite dich, Zion*
no. 5 Chorale: *Wie soll ich dich empfangen*
Group II:
no. 6 Recitativo secco (narrative): *Und sie gebar ihren ersten Sohn*
no. 7 Chorale and recitativo accompagnato: *Er ist auf Erden kommen arm*
no. 8 Aria: *Großer Herr, o starker König*
no. 9 Chorale: *Ach mein herzliebes Jesulein*.

The Evangelist's narration (nos. 2 and 6) is commented upon in three movements: two new texts set respectively as (accompanied) recitative and aria, and a chorale to conclude.

The succession of four contrasting movements (the story in recitativo secco, and the commentary in recitativo accompagnato, aria and chorale) can be seen as a musical realization of what the theologian August Hermann Francke praised as the ideal manner of reading the Bible.[84] After a reading of the Bible text, the 'dictum' (recitativo secco, nos. 2 and 6), comes the 'explicatio,' an interpretation (recitativo accompagnato, nos. 3 and 7), followed by the 'applicatio,' the concrete application to the Christian life (aria, nos. 4 and 8) and finally the affirmation by the

---

[84] In his text *Einfältiger Unterricht, wie man die Heilige Schrifft zu einer wahren Erbauung lesen solle*, Halle, 1694. ('A simple lesson in how Holy Scripture should be read for true edification'). Cf. Francke 1969 en Peschke 1970.

congregation of the faithful (a prayer, a plea or thanksgiving in the form of a chorale, nos. 5 and 9).[85]

The first group of texts (nos. 2 to 5) deals with the imminent coming of Christ. The second (nos. 6 to 9) concentrates on the birth of Jesus: after Advent, the time of 'expectation,' comes Christmas, the fulfillment of the Incarnation of God's son.[86] The first recitative (no. 2) tells of the census ordered by Emperor Augustus, as well as Joseph's departure from Nazareth for Bethlehem together with his pregnant wife Maria. The story breaks off just before the birth ("...kam die Zeit, dass sie gebären sollte"). The second phase (no. 6) begins with the birth ("Und sie gebar ihren ersten Sohn...") and briefly sketches the unusual circumstances (the manger and the inn).

In the second cycle of four movements, Bach builds up to a climax, relative to the first cycle, by applying the 'combination technique' to two movements, a favorite procedure of the composer's whereby very different genres or scorings are mixed. In the second recitativo accompagnato (no. 7), he adds a chorale melody. Moreover, the parts of the added wind instruments (two oboes d'amore) are quite independent. The concluding chorale (no. 9) is, like no. 5, written in Cantionalstil, but the chorale phrases are here separated by instrumental intermezzos for trumpets and timpani. In this way Bach makes a link between this final chorale and the jubilant introductory chorus in which trumpets and timpani also play a prominent role.

This first cantata convincingly illustrates the relationship with the genre of oratorio. Only two of the nine movements (2 and 6) are based on original Bible texts; the other seven are all 'libretto' in the form of commentaries with non-biblical texts. Typical for Bach is the prominent place of chorale melodies (in three movements: 5, 7 and 9), a repertoire close to his heart, which also held a central place in his passions, cantatas and organ works.[87]

---

85 Blankenburg 1982, p. 305.
86 Dürr 1999, p. 133.
87 Especially in the larger collections of organ works, the *Orgelbüchlein* (BWV 599-644), the so-called *Achtzehn Leipziger Choräle* (BWV 651-668) and the *Clavier-Übung III* (BWV 669-689).

1 *Jauchzet, frohlocket, auf, preiset die Tage*

>Jauchzet, frohlocket, auf, preiset die Tage,
>Rühmet, was heute der Höchste getan!
>Lasset das Zagen, verbannet die Klage,
>Stimmet voll Jauchzen und Fröhlichkeit an!
>Dienet dem Höchsten mit herrlichen Chören,
>Lasst uns den Namen des Herrschers verehren!

>Rejoice, be glad! Come, praise the days!
>Glorify what the Lord has done this day!
>Set fear aside, banish lamentation!
>Strike up a song of rejoicing and merriment!
>Serve the All Highest with glorious choirs!
>Let us worship the name of the Lord!

The introductory chorus immediately sets the tone for the first cantata and for the *Christmas Oratorio* as a whole: it recalls the joyful event that is the Incarnation of Christ, the Redeemer, who is announced as "the hero of David's line" ("der Held aus Davids Stamm," as he is referred to in the recitative no. 3). For this mighty chorus, Bach took as his fitting model the opening chorus from his secular cantata *Tönet, ihr Pauken* (BWV 214), which he had performed for the first time a year previously, on 8 December 1733, for the birthday of the electress of Saxony, Maria Josepha, who was also queen of Poland (see above).[88] The original text proceeds as follows:

A section:

Tönet, ihr Pauken! Erschallet, Trompeten!	(rhyme: a)
Klingende Saiten, erfüllet die Luft!	(b)
Singet itzt Lieder, ihr muntren Poeten!	(a)
Königin lebe! wird frölich geruft.	(b)

(Resound, ye drums! Ring out, ye trumpets!
Resonant strings, fill the air!
Glad poets, sing your songs now!
'Long live the Queen!' is joyfully cried).

---

88 For an analysis of this cantata, see Dürr 1999, pp. 903-908.

B section:
Königin lebe! dies wünschet der Sachse, (c)
Königin lebe und blühe und wachse! (c)

('Long live the Queen!' is the Saxons' wish,
May the Queen live and bloom and thrive!).

For the *Christmas Oratorio*, this text is replaced by:
A section:
Jauchzet, frohlocket, auf, preiset die Tage, (rhyme: a)
Rühmet, was heute der Höchste getan! (b)
Lasset das Zagen, verbannet die Klage, (a)
Stimmet voll Jauchzen und Fröhlichkeit an! (b)
B section:
Dienet dem Höchsten mit herrlichen Chören, (c)
Lasst uns den Namen des Herrschers verehren! (c)

The transplantation of existing music into a new composition must meet two main requirements:
(1) the formal adaptation to the new text (the external aspect), and
(2) respect for the relationship between the new text and the affect expressed by the music (the internal aspect).
The birthday celebration of a royal personage inspired Bach to write triumphant and celebratory music, in a dancing ternary meter (3/8) and a festive key (D major), for which he calls on an extensive orchestra of strings, two oboes, two flutes, three trumpets and timpani, with basso continuo and four-voice chorus. In terms of content, this brilliant, extroverted music is a perfect fit with the new context, the welcoming of the heavenly king, Christ, whose name is honored ("Lasst uns den Namen des Herrschers verehren"). The poet adapts the text in terms of content and ensures that the structure, the rhyme scheme and the meter correspond with the original. The structure of six lines, divided into four (A) plus two (B), with a repetition of the first four in function of the da capo form (A, see above) is respected, as is the rhyme scheme (a - b - a - b - c - c), the dactylic meter long-short-short ("*Tö*-net ihr *Pau*-ken! Er-*schal*-let, Trom*pe*ten!" = "*Jauch*-zet, froh-*lo*-cket, auf,

prei-set die *Ta*-ge") and the accented or unaccented final syllables of the lines (b accented, a and c unaccented).[89]

The cantata text inspired Bach to a literal interpretation of the instrumental entries: first the timpani, then the trumpets, and finally the strings ("Saiten"). The flutes and the oboes, which make their appearance in the first measures together with the trumpets and drums, are not mentioned in the text. Bach realized that this colorful opening chorus lent itself naturally to the *Christmas Oratorio*, since the emotional atmosphere of triumph and royal celebration accord perfectly with the new subject matter, completely apart from the instrumentation. On the autograph score of the *Christmas Oratorio*, it is clear that Bach originally copied the first words of the cantata text, but later scrapped them in favor of the new, more universal text, less associated with a one-off occasion.[90] This is one of the many examples that indicates that representing details or expressively illustrating individual words was less important to Bach than conveying the general idea or basic affect of the text. His son Carl Philipp Emmanuel Bach mentions this in a 1774 letter to Johann Nikolaus Forkel, the author of the first Bach biography,[91] writing that "as to the church works of the deceased [Johann Sebastian Bach], it may be mentioned that he worked devoutly, governing himself by the content of the text, without any strange misplacing of the words, and without elaborating on individual words at the expense of the sense of the whole, as a result of which ridiculous thought often appear such as sometimes arouse the admiration of people who claim to be connoisseurs and are not."[92] This does not mean that Bach never specifically accentuates a particular word (there are examples enough, as we shall see); rather, this never occurs at the expense of the larger idea.

Bach first worked out the prototype of this kind of jubilant chorus in D major with trumpets and timpani, themes based on triads (ideal for the trumpet) and in da capo form, in the Pentecost cantata, *Erschallet, ihr Lieder, erklinget, ihr Saiten!* (BWV 172),

---

89 Wolff 2000, p. 384.
90 Facsimile of the autograph in Blankenburg 1999, p. 49.
91 Forkel 1802.
92 Cited by Wolff 2000, pp. 384-385, after NBR 1998, p. 396. The original text, is as follows: "Bey des seeligen Kirchensachen kan angeführt werden, dass er devot u. dem Inhalte gemäss gearbeitet habe, ohne comische Verwerfung, ohne einzelne Worte auszudrücken, mit Hinterlassung des Ausdruckes des ganzen Verstandes, wodurch oft lächerliche Gedancken zum Vorschein kommen, welche zuweilen verständig seyn wollende und unverständliche zur Bewunderung hinreissen" (JSB 1975, p. 195, partly cited by Forchert 2000, p. 206).

which he wrote in 1714 in Weimar. The music proceeds chordally, for the most part, with a degree of imitative or free counterpoint in the central B section, in which, moreover, the scoring is reduced (without trumpets and drums).[93] *Tönet, ihr Pauken* and *Jauchzet, frohlocket* are perfectly modeled on this example. The orchestral ritornello begins with a broken D-major chord (*d - f-sharp - a - d'* in timpani and trumpets), accompanied by woodwinds and strings. The actual melodic theme of the A section is heard first in the woodwinds and then completed by the trumpets and the violins (music example 10, m. 9 ff.). Swirling sixteenth- and thirty-second-note figures round off the ritornello. This is followed by the first Choreinbau, as the voices completely take over the introductory triadic motif on the first phrase, "Jauchzet, frohlocket, auf, preiset die Tage." The first two lines pick up on the A theme, which appears complete in the voices. In the instruments it is distributed over the woodwinds, the trumpets and the violins, as in the introductory ritornello. The third line, "Lasset das Zagen, verbannet die Klage," carries over a motif that is played in the first measures of the ritornello by the flutes and the oboes (music example 10, mm. 2-4). This example clearly shows how Bach leaves nothing to chance, carefully combining all the elements. After a shortened intermediary ritornello, the whole process is repeated with minor variations. The middle section B ("Dienet dem Höchsten") begins with imitation, but after the ritornello on the final phrase ("Lasst uns den Namen des Herrschers verehren") returns to a more chordal style (see above for the structure of this movement).

Bach's main aim is to create an atmosphere of festive jubilation, in an extroverted, tumultuous chorus in which the text remains clear and intelligible. The intentions are clear and need little interpretative commentary. Once again, Bach is revealed as the master of total coherence: the instrumental ritornello holds in it the musical material for the whole movement (note for example the seemingly ungainly motif in the woodwinds, which eventually forms the central motif on "Lasset das Zagen"; equally, the ritornello theme from A also forms a link with the B section, where it also appears in the ritornello). The harmonic structure is logical and well thought-out: the first part (A) revolves around the tonic and dominant keys, D major and A major, while in the second (B) the parallel keys of B minor and F-sharp minor predominate.

---

93 Geck 2000, p. 341 and Dürr 1999, p. 394.

The da capo structure with ritornello and the concerted participation of the instruments points to the influence of Italian music, especially the opera and concerto. The opening chorus of the cantata *Erschallet, ihr Lieder*, which was a model for the festive cantata for the electress from Dresden and for the *Christmas Oratorio*, was one of Bach's first cantata movements to be based on these principles of composition. Bach kept himself up to date with the latest Italian music, which circulated in Germany in manuscripts and editions. A prime example of this interest was his intense study of Antonio Vivaldi's series of twelve concerti opus 3, *L'estro armonico*, published in Amsterdam in 1711. In July of 1713, a young member of the duke of Weimar's family brought a printed copy of this music home with him upon his return from a two-year study trip through Europe. Bach made transcriptions of a number of concertos from this collection when he was employed at the Weimar court. This was, however, not Bach's first encounter with the genre of the Italian concerto; he had previously studied and assimilated the work of Arcangelo Corelli, Giuseppe Torelli, Alessandro and Benedetto Marcello and Tomaso Albinoni.[94] It was undoubtedly Vivaldi's popular work, however, that intensified Bach's predilection for the concerted style and a structure framed by instrumental ritornellos.[95] Precisely in the years 1713-1714, when he had become absorbed in Italian music, he composed the first cantatas in which this style is clearly present, including *Erschallet, ihr Lieder* (performed on 20 May 1714).

Striking in the choruses *Tönet, ihr Pauken!* and *Jauchzet, frohlocket* is the 'modern' style that a somewhat different Bach would display in his many church cantatas: the style is simplified, with less complex counterpoint, and is even strongly homophonic, often with a structure built up out of symmetrical-periodical phrases (four to eight measures or multiples thereof), combined with the greatest of care for the clarity of the text. In this celebratory music, Bach opts for a direct musical language that can be enjoyed with little intellectual effort, music which is easy on the ear, rather than a demonstration of his great erudition. In this he met the requirements of what was termed 'dem neuesten Geschmack', the latest taste, which seemed to him appropriate for such an occasion.[96] Even though Bach regularly catered to 'the

---

94 BWV 972-987 are sixteen keyboard arrangements of concertos by, among others, Vivaldi and Benedetto and Alessandro Marcello. BWV 579 is an organ fugue on a theme by Corelli, BWV 946 and 951 are fugues for keyboard on a theme by Albinoni.
95 In connection with Bach and the Italian concerto, see especially Rampe 2000, pp. 65-79.
96 Geck 2000, pp. 455-458. In connection with characteristics of the 'modern style' in Bach's work,

latest taste' (in particular, a predilection for 'Anmut der Melodei' or 'charming melodies') when he deemed it fitting, he cannot be accused of taking a simplistic approach. This would have been at odds with Bach's own nature, with the honor of his profession and love for his 'craft,' and with his ideal of combining 'Art' (technical skill and control over the process of composing) and 'Nature' (spontaneous melodic invention and lucid structures).[97] The choruses *Tönet, ihr Pauken!* and *Jauchzet, frohlocket,* modeled on *Erschallet ihr Lieder,* are more than simply bits of *galant* froth: the monumental scoring, the interaction inherent in the concerted style, the regular (if fragmentary) appearance of imitative counterpoint and the thematic development of the ritornello – all these elements are evidence to the contrary.[98]

2 Es begab sich aber zu der Zeit

> Es begab sich aber zu der Zeit, dass ein Gebot von dem Kaiser Augusto ausging, dass alle Welt geschätzet würde. Und jedermann ging, dass er sich schätzen ließe, ein jeglicher in seine Stadt. Da machte sich auch auf Joseph aus Galiläa, aus der Stadt Nazareth, in das jüdische Land zur Stadt David, die da heißet Bethlehem; darum, dass er von dem Hause und Geschlechte David war: auf dass er sich schätzen ließe mit Maria, seinem vertrauten Weibe, die war schwanger. Und als sie daselbst waren, kam die Zeit, dass sie gebären sollte.

> And it came to pass in those days that there went out a decree from Caesar Augustus, that all the world should be taxed, and all went to be taxed, everyone to his own city. And Joseph also went up from Galilee, out of the city of Nazareth, into Judaea, unto the city of David, which is called Bethlehem; because he was of the house and lineage of David; to be taxed with Mary his espoused wife, being great with child. And so it was that, while they were there, the days were accomplished that she should be delivered.

The first secco recitative is the most extensive of all the narrative fragments in the *Christmas Oratorio*. It is based on verses 1-3 from chapter 6 of the Gospel according

---

     see also the chapter 'Stilfragen' in Forchert 2000, pp. 243-249.

97 See in this connection the section entitled 'Zwischen Kunst und Natur' in Forchert 2000, pp. 150-165.

98 In connection with this chorus Geck 2000, p. 458 remarks that "This highly organised composer would not be denied!' Forchert 2000, p. 165 notes that 'for [Bach], agreeableness ... could never be the sole driving force of his creativity; but was only a secondary aspect of artistic perfection."

to Luke.[99] Bach ensures the story's continuity through the use of systematic musical formulas in his recitatives. In contrast with choruses and arias, a recitative does not present musical themes that return later in the movement or are developed in order to create tightly-knit structure. In the recitatives, Bach's main guiding principle is the syntax of the text, where the beginning of each line is often demarcated by a recurring (albeit variable) melodic formula. In this way the successive and differing phases are accorded a 'fixed form' and the different phases of the narrative are welded into one coherent whole. Each of the five lines begins with an identical or similar melodic pattern consisting of a rising interval of a fourth followed by a further movement upwards by a third, usually in stepwise motion (music example 11):

line 1: "Es begab sich aber zu der Zeit": *f-sharp - b - c-sharp' – d'*

line 3: "Und jedermann": *f-sharp' - b - c-sharp - d* (here the first note is shifted to the upper octave, changing the usual rising fourth to a falling fifth)

line 4: "Da machte sich auch auf": *a - d' - e' - f-sharp'*

line 5: "Auf dass er sich schätzen ließe": *b - e-sharp' - f-sharp' - g-sharp'* (the perfect fourth *b - e'* is stretched to an augmented fourth, creating a feeling of tension)

line 6: "Und als sie daselbst": *c-sharp' - f-sharp' - a'* (leap of a third, rather than a second, after the *f-sharp'*).[100]

The conclusion of the lines is also based on a recurring melodic formula, a descending interval of a fourth and a rising (minor or major) second:

line 1: "... geschätzet würde": *f-sharp' - c-sharp' - d'*

line 3: "... in seine Stadt": *a' - e' - f-sharp'*

line 4: "... David war": *f-sharp' - c-sharp' - d'*

line 5: "... die war schwanger": *c-sharp' - g-sharp - a*

Line 6 ends on "... sollte" with a falling fourth (*a - e*), the typical conclusion for a recitative. A V-I cadence then follows as usual in the basso continuo. The word *attacca* indicates that the following fragment follows immediately,[101] a course of action suggested by Bach since the two cadential notes are divided between this

---

99 The second verse, which provides more historical detail and is less relevant to the story, has been omitted ("This was the first census that took place while Quirinius was governor of Syria").

100 Küster 1999 discusses these typical opening formulas in the St. Matthew Passion (pp. 462-464) and refers to their use in the *Christmas Oratorio* (p. 476). See also his article in Küster 1995.

101 The *attacca* indication has been added by the publisher (for the edition of the score, see bibliography). All editorial additions to the score are printed in italics, while Bach's original indications are printed normally.

movement and the following one: the secco recitative ends on an E-major chord (V), resolving to the A-major chord (I) with which the following movement begins.

The typical melodic formulas used at the beginnings and ends of recitatives are avoided in other places, so that they remain associated with syntactical caesuras. A variant with a rising fifth followed by a rising second is found on "darum dass er von dem Hause ..." in line 4. As an explanation of what goes before (why does Joseph go to Bethlehem?), it functions as a separate element, justifying such an opening formula (which remains a variant form).

Characteristic of Bach's recitatives in general is the rich melodic development, with relatively few repeated notes and often with large leaps that enhance the expressive content of the music. At the beginning, Bach avoids repeating the note *b* five times by lowering the second note by a minor second, and thus setting up the word "aber" for added accentuation. Repeated tones tended to be avoided because they recalled too vividly the liturgical reciting tone used in chanting prayers and Bible texts. In the 18th century, such a 'churchy' sound was not found desirable for recitative.[102] By constructing a melodic line which continually alternates between rising and falling figures, either small or large, Bach creates inspired and captivating recitatives.

In the first line there is clearly a melodic climax reached on the verb "ausging" (on a *g'*, the highest note in this line) which functions as a high point in the tension, as if the question 'which command?' were being asked. The answer "dass alle Welt geschätzet wurde" completes the line.

The second line proceeds somewhat differently: here Bach seeks to emphasize the fact that each person was expected to go specifically to his or her own city, which explains why Joseph has set out for Bethlehem. He achieves this with an octave leap on "seine," with a melodic high point towards the end of the line, an effect that comes across that much more forcefully because the first half of the line ("und jedermann ging, dass er sich schätzen ließe") ends on a very low note (an *e*, the final note of the whole recitative).

The next line is characterized by a constant wave-like motion, rising to *a'* in the highest register and subsiding to *d-sharp* in the lowest. The recitative immediately

---

102 This is one of the rules for a good recitative as laid down by Stölzel (Küster 1999, p. 476).

ascends to its highest note, *a'*, highlighting the name of Joseph. Soon after this the melody reaches its lowest point on the word "Nazareth," on a somewhat unusual *d-sharp*, a note which occurs only once in this recitative. This 'lowly' note may be a reference to the insignificance of the city of Nazareth, as suggested by the question asked in John's Gospel: "Can anything good come from there?"[103]

In the last line the recitative quickly rises to the last high note *a'* on the word "daselbst," drawing attention to the place where Christ will be born. A not insignificant detail is the interruption of the syllabic declamation on the word "gebären," as two notes are accorded to the accented syllable, and not just one: a subtle and efficient way of expressing the word. In his recitatives, Bach does not limit himself to "animated declamation," but strives to interpret the story.[104]

3   Nun wird mein liebster Bräutigam

> Nun wird mein liebster Bräutigam,
> Nun wird der Held aus Davids Stamm
> Zum Trost, zum heil der Erden
> Einmal geboren werden.
> Nun wird der Stern aus Jakob scheinen,
> Sein Strahl bricht schon hervor.
> Auf, Zion, und verlasse nun das Weinen,
> Dein Wohl steigt hoch empor!
>
> Now shall my most beloved bridegroom,
> Now shall the hero of David's line,
> For the solace and salvation of all the earth,
> At last be born.
> Now shall the star of Jacob shine,
> Already its light is breaking forth.
> Arise, Zion, and leave weeping now,
> Thy salvation rises up on high.

The first recitativo accompagnato follows without interruption, functioning as something of a continuation of the Gospel text.[105] A 'third person,' not explicitly

---

103   John 1:46.
104   Dürr 1967, p. 17, writes: "If Schütz was able to reach the heights of animated declamation using the formal means of his time, Bach wished to add to this a musical interpretation of the events."
105   Küster 1999, p. 476.

named, announces the birth of Christ, referring to his descent from the house of David (and of Jacob)[106] and reveals God's intention: Christ is born "for the solace and salvation of all the earth" ("zum Trost, zum Heil der Erden)". He approaches like a shining star,[107] and Zion is exhorted to put aside all sorrow. The text picks up on the Evangelist's narrative, but carries it further, answering the questions: Why this Incarnation? How should we react to it? Christ is compared with the bridegroom for whom the bride is waiting, an ancient Christian symbol that harks back to an interpretation of the Song of Songs (4:8, "Come with me from Lebanon, my bride") and that was also kept alive in chorale texts. In *Wie schön leuchtet der Morgenstern* (1599), the melody that Bach took as his point of departure for Cantata BWV 1, this symbolism is found in the first verse: "O son of David from the root of Jesse, my king and my bridegroom, you have captured my heart."[108]

The German theologian and musicologist Blankenburg attributes the words of the accompagnato recitative to the Virgin Mary, who is here accompanied by an appropriate musical attribute, the oboe d'amore, serving as a symbol of love. She can also be seen symbolically as the bride awaiting Christ's arrival, since she was the first human associated with Jesus and thus is seen as the original emblem for belief and the congregation of the faithful. For Zion, the Jewish nation, Christ is the bridegroom who comes to meet his people, an image which is again drawn from the Christian view of Bach's time. The intention of these commenting recitatives is to interpret the word of the Bible in order to translate it to the contemporary situation.[109]

In the musical setting, this accompanied recitative (music example 7) is related to the preceding secco recitative: here too Bach begins with the typical rising interval of a fourth, followed by a further ascent (*e' - a' - c-sharp"*). The text is a poem of eight lines (rhyme-scheme aabbcdcd), the verse structure of which is not only underlined by the pauses in the vocal part, but also – and especially – by a recurring motif in the two oboes d'amore that bridge the lines (except in one place, at the end of the line "zum Trost, zum Heil der Erden"). Since Christ has humbled himself to become

---

106 David was the second king of Israel, and lived approximately 1000 years before Christ. He was the son of Jesse of Bethlehem, from the tribe of Judah. Judah was the fourth son of Leah and Jacob. Jacob was the son of Isaac, who in turn was the son of Abraham, the father of the Jewish people. Excellent introductions to the Old-Testament figures are found in Comay 2001.
107 Cf. the symbol of the star in cantatas V and VI (the story of the Wise Men).
108 Blankenburg 1999, pp. 40-42 and Dürr 1999, p. 737 ff. (discussion of Cantata 1). For more in connection with the mysticism of the bride, see Steiger 2002, pp. 163-174 (examination of the cantata *Ich geh und suche mit Verlangen*, BWV 49) and pp. 250-254.
109 Blankenburg 1999, p. 42.

a human on earth, at the word "Erden" the melody appropriately descends to its lowest point, the note *d-sharp'* (by chance or design the same note given to "Nazareth" in the previous recitative?). During the last, 'positive' line "Dein Wohl steigt hoch empor," the oboes, by contrast, continue unabated. The descending melodic line that finishes on "Erden" makes up the interval of a diminished fourth (*a' - f-sharp' - d-sharp'*): the 'perfect' fifth *a' - d'* becomes 'imperfect,' as it were.[110] Again, on the word "Weinen" at the end of the penultimate line, the melody descends in a similar line: *c' - b - g-sharp* (a diminished fourth rather than the perfect fourth of *c' - g*). Striking here is also the chromatic motion on "verlasse nun das Weinen," with *D-sharp - D* in the basso continuo and *f-sharp' - f* in the oboe d'amore: Bach first focuses the attention on the negative ("das Weinen"); as a result, the ensuing contrasting effect with the positive ("dein Wohl") is that much starker. With "Wohl" and "empor," the melodic high point (*e"*) has been reached, heights previously attained on "David" (the melodic conclusion of a rising line on the words "nun wir der Held aus Davids Stamm") and on "Strahl" (with a bold leap of a seventh, *f-sharp' - e"*).

4   Bereite dich, Zion

> Bereite dich, Zion, mit zärtlichen Trieben,
> Den Schönsten, den Liebsten bald bei dir zu sehn!
> Deine Wangen
> Müssen heut viel schöner prangen,
> Eile, den Bräutigam sehnlichst zu lieben!
>
> Prepare thyself, Zion, with tender affection,
> Soon to behold the fairest and dearest!
> Your cheeks
> Today must be more radiant,
> Hasten to the Bridegroom with most ardent love.

The first aria goes further into the symbolism of bride and bridegroom, a favorite theme in Pietistic literature, as we have seen: Zion, prepare to receive "den Schönsten, den Liebsten," go quickly to him to show him your passionate love ("eile, den Bräutigam sehnlichst zu lieben"). According to Blankenburg, these words may also

---

110   Blankenburg 1999, p. 43.

be ascribed to Mary, as the logical continuation of the recitativo accompagnato for the same voice.[111]

For this aria, Bach turned to another cantata, also mentioned above, the 'dramma per musica' *Lasst uns sorgen, lasst uns wachen* (BWV 213), a work on a libretto that the poet Picander entitled *Hercules auf dem Scheidewege* ('Hercules at the crossroads'). The subject matter is the choice that the classical hero Hercules must make between a virtuous and demanding life, and a life of pleasure and ease. After both 'Tugend' ('virtue') and 'Wollust' ('pleasure') have made their cases, Hercules (naturally) chooses virtue, resolutely rejecting pleasure in the aria *Ich will dich nicht hören, ich will dich nicht wissen*.[112]

This aria is an excellent example of the way Bach adapts an existing composition to a new context, without making spectacular changes and yet achieving a quite different result. The most important task facing the composer here is the creation of a new affect: he must transform Hercules' firm, forceful rejection of pleasure to the appeal to love represented in the *Christmas Oratorio*. A first alteration is an addition of an oboe d'amore, the 'love instrument' from the preceding recitative, to the first violin part from the cantata. This oboe simply doubles the violin part, but helps to create the appropriate atmosphere through its specific, intimate tone color. The different articulation in the instruments is another essential change. In the cantata, the violins are instructed to play *staccato*, whereby the separate notes are played short and sharp, giving Hercules' determined reaction a 'snappy' quality. This indication is absent in the oratorio version. From the first measure the slurs indicate a flowing *legato* that ideally fits the portrayal of a loving appeal.

In the B section of this da capo aria, Bach finds a more drastic intervention necessary in order to change in the affect, this time mainly in the vocal part. Below, the two texts, beginning with the Hercules cantata:

Denn die Schlangen,
So mich wollten wiegend fangen,
Hab ich schon lange zermalmet, zerrissen.

---

111 Blankenburg 1999, p. 40.
112 For a discussion of this cantata, see Dürr 1999, pp. 897-903 and Küster 1999, pp. 410-412. The story comes from the Greek sophist Prodikos of Keos (5th century B.C.). The 'Scheideweg' is a fork in the road at which two women confront Hercules with the choice between an easy and a difficult path. See also Steiger 2002, pp. 260-263.

(For the serpents
that sought to twine themselves around me
I long ago crushed and tore apart.)
And the *Christmas Oratorio*:
Deine Wangen
Müssen heut viel schöner prangen,
Eile, den Bräutigam sehnlichst zu lieben.

In the cantata text, Hercules refers to the snakes that the goddess Hera sent to kill him shortly after his birth, but that the child strangled while still in the crib ("zermalmet" and "zerrissen": "crushed" and "tore apart").[113] This fierce, heroic accomplishment of the young Hercules would appear difficult to reconcile with the happy welcome awaiting the bridegroom! The last sixteen measures of the B section of both versions clearly show that Bach rethought the vocal part in function of the new affect (music example 12a and 12b). Hercules sings passionately, with many leaps in the melody (from thirds to octaves, with a striking seventh, followed by a pause on the word "zerrissen") and with an appropriately long note and a melisma on the word "lange" (music example 12a). In the *Christmas Oratorio* aria, the alteration is audible right from the first words: we hear a more flowing melodic line, with smaller intervals, reaching its dramatic high point on the 'shining' melisma of the word "prangen." The descending line on "lange" is replaced by a rising melody stretching from "eile" to "Bräutigam," expressing the urgency with which the bride hurries towards her betrothed. The instrumental parts, too, are adapted to the new mood (music example 12b).

It is astonishing how Bach succeeds in adapting previously composed music effectively in a new composition, using a minimum of means. These minimal changes are sometimes made at the expense of the original meaning, which is, for example sometimes linked to a particular word, but in general the composer convincingly manages to marry new text to old music. As an illustration, we may consider a detail from these arias. In the Hercules version, the sinewy instrumental bass line on the words "Denn die Schlangen…" (in their first appearance in the B section) can be interpreted as a representation of the writhing snakes. This type of text expression is, however, relatively neutral and not strictly linked to one concrete

---

[113] Hera hated Hercules because he was the son of her husband Zeus by another woman (Alcmene).

intention; thus the same bass figures, once transplanted, succeed on their own purely musical terms without any obvious symbolism. These very same notes in no way disturb the mood suggested by the words "Deine Wangen müssen heut...". Indeed, the rapid figures, now removed from their former context, nicely support the joy and happy expectation expressed by the words.[114] In that same B section of the aria, Bach is more than once confronted with a problematic setting of the words "zermalmet, zerrissen." At one point he goes beyond simply smoothing out the sharp edges of the melodic line, and composes a number of new measures of music in order to do justice to the new text (music examples 12a and 12b). Bach does not lose himself in the details: once he determines that a word has been sufficiently emphasized, he does not repeat the 'effect' ad nauseam but allows that word to take its place in the larger whole. In the music example, the long tone illustrating the word "lange" in the Hercules cantata is equally appropriate to the less neutral and emotionally-laden word "sehnlichst," where this drawn-out note is now literally a 'longing'. When the same word appears several measures later, it is no longer so clearly in the foreground, but is an integral part of a sentence in which rhythmic contrasts are avoided. In the B section of the aria, the word "sehnlichst" occurs four times; only once on the extended 'longing' note. Bach applies the same technique to the word "prangen," saving the melisma for the concluding climax (music example 12b); prior to this, the word draws little attention to itself.

This aria also nicely illustrates well how Bach creates a coherent musical structure on the basis of the material he uses in the instrumental ritornello. A closer analysis of the A section of this da capo aria offers an illustration (music example 13). The movement has a three-fold, symmetrical structure: the introductory ritornello is followed by an extended fragment for the voice, after which a repetition of the ritornello rounds off the A section. The ritornello itself is also very clearly organized, with sixteen measures divided into a first half of eight measures (1: mm. 1-8) and a second half of eight measures (2: mm. 8-16). The second half is an 'answer' to the 'question' posed in the first – a question suggested by the cadence on the dominant scale-step *e* at the end of the first half – as the tension is resolved by a return to the tonic *a* in the final measure. Each eight-measure phrase can likewise be divided into

---

114 Küster 1999, p. 412, compares the Hercules cantata and the *Christmas Oratorio* in terms of this issue. He writes that "the music is so 'ideal' that even after the remodeling, not all of the particular details necessarily need an interpretation."

two halves of four measures each (1a and 1b, 2a and 2b), the first half dominated by eighth-note figures, and the second by running sixteenth notes.

This orderly construction points in the direction of dance, an element that is always strongly present in Bach's (secular *and* sacred) music. The melody, too, has a strong dance-like character, with an agreeable melody and a rhythm laid down with precise regularity. In the secular context for which the original cantata was written – a celebratory work presented to the young Saxon prince by Bach's Collegium Musicum – this was a fitting style, which also nicely suited the Christmas mood associated with Christ's birth. The light-footed, *galant* and – for Bach – modern feel of this music is reinforced right from the beginning through the doubling of the vocal part by instruments (*all'unisono*), a procedure more typical of Bach's contemporary, Georg Philipp Telemann, than of Bach himself (mm. 16-24).[115] Bach (being Bach) does not maintain the arrangement for the whole aria, however; soon enough, he begins a dialogue between the instruments and the voice, through the exchange and redistribution of the musical ideas. In mm. 24-25, he inserts a supplementary measure for the words "den Schönsten," which then links directly to phrase 2a of the instrumental ritornello (mm. 25-29). The voice continues with the text and even with the recapitulation of the opening text, "Bereite dich, Zion" (m. 28), resulting in a more contrapuntally conceived vocal-instrumental duet. The main motif of the ritornello is clearly recognizable (mm. 29-34). The voice picks up the thread in m. 36 with a complete repetition of 1a and 1b (mm. 36-44), while the violins and oboe d'amore make reference to both 1 and 2 (sixteenth-note runs). Here again we encounter one of Bach's typical traits: he likes to take elements presented successively throughout a movement and stack them up for simultaneous performance. The all'unisono fragment in mm. 44-52, on the text of the first two lines, is comparable with mm. 16-24. Interestingly, Bach takes the rhythm of 1 (in eighth notes) and combines it with a melody inspired by 2 (reduced to its essential notes). The continuation also proceeds in parallel with m. 24 and following measures: the voice temporarily interrupts the ritornello (mm. 52-53) and the instruments join in with the alto voice at 2a. The combination of 1 in the vocal part and 2 in the instruments in mm. 62-72 proceeds similarly to mm. 34-44. The full instrumental ritornello completes the A section (mm. 72-88). In harmonic terms, the music begins to go places starting in m. 53, when the home key of A minor

---

115 Bossuyt 1995, pp. 45-46.

momentarily gives way to the subdominant D minor. A minor is re-established by m. 72. The tonic and subdominant keys are the two harmonic poles of this A section, in which Bach also continually touches on other tonal centers in order to spice up his harmony. The result is a constantly modulating musical story, with gradual – not abrupt – transitions, so that forays off the main harmonic path do not upset the flow of the musical story. The tightly-woven thematic coherence ensures that the listener never loses the way, as the material from the ritornello plays a part in every measure. This procedure has the effect of constantly reminding the listener of the text's leading idea ('prepare for the arrival of your beloved'), thus making a lasting impression on the congregation. The B section of the aria, which further develops the basic idea of the text, clearly carries on with the material from the ritornello (especially in the instrumental parts).

The following is a schematic overview of the A section of this da capo aria:
    mm. 1 - 16: Ritornello: 1a - 1b - 2a - 2b

    mm. 16 - 72: Ritornello + Vokaleinbau
        mm. 16 - 44:
            mm. 16 - 24: 1a - 1b (voice and instruments all'unisono)
            mm. 24 - 29: 2a (instruments)
            mm. 29 - 34: 1a (head motif)
            mm. 34 - 44: 1a - 1b in the voice; 1 + 2 (variant) in the instruments
        mm. 44 - 72:
            mm. 44 - 52: 2 ('reduction' in voices and instruments all'unisono)
            mm. 52 - 57: 2a (instruments)
            mm. 57 - 62: 1a (head motif, melodic variant, rhythmically identical)
            mm. 62 - 72: 2 ('reduction' in voice, recognizable in the instruments).
    mm. 72 - 88: Ritornello (= mm. 1 - 16).[116]

---

[116] Dürr 1967 provides a detailed analysis of this aria (pp. 29-32). Dürr, too, remarks that "in the whole A section – and this confirms our assertion concerning the thematic density of Bach's composing style – there is not one single measure which cannot be traced back to the thematic-motivic material found in the introductory ritornello."

5   Wie soll ich dich empfangen

> Wie soll ich dich empfangen
> Und wie begegn' ich dir?
> O aller Welt Verlangen,
> O meiner Seelen Zier!
> O Jesu, Jesu setze
> Mir selbst die Fackel bei,
> Damit, was dich ergötze,
> Mir kund und wissend sei!
>
> How shall I receive Thee,
> And how encounter Thee?
> O Thou, desired by all the world,
> O Thou, the jewel of my soul!
> O Jesus, Jesus, set down
> The torch beside me here,
> Whereby that which pleases Thee
> May be manifest and known to me!

In this chorale, a congregational song, Christian believers confirm their readiness to accept Christ's arrival, albeit with a degree of uncertainty and humble powerlessness, as suggested by the question with which it begins: "How shall I receive Thee, and how encounter Thee?" ("Wie soll ich dich empfangen, und wie begegn'ich dir?"). The first-person-singular perspective of the chorale is, as mentioned, characteristic of the poems of Paul Gerhardt. The 'ich' here stands as much for each individual (Christian) as it does for all of God's people taken together.[117]

Mention has already been made of the special care with which Bach reworks these chorales into a harmonically rich Cantionalstil movement in four voices. The first chorale is no exception to this approach. The first phrases (music example 3) are a perfect illustration of Bach's refined harmonic language in the chorale settings. Note especially the stepwise eighth-note motion in the alto part, with dissonant suspensions (third and fourth beats of m. 1, first beat of m. 3) or passing notes (m. 2, second beat). The first chord of m. 1 includes a seventh, a dissonant interval. A comparison of this with the harmony of the first phrase in the concluding chorale of the *Christmas Oratorio*, the same melody with a different text ("Nun seid ihr wohl

---

117   Blankenburg 1999, p. 44.

gerochen"), reveals how Bach carefully responds to the text and context in his harmonizations. The uncertainty, agitation and questioning with which *Wir soll ich dich empfangen* begins is reflected in the dissonant chord. In the first measure of the concluding chorale, the brilliant conclusion of the whole work (with a virtuoso trumpet part), the harrowing, dissonant seconds are nowhere to be found (music example 14). In some places, Bach pushes the complexity to the limit, as in the 'glowing' harmonic sequence on "mir selbst die Fakkel bei" (achieved partly through the use of the accidentals *b-flat, c-sharp* and *g-sharp*) (music example 3). This is the only place in the whole chorale in which the notes *b-flat* and *c-sharp* appear.[118]

Opinions differ concerning the question of why Bach chooses this melody precisely here. Some scholars are convinced that the two uses of this chorale, at the beginning and at the end of the *Christmas Oratorio*, link Christ's Incarnation with his Passion, since the same melody is used for the Passion chorale *O Haupt voll Blut und Wunden* (again a text by Paul Gerhardt), which appears several times in the *St. Matthew Passion*. Others dispute this intention. It is a fact that in contemporary theological writings and prayer books, the association between Christ's Incarnation and Atonement is prominent, so that listeners could easily have (consciously or not) made the link suggested by the use of this melody here. On the other hand, it can be argued that Bach could have made his intentions much clearer through the use of other, more obvious Passion melodies, and that the context of the eager anticipation of Christ's coming is not the right moment to arouse intimations of his later suffering.[119]

---

118 For a thorough discussion of Bach's chorale settings, see Seidel 1998.
119 This is the view taken by Leaver 1997b, pp. 98-99. The link is also disputed by Küster 1999, p. 477, who notes that this melody was often used during the Christmas season; Blankenburg 1999, pp. 46-47 concurs ("A reminder of Jesus' death would hardly be appropriate in the conceptual context of part I of the *Christmas Oratorio*, which deals with the inner preparation for the receiving of the savior"). Likewise, Dürr 1967, pp. 42-43 rejects the theory that the chorale looks ahead to Christ's suffering and death ("If Bach had wanted to foreshadow the Passion in his *Christmas Oratorio*, he could have chosen from a great number of less ambiguous Passion melodies which would have left no room for uncertainty"). All the same, it is worth mentioning the tradition, which went back to Luther's time, of stressing the connection between the 'theologia gloriae' and the 'theologiae crucis', between joy and suffering, victory and the cross. Luther made an analogy with music: "Cantare domino non semper est letari et gaudere, immo canticum novum est canticum crucis" ("Singing for God is not always about singing a song of happiness and joy; rather, a new song is a song of the cross"). This double theme of joy and suffering regularly appears in Bach's cantatas and Passions. In this connection see Geck 2000a, pp. 85-86. See also Steiger 2002, pp. 180-181, who in cantata IV draws attention to the link between Jesus' Naming, Circumcision and the Redemption by his blood (and thus his Passion; see below).

However this may be, this example is representative for the continuing discussions around the possible symbolic and referential intentions in Bach's vocal (and instrumental!) music.[120] Considering the generally accepted profundity of his work, both in terms of content and pure music, it remains enticing to 'discover' extraordinary connections and sometimes surprising associations. Leaving aside for the moment the question of whether such speculations have any bearing on a listener's experience of the music, it remains intriguing to attempt to explore the intellectual, social and theological movements influencing Bach's biography and oeuvre, in order to gain a deeper understanding of 'the Bach phenomenon' and the extent to which it was characterized by symbolism. Personally, I am drawn to the notion that Bach's music did indeed draw on different movements, although I am aware of the need to beware of certain, surely absurd interpretations, for instance in connection with number symbolism.[121]

6 Und sie gebar ihren ersten Sohn

> Und sie gebar ihren ersten Sohn und wickelte ihn in Windeln und legte ihn in eine Krippen, denn sie hatten sonst keinen Raum in der Herberge.

> And she brought forth her first-born Son, and wrapped him in swaddling clothes, and laid him in a manger, because there was no room for them in the inn.

---

120 See for example Marissen 1999 in connection with the Brandenburg Concertos.

121 Concerning the tricky area of number symbolism, see especially Tatlow 1991, who writes that (p. 1) "Bach's use of the number alphabet is a highly controversial topic, kept alive today by a few writers who continue to wrench ideas from their original context in Smend's theory and exaggerate them to the point of academic absurdity" (an accusation which can with justification be leveled at the controversial book by Van Houten 1985). (Friedrich Smend was one of the first scholars to look at this issue). For an overview of the subject, see M. Heineman, *Zahlensymbolik*, in Bach H, pp. 573-575. Other sources include Prautzsch 1980 and Prautzsch 2001, passim. In this connection, see also the article *Ästhetisches Bedeuten und symbolisches Meinen* in Eggebrecht 1994, pp. 136-142. The author writes here that "regarding number symbolism, three observations may be made: Caution, not completely demonstrable! – nevertheless possible – but not to be considered independent of the aesthetic significance!" (p. 139). This article originally appeared in H.H. Eggebrecht, *Bachs Kunst der Fuge - Erscheinung und Deutung*, reprint of the second ed. of 1985, Munich-Mainz, 1988. The research into the theological background to Bach's work has recently been collected in the monumental and richly documented study by Steiger 2002.

After the news of Christ's coming, the 'joyous expecting' (both ours and the mother's) and the preparations for welcoming the 'bridegroom,' comes the great moment itself: the birth, as related by Luke in one single verse (2:7), with the astonishing qualification that the child was laid in a manger, "because there was no room for them in the inn." This signals the beginning of the second half of the cantata, the second group of four movements, which sets out from a second element of the story and offers commentaries on it. The short recitativo secco has already been discussed above (music example 1).

Bach modulates to the key of G major by way of this recitative. A recitativo secco, which presents a linear narrative, without repetitions or a return to previous material, does not have a closed form: it drives the action forward, creating a bridge between the meditative moments, such as arias and chorales, which do follow particular, sometimes symmetrical (e.g., da capo in the aria) patterns, thanks to repeats and a unifying tonality. Recitatives function musically as modulating, transitional passages to other related keys. After the opening chorus in D major (no. 1), the recitatives (no. 2, secco, and no. 3, accompagnato) evolve through an ever-changing series of keys towards A minor, the key of the first aria (no. 4). The chorale (no. 5) is a melody in the *mi mode*. In terms of melody, the chorales of the 16th and 17th centuries obeyed different laws to those of Bach's time. One of Bach's aims was thus to adapt the harmonization of these older melodies to the more modern tonal system.[122] Essentially, this chorale revolves around the note *e* (the fifth from the preceding key of A minor). The recitative no. 6 provides a modulation to G major, the subdominant of D major (the central key of the whole cantata).

7   *Er ist auf Erden kommen arm*

>Er ist auf Erden kommen arm,
>>Wer will die Liebe recht erhöhn,
>>Die unser Heiland vor uns hegt?
>
>Dass er unser sich erbarm,
>>Ja, wer vermag es einzusehen,
>>Wie ihn der Menschen Leid bewegt?
>
>Und in dem Himmel mache reich
>>Des Höchsten Sohn kommt in die Welt,
>>Weil ihm ihr Heil so wohl gefällt,

---

122   We shall not pursue this purely technical question further here. For more, see Boyd 1999.

> Und seinen lieben Engeln gleich.
>> So will er selbst als Mensch geboren werden.
> Kyrieleis!

> He came to earth in poverty,
>> Who can fully extol the love
>> Which our Savior feels for us?
> To have mercy upon us,
>> Yea, who is capable of comprehending
>> How man's distress has moved Him so?
> And make us rich in Heaven,
>> The Son of God comes into the world,
>> Because it so pleases him to save it,
> And make us like His dear angels.
>> Thus would He Himself be born a man.
> Lord have mercy on us!

After the announcement of Christ's birth, Bach surprises us with an exceptional moment: a combination of a recitativo accompagnato with a chorale melody, supplemented by an instrumental trio of two oboes d'amore (the word "Liebe" appears right in the first phrase of the recitative) and basso continuo, which play an independent, concerted role. After an instrumental introduction, a ritornello, come four chorale phrases, each of which is interrupted by a fragment of accompanied recitative. The movement is rounded off with a repeat of the ritornello. The chorale phrases are a sort of Vokaleinbau within the instrumental refrain.

The tempo is *andante*, a moderate speed somewhere between slow and fast. The indication *arioso* is a term that was used for recitative accompagnato in Bach's time.[123] Today, the word *arioso* usually refers to fragments in recitatives in which a syllabic setting temporarily gives way to a more melismatic melodic line.

Both the chorale and recitative texts reflect on the difficult circumstances surrounding Christ's Incarnation. The chorale begins fittingly with the words "He came to earth in poverty" ("Er ist auf Erden kommen arm") and goes on to point to Jesus as the one who has pity on us and opens for us the kingdom of heaven. This is the sixth verse of Luther's Christmas song, *Gelobest seist du, Jesu Christ*. This

---

123 Küster 1999, pp. 120-121.

melody also provides the basis of Bach's similarly named Cantata 91, composed for Christmas Day, 1724.[124]

The soprano expresses the reaction of faithful Christians, while in the recitative fragments the bass interprets the divine events in question-and-answer form: "Who is capable of comprehending how man's distress has moved Him so?...The Son of God comes into the world, because it so pleases him to save it". In the first recitative fragment, the melody ascends in seconds to its melodic climax on the word "Heiland" ("savior"). In the second fragment, the burning question "Yea, who is capable of understanding how man's distress has moved him so?" ("Ja, wer vermag es einzusehen, wie ihn der Menschen Leid bewegt?") is underlined dramatically by dissonant intervals: a major seventh on "einzusehen" (*d - c-sharp'*) and a diminished seventh on "Menschen Leid" (*c-sharp - b-flat*). The series of modulations moves constantly 'downwards,' as if to indicate that God had to lower himself to the level of humanity. The central key of this movement, G major, is itself the *sub*dominant of D major. Through E minor, the relative minor of G major, Bach makes his way to D minor, as the harmonic line takes a drastic plunge downwards (the subdominant of G major is C major, the subdominant of C major is F major, D minor is the relative minor of F major).[125] From this 'harmonic low point,' the harmonies then begin to turn 'upwards' again, wending their way back to the starting point of G major.[126] In the third recitative fragment, the descent of the "son of the Highest into the world" is expressed by a descending line (over an octave from *d' to d*). In a surprising paradox, Bach stresses the word "Mensch" with an octave leap upwards (*e - e'*) in the bass's final intervention; a very strong effect, both through the size of the

---

124 In the chorale cantatas of the second yearly cycle, which Bach composed in Leipzig (1724-1725), the composer takes as his basic material a chorale with several verses, a number of which are cited literally, while others are paraphrased (and worked out musically as recitatives and arias). *Gelobest seist du Jesu Christ* is a chorale cantata in six movements, with the first and last verses of the cantata imported whole, and the others adapted. Verse six, which appears here in the *Christmas Oratorio*, becomes an aria in the cantata. The text, in which the original is clearly present, begins "Die Armut, so Gott auf sich nimmt, hat uns ein ewig Heil bestimmt, den Überfluss an Himmels-schätzen" ("The poverty that God has assumed, has bestowed on us eternal salvation, the brimming store of heaven's treasures"). Cf. Dürr 1999, pp. 49-56, on the chorale cantatas of the second Leipzig series and pp. 122-126, on Cantata 91. Bach also quotes the melody (and the text of the last verse "Das hat er alles uns getan") in the cantata for the Third Christmas Day, 1723, *Sehet, welch ein Liebe hat uns der Vater erzeiget* (BWV 64, see Dürr 1999, pp. 152-155). He included a version for organ in the *Orgelbüchlein* (BWV 604).

125 Blankenburg, 1999, p. 47, sheds light on this modulation.

126 For other examples of modulating 'descents' and 'ascents', see Steiger 2002, pp. 142-143 and pp. 338-340 (including examples from the *St. Matthew Passion*).

ascending interval and the sudden breaking off of the melody at this high point.[127] The effect is to fix our attention firmly on the extraordinary nature of this news. Unlike an aria, a recitative must make do with just one appearance of each word, allowing one chance for it to achieve its effect. This situation gives Bach the opportunity to demonstrate his musical-rhetorical talents. The fragment ends with the chorale statement of the text "Kyrieleis" and the flowing, instrumental ritornello. "Kyrieleis," an abbreviation of the Greek *Kyrie eleison* ('Lord, have mercy'), had been used from as early as the Middle Ages in German liturgical music as a recurring refrain at the end of a verse, a practice which resulted in the name *Leisen* for such pieces.[128] Bach's transformation of the chorale melody from a duple to a triple meter is seen by Blankenburg as a reference to the Holy Trinity, although the Trinity would not at first sight seem relevant to this context.[129]

8   Großer Herr, o starker König

> Großer Herr, o starker König,
> Liebster Heiland, o wie wenig
> Achtest du der Erden Pracht!
> Der die ganze Welt erhält,
> Ihre Pracht und Zier erschaffen,
> Muß in harten Krippen schlafen.

> Great Lord and mighty King,
> Dearest Savior, oh how little
> Dost Thou esteem earthly splendor!
> He who supports the whole world,
> And did create its splendor and beauty,
> Must sleep in a hard manger.

In this aria, which sings of God's majesty and glory, but also, as so often in this work, of how he humbled himself to the lowest estate ("...muß in harten Krippen

---

127 Blankenburg 1999, p. 48.
128 Such songs were often translations of Latin hymns, such as *Christ ist erstanden* (*Victimae paschali laudes*) and *Nun bitten wir den heiligen Geist* (*Veni Sancte Spiritus*). Luther's Easter song, *Christ lag in Todesbanden*, the basis of one of Bach's earliest cantatas (BWV 4, 1707/1708) is in fact a reworking of *Christ ist erstanden*, a text that first emerges in the 12th century. See Lipphardt 1960.
129 Blankenburg 1999, p. 48: "The change in the setting from a duple to a triple meter may be a reference to God's Trinity."

schlafen"), the oboe disappears in favor of the trumpet, the instrument that symbolized power and royal dignity. The movement returns to the cantata's opening key of D major, one of the most suitable keys for the trumpet. By choosing as his model an aria for the same scoring, taken from the celebratory cantata for the Polish queen, *Tönet, ihr Pauken*, Bach precluded the need for any substantial changes in this parody work. In that version, the aria begins with the words "Kron' und Preis gekrönter Damen, Königin!" ("Glory of all crowned ladies, O Queen!"). The poet needed only compose a fitting text.

In the instrumental ritornello, the solo trumpet plays a prominent role, together with the first violins, which, in contrast to the earlier version, are here complemented by a solo traverso. When the voice enters, the trumpet recedes to the background, allowing the vocal part to come through clearly.[130] The solo instrumental part is limited to *arpeggios* (broken chords), which themselves may be symbolically interpreted, since they are 'perfect' chords (d' - f-sharp' - a' - d"- a' - f-sharp' - d'), possibly suggesting God's perfection. Both the beginning of the ritornello in the continuo and the entry of the voice are marked by striking octaves, again 'perfect,' consonant intervals.[131]

Although this aria draws its powerful expression partly from the emphatic presence of the solo trumpet and from the melodic lines with their strong arpeggios, it is the syncopated rhythms (short - long - short, eighth-note - quarter note - eighth note) that drive the music resolutely forward right from the first measure. The bass voice entry on "Großer Herr" is 'on the beat,' but the syncopations soon enough become part of the vocal line as well ("o starker König"); this rhythmic shift continues to dominate the aria into the B section (beginning with the words "Der die ganze Welt erhält"). Bach is quite flexible in his handling of the da capo form of this aria: the recapitulation of the instrumental ritornello at the end of A, though the same length as the first time around (16 measures), is not an identical repetition, but a variant of the opening ritornello (the beginning is an inversion of the original), with a more pronounced trumpet solo. The recurrence of the striking syncopated rhythms ensures the sense of return.

Bach constantly varies the motivic cells, the material that helps to create coherence throughout the whole musical narrative. When texts are repeated, there is often both a previously heard element and new material, so that on the one hand

---

130 Küster 1999, p. 477.
131 Blankenburg 1999, p. 50.

the listener's expectations are satisfied (same text = same melody and/or rhythm), while on the other, the music continues to surprise. As an illustration, consider the four fragments from the A section of this aria, all of identical length (four measures = point of recognition), on the words "Großer Herr, o starker König," together with the instrumental parts. The common element is the descending broken chord on "Großer Herr," while the setting of "o starker König" is less predictable, as it varies each time. The instrumental accompaniment also varies:

- 1 is characterized by the D major arpeggio in the trumpet and short rhythmic accents in the strings (music example 15a),
- in 2 the trumpet is silent; the violins play a descending scalar figure and the continuo part is altered (music example 15b),
- in 3 the voice enters with syncopations, the violins have accents on the beat while the first violin plays a rising scalar pattern (music example 15c),
- in 4 the entry of the voice comes one measure after the beginning of the ritornello motif in the strings and the trumpet's arpeggio (instead of beginning together) (music example 15d).[132]

The trumpet motif with its arpeggio in music example 15a, which returns in a varied form in music example 15d, is remarkable for its characteristic 'signal character'. This was perhaps intended by Bach as a conscious reference to an existing fanfare motif, characterized by three eighth-note upbeats at the beginning and sixteenth notes (sometimes triplets) at the end. Bach cites the same melody even more clearly in the first movement of the Brandenburg Concerto No. 1 (BWV 1046) and in the string part of the Gavotte II from the Orchestral Suite No. 1 (BWV 1066). In royal and noble circles, which had a monopoly on the use of trumpets and horns as symbols of power, specific events were linked to particular signals, such as the arrival of a member of royalty, the beginning of a dinner, a military ceremony or a hunting party. Each signal had its own function and was not interchangeable with another. The motif quoted by Bach may have been a typical musical greeting, in this case for the electress of Saxony and queen of Poland. Within the context of the *Christmas Oratorio*, the symbolism is transposed to the welcoming of Christ as the "Großer Herr" and "Starker König."[133]

---

[132] Concerning this aria, Jena 1999, p. 60 writes: "As in the formation of crystals one sees on the one hand a high degree of adherence to laws with simple proportions, and on the other, organic blossoming in all its naturalness and randomness."

[133] Hofman 1995.

9   Ach mein Herzliebes Jesulein

>Ach mein herzliebes Jesulein,
>Mach dir ein rein sanft Bettelein,
>Zu ruhn in meines Herzens Schrein,
>Dass ich nimmer vergesse dein!

>Ah, my dearest little Jesus!
>Make Thyself a clean soft cradle,
>To rest in my own heart's shrine,
>That I may never forget Thee!

A chorale concludes the first cantata in the six-part cycle. The movement is in the Cantionalstil, but is here more festive and grand with its intermezzos for the three trumpets and timpani, as befits a cantata for Christmas Day. In this way, Bach links the conclusion with the joyful opening chorus. The brilliant instrumentation was undoubtedly more inspired by this consideration than by the text itself, an introverted and gentle verse from Luther's Christmas hymn, *Vom Himmel hoch da komm ich her*, which Bach also used in the first version of his Magnificat (BWV 243a): 'Ach mein herzliebes Jesulein...'.[134] Besides the trumpet motifs, the many octave leaps in the bass suggest the majesty and glory of God as king and ruler.[135]

---

134 Blankenburg 1999, pp. 50 and 52, refers to the mystical image of the heart as a shrine in which to preserve a treasure.

135 Jena 1999, p. 62. In connection with the opposition between the content of the text and its musical 'translation', Walter 1999, p. 60 writes that "the concluding chorale of the first part ...is surprising in its contrast between words and music: the majestic role of the trumpets and timpani do not seem to rhyme with the text "Ach mein herzliebes Jesulein, mach dir ein rein sanft Bettelein ...", a verse today often considered precious or mannered. However, precisely this lack of correspondence may perhaps be heard and interpreted as an attempt by Bach to artistically reconcile two opposites in his musical exegesis of Christmas (compare also "starker König" – "harte Krippe" in the preceding aria); in this way, the musical integration becomes a symbolic emblem of the religious content: from the most tender proceeds the most mighty."

II Sinfonia - Und es waren Hirten in derselben Gegend

Introduction

The theme of the second cantata is the annunciation of Christ's birth to the shepherds, as told by Luke in chapter 2, verses 8-14. The shepherds, tending their flock at night, are frightened by a bright light shining from the sky (vv. 8-9, recitative no. 11). An "angel of the Lord" calms their fears with the joyful news of the birth of Christ, the Savior (vv. 10-11, recitative no. 13). As a sign they will find a child in a manger (v. 12, recitative no. 16). This news is confirmed by a song of praise sung by "the heavenly host" who join the angel: "Glory to God in the highest and on earth peace, good will toward men" (vv. 13-14, recitative no. 20 and chorus no. 21).

On closer examination, the musical-dramatic possibilities of this annunciation are somewhat limited. A subject that would be well suited to a normal Sunday cantata, with its series of meditative reflections, is less suitable to a genre in which narrative and action are crucial ingredients. In order to increase the drama, the poet and the composer insert a scene anticipating the adoration of the shepherds, which is in fact the theme of the third cantata. Before the angel reveals the 'sign' intended to convince the shepherds (no. 16), they are exhorted in an aria – slightly prematurely – to hurry to see the child (*Frohe Hirten, eilt, ach eilet*, no. 15). The chorale *Schaut hin, dort liegt im finstern Stall* (no. 17) that follows the 'sign' also anticipates the events. It is immediately followed by another appeal to set off for Bethlehem, this time in a recitativo accompagnato (*So geht denn hin, ihr Hirten, geht*, no. 18); and there is more: at the end of the recitative there follows the invitation to sing a lullaby ("Lied der Ruhe") for the child which accordingly follows in the form of the aria *Schlafe, mein Liebster, genieße der Ruh* (no. 19). Only then does the story continue with the arrival of the heavenly host (no. 20) with their song of praise (no. 21). One has the impression that Bach was determined to create a suitable context for the two (admittedly superb) arias! The insertion of the shepherds' scene may also be related to the fact that the following cantata, on the adoration of the shepherds, was only performed in the Nikolaikirche and not in the Thomaskirche (see above). This solution allowed the congregation that only went to the Thomaskirche to hear practically the whole Christmas story. The added bass recitative *So geht denn hin ihr Hirten* (no. 18), thus functions as a sort of continuation of the story that does not appear in the Gospel text.[136]

Taking as the point of departure the basic pattern of four sections used in the first cantata in its pure form (1 Gospel text as secco recitative, 2 recitativo accompagnato, 3 aria, 4 chorale), but which Bach and his librettist apply quite flexibly, the structure of the second cantata is as follows (I here use the numbers 1 to 4 as a reference to the four basic sections):

I First phase

1 Gospel text: the shepherds in the field are overcome by the "glory of the Lord" and are "sore afraid" (*Und es waren Hirten*, no. 11), when an angel comes to comfort them with the news of the Savior's birth (*Und der Engel sprach zu Ihnen*, no. 13). Bach interrupts the two narrative fragments by a suitable chorale (*Brich an, o schönes Morgenlicht*, no. 12), which on the one hand alludes to the shepherds' fear ("You shepherd folk, be not afraid" in line 3) and on the other looks forward to the joyful message of the angel ("because the angel tells you that this weak infant boy shall be our comfort and joy," lines 4-6). In this way, the events are related to the present situation of the listeners, who need fear no longer, since Christ is the Comforter and bringer of peace ("und letzlich Friede bringen!": "and bring peace at last", final line).

2 Recitativo accompagnato (*Was Gott dem Abraham verheißen*, no. 14). This theological commentary underlines the notion that lowly shepherds were chosen as the first witnesses to the fulfilling of God's promise to Abraham. In Genesis 12:2, God promises the patriarch Abraham that "I will make you a great nation and I will bless you; I will make your name great and you will be a blessing." Abraham is considered the forefather of the Jewish people, from whom Christ descended. Because of his unconditional belief in the word of God, Abraham was named the 'father of all believers' by St. Paul and the Fathers of the Church.[137]

3 Aria (*Frohe Hirten, eilt, ach eilet*, no. 15): an appeal to the shepherds to make haste to go in search of the child (since they had been chosen as the first witnesses).

Gospel text (=1): before the chorale is sung, the 'sign' is announced by the angel who had been interrupted in no. 13: the child will be found wrapped in swaddling clothes, lying in a manger (*Und das habt zum Zeichen*, no. 16).

---

136 Küster 1999, pp. 478-479.
137 See 'Abraham', in Comay 2001.

4 This remarkable situation gives rise to the chorale *Schaut hin, dort liegt im finstern Stall*, both an explanation and a confirmation (no. 17): what was a feeding-trough for livestock in a dark stable has now become the bed for Mary's child.

In this first phase, Bach follows the basic four-part pattern, with the Gospel text distributed over three moments and interrupted, at the beginning, by a chorale.

II In a second phase, Bach goes further into the 'sub-plot' of the added shepherd's scene, which is not included in the Gospel version; here the shepherds are urged to sing a song "in a sweet voice" for the "son of the Most High." This phase is limited to moments 2 and 3: the accompagnato recitative (*So geht denn hin, ihr Hirten, geht*, no. 18) and the aria (*Schlafe, mein Liebster*, no. 19).

III The third phase picks up the thread of the Gospel story, acting logically as something of a climax to the added phase II: the shepherds' song (= the song of faithful believers) is followed by the song of praise of the heavenly host (*Ehre sei Gott in der Höhe*, no. 21), as described in the Bible (recitative *Und alsobald war da bei dem Engel*, no. 20). After this chorus, the content of which speaks for itself, the story is rounded off and Bach decides that no further interpretative commentary is necessary (a solo aria would be an anticlimax). A chorale, on the other hand, is most fitting at the end of a cantata, as the people embrace the religious message, and heaven and earth, angels and mortals join together as one jubilant congregation: *Wir singen dir in deinem Heer, Aus aller Kraft Lob, Preis und Ehr* (no. 23). Bach found it problematic to allow a chorale in Cantionalstil to follow immediately on the heels of another chorus, especially one so monumental, in motet style. To avoid this, he inserts a short secco recitative for the bass, exhorting the people to join with the heavenly choir (*So recht, ihr Engel, jauchzt und singet*, no. 22). This third phase contains the essential moments, 1 (nos. 20 and 21) and 4 (no. 23), preserved from the basic pattern and linked by moment 2, no. 22.

10 Sinfonia

The only instrumental movement in Bach's *Christmas Oratorio* is a masterpiece, pure and simple, which astonishes time and again with its spontaneous expressive power, together with a transparent and ingenious structure that beautifully reflects the central idea of the cantata. The term 'sinfonia' is used frequently by Bach for the instrumental introductions to cantatas. As mentioned, this sinfonia is a sort of pastorale, the high point in a long tradition in the vocal and instrumental repertoire of the Baroque. The standard ingredients of such pieces include: the key of G major, the siciliano rhythm in 12/8 (triplet rhythm) with dotted eighth notes, the parallel third and sixths, and the organ points ('drone bass line'). One of the best-known examples of the genre is the concluding movement from the Concerto grosso opus 6, no. 8 by Arcangelo Corelli. The subtitle of this concerto, "fatto per la notte di natale" ("written for Christmas Eve"), points to the function of this work as an instrumental composition intended for a church service. The last movement is labeled a "Pastorale ad libitum" ("Optional Pastoral"). Equally famous is the so-called 'Pifa' from *Messiah* by Georg Friedrich Handel. The word *pifa* refers to the Italian *piffero* (or *piffaro*), *piva* and *pifferari*. *Piffero* was the name given to a folk wind instrument, the shawm, played by shepherds. *Piva* refers to the bagpipe, a similar, popular instrument with a blowpipe. The *pifferari* were the Italian country folk who, according to ancient tradition, trekked to Rome on Christmas Eve to play their instruments in (supposed) imitation of the shepherds in the Bible.[138] While Corelli and Handel wrote their pastorales for strings only, Bach adds four oboes (two oboes d'amore and two oboes da caccia). Two traversos double the violin parts.

The characterization of Bach's sinfonia as 'heavenly' music is intended in all possible senses of the word. The strings symbolize the heavenly choir of angels, the oboes the earthly family of shepherds. The movement begins with the strings alone, followed by the winds alone, after which the two groups gradually join forces. Without words, but nonetheless very convincingly, the sinfonia explicates the essence of the Christmas message: divine glory enters into the realm of mortals and becomes part of it. Bach develops a specific motif for each of the two worlds: a rising motif in the violins for the heavenly (music example 16a) and a descending oboe motif for the earthly (music example 16b). The process of invention is clearly audible. Bach repeats this two times, creating a tripartite structure with the scheme A (mm. 1-23) - A' (mm. 23-44) - A" (mm. 44-63). A' and A" are varied repetitions of A. The third fragment is a shortened repetition of A. In harmonic terms as well, A" is a return to the home key of G major, which Bach reaches through that key's relative minor (E minor, at the end of A) and modulating explorations into related keys in A' (especially the dominant D major and its relative minor of B minor). The

---

138 Geller 1954. See Jung 1980 in connection with the pastorale in music (from antiquity up to Bach and Handel).

build-up and release of tension unfolds according to the 'classic tonal arch': establishment of the basic tonality (G major) with a first move away from the home key (to E minor) in the A section and more excursions and a climax in the central section A' (D major, B minor), and finally a relaxation and reconfirmation of the home key (G major) in the tonal reprise of section A".[139]

Typical for Bach's manner of working is the extreme economy of means: in the first measure of the violin motif he foreshadows the melody and the rhythm of the oboe motif, in which after one measure the rhythm of this violin motif is heard. In comparison with other pastorales – by Corelli and Handel, for instance – Bach avoids parallel thirds and sixths and demonstrates once again his unrivaled mastery of counterpoint, as all the parts function as equal partners (note the violin motif in the bass from m. 4, music example 16a). Moreover, he also avoids regular rhythmic patterns, a normal characteristic of the pastorale, through constant syncopation. The conclusion is a brilliant touch: the union between God and man is musically illustrated by the distribution of one of the motifs between the (heavenly) strings and the (earthly) oboes: the strings begin with the motif, the oboes take it over and then together they bring the movement to a close on the final chord.[140]

A similar pastoral atmosphere appears regularly in other cantatas by Bach, especially in connection with the Christian symbolism of Christ as the Good Shepherd, a form of imagery which draws on Psalm 23 ("The Lord is my shepherd, I shall not want")[141] and on the words of Jesus, who compares himself with a shepherd and the people with his flock (John 10:1-19: "I am the good shepherd"). Luke's Gospel relates the parable of the lost sheep (15:3-7). It is thus hardly surprising that the musical ingredients found here in the Christmas pastorale are also found in other cantatas: these include organ points, triplet rhythms, winds (oboe, including oboe d'amore as a symbol of the loving shepherd, traverso and also the recorder with its soft, sweet sound).[142] Examples are found in the cantatas *Du Hirte Israel, höre* (BWV 104) and *Ich bin ein guter Hirt* (BWV 85) for the second Sunday after Easter, as well as

---

139 For a detailed discussion of this tonal arch, see Bossuyt 2000, pp. 38-42.
140 Dürr 1967, pp. 38-40, provides a detailed analysis of this sinfonia. See also Blankenburg 1999, pp. 53-57.
141 See Tromp 2000, p. 148: "'Shepherd' is the normal honorary title for the king who watches over his *people*, leads them into battle, stands by them, protects them, feeds them and brings them safely home; the Psalm transfers this to the relationship between God and the *individual*." For more on the image of the shepherd, see Steiger 2002, pp. 254-259.
142 The recorder was often called the *flauto dolce*.

Erwünschtes Freudenlicht (BWV 184) and *Er rufet seine Schafen mit Namen* (BWV 175) for the Third Pentecost Day. On both feasts, the Gospel of the day is taken from chapter 10 of John (vv. 1-11 and vv. 12-16).[143]

11 Und es waren Hirten

> Und es waren Hirten in derselben Gegend auf dem Felde bei den Hürden, die hüteten des Nachts ihre Herde. Und siehe, des Herren Engel trat zu ihnen, und die Klarheit des Herren leuchtet um sie, und sie furchten sich sehr.

> And there were in the same country shepherds abiding in the field, keeping watch over their flock by night. And lo, the angel of the Lord came upon them, and the glory of the Lord shone round about them: and they were sore afraid.

The first narrative recitative (from Luke 2:8-9) begins with the typical melodic formula: a rising fourth followed by a further stepwise ascent of a third, as in the recitative no. 2 (*b - e' - f-sharp' - g'*). This formula gets the story going, often appearing at the beginning of a line, so that it also has a structural function. In the second verse "Und siehe, des Herren Engel" ("And lo, the angel of the Lord") Bach separates the words "Und siehe" from the rest through the use of an unexpected falling third, followed by a short pause: in this way he fixes our attention on the appearance of the angel. Only on "des Herren Engel" do we hear the leap of a fourth that immediately leads to the melodic high point of the whole recitative (*a'*), not by chance on the word "Herren."[144] The melody rises to a second high note (*g'*) on "Klarheit" ("glory"). Descending lines, melodic low points and strange combinations of intervals are reserved for passages with negative connotations: "Nachts" (the darkness of the night, or, in other words, the darkness of humanity before Christ's arrival) and "sie furchten sich sehr" (the shepherds, seized with fear). On "hüteten des Nachts," the melody descends from an *a* to the lowest note, a *d-sharp*, which constitutes a diminished fifth (an interval consisting of two successive minor thirds: *a – f-sharp – d-sharp*). The same process is repeated on

---

143 Dürr 1999, pp. 339-345 and pp. 413-420, and Jung 1980, pp. 205-212 (see also pp. 201-205 and pp. 212-218 for examples of the 'heavenly pastorale' – in which paradise on earth is invoked – in Bach's work, and the 'earthly pastorale' in the secular cantatas). The second Sunday after Easter is also known as *Misericordias Domini*, after the opening words of the traditional introit for the day. For an overview of the Lutheran liturgical calendar, see Wolff 2000, pp. 543-544.

144 Küster 1999, p. 479.

"leuchtet um sie" and "und sie furchten": *e' - c-sharp' - a-sharp* and *b - g-sharp - e-sharp*. The word "leuchtet" ("shone") is experienced as frightening. Exactly at this place the basso continuo intensifies the shepherds' fear through an outburst in quickly descending notes which once again span dissonant intervals: *g - G-sharp* (diminished octave) and *d - E-sharp* (diminished seventh).[145] This is coupled with a modulation from D major (major key = positive) to the relative minor of E minor (minor key = negative; music example 17). A diminished or augmented interval was known as a *saltus duriusculus*, a 'hard leap,' and often associated with negative affects (pain, suffering, sorrow, fear, weakness).[146]

12 Brich an, o schönes Morgenlicht

Brich an, o schönes Morgenlicht,
Und laß den Himmel tagen!
Der Hirtenvolk, erschrecke nicht,
Weil dir die Engel sagen,
Dass dieses schwache Knäbelein
Soll unser Trost und Freude sein,
Dazu den Satan zwingen
Und letzlich Friede bringen!

Shine forth, beauteous morning light,
And let the heavens dawn!
You shepherd folk, be not afraid,
Because the angels tell you:
That this weak infant boy
Shall be our comfort and our joy,
That He will also conquer Satan
And bring peace at last!

The chorale, *Brich an, o schönes Morgenlicht* interrupts the story to comment on the two contrasting situations: on the one hand the "Klarheit des Herren," the appearance of the light symbolizing the Incarnation of God, and on the other the fearful reaction of the shepherds, representing the apprehensive astonishment of the

---

145 Blankenburg 1999, pp. 56 and 58.
146 See especially Senden 1995. Steiger 2002 provides several striking examples from the St. Matthew Passion (the 'cross motif') and cantatas (pp. 14, 148, 217, 278 and 291).

faithful. The chorale text deals with both elements ("Brich an, o schönes Morgenlicht" – "Du Hirtenvolk, erschrecke nicht") and thus anticipates the calming words of the angel in recitative no. 13. The text is the ninth verse of the chorale *Ermuntre dich, mein schwacher Geist* (1641) by Johann Rist, sung on a melody by Johann Schop.[147]

In setting this chorale as a harmonically enriched and refined Cantionalsatz, Bach accentuates certain words with striking melodic turns, especially in the bass part, such as the octave ascent on "Himmel" (the second time on "Engel"), the descending 'saltus duriusculus' *a - d-sharp* (diminished fifth) on "schwache Knäbelein" ("weak infant boy"), the 'beseeching' chromatic rise on "soll unser Trost und Freude sein" ("shall be our comfort and our joy") (*g - g-sharp - a - a-sharp - b*) and the melisma on the verb "zwingen," which reflects the sense of 'coercion' ("dazu den Satan zwingen").

Bach may have inserted a choral fragment here in the interest of variety, since the cantata begins with an instrumental introduction. Otherwise, the first choral movement would have come only at no. 17, a chorale in Cantionalstil.

13 *Und der Engel sprach zu Ihnen*

> Und der Engel sprach zu ihnen: Fürchtet euch nicht, siehe, ich verkündige euch große Freude, die allem Volke widerfahren wird. Denn euch ist heute der Heiland geboren, welcher ist Christus, der Herr, in der Stadt David.
>
> And the angel said unto them: Fear not, behold, I bring you good tidings of great joy, which shall be to all the people. For unto you is born this day in the city of David a Savior, which is Christ the Lord.

In order to give added emphasis, the Evangelist announces the angel's message, "Und der Engel sprach zu ihnen," starting with a slightly altered formula: a rising fifth plus a third instead of a fourth plus a third (*a - e' - g'*, with "sprach" on the highest note). The solemnity of the angel's words, "Fürchtet euch nicht" ("Fear not"), in effect God's words (sung by a soprano), is underlined by the held chords in the strings. In the *St. Matthew Passion*, Bach reserves the recitativo accompagnato for the words of Christ (all other soliloquentes are given secco recitatives).[148] Especially

---

147 Dürr 1967, p. 45.
148 Platen 1999, p. 78. This is the simplest from of accompanied recitative, the so-called *ausinstrumentiertes Secco* (see footnote 67).

striking is the high note (*a"*) on "große Freude" (once again in the 'bright' key of D major). Octave leaps also draw attention to particular words: "der Heiland" (*d' - d"*) and "Christus, der Herr" (*f-sharp' - f-sharp"*). Here, "Der Herr" is set apart by short pauses before and after it.[149]

14 Was Gott dem Abraham verheißen

> Was Gott dem Abraham verheißen,
> Das lässt er nun dem Hirtenchor erfüllt erweisen.
> Ein Hirt hat alles das zuvor
> Von Gott erfahren müssen.
> Und nun muß auch ein Hirt die Tat,
> Was er damals versprochen hat,
> Zuerst erfüllet wissen.
>
> That which God promised Abraham,
> He now shows to the shepherd band,
> That it has come to pass,
> It was a shepherd who, a long time ago,
> First heard it from the lips of God.
> And now again a shepherd
> Learns that the promised act
> Is come to pass.

The bass voice in the accompagnato recitative *Was Gott dem Abraham verheißen* represents God's voice. In the choice of the shepherds as the first witnesses, the Old Testament promise to Abraham is fulfilled (see above). Abraham, too, was a shepherd, like David, from whom Christ descended.[150] The shepherds' instruments from the sinfonia, the two oboes d'amore and the two oboes da caccia, are strategically employed to accentuate certain words ("verheißen," "Hirtenchor," "erweisen," "zuvor," "müssen," "Hirt"). In the final phrase ("zuerst erfüllet müssen") they play on every beat of the (penultimate) bar, helping the recitative to build to a climax.

This fragment illustrates once again the highly varied melodic development in Bach's recitative, requiring the listener to pay close attention. The different phrases

---

149 Blankenburg 1999, p. 60.
150 Ibid.

follow constantly changing melodic patterns (music example 18).

1) "Was Gott dem Abraham verheißen": inverted-arch form (descending - ascending, from *d'* through *g* to *c'*), starting from a melodic high point on "Gott" (the exalted one, whom Abraham meets on the earth?).

2) "Das lässt er nun dem Hirtenchor erfüllt erweisen": again inverted-arch form, a major second lower (from *c'* through *f-sharp* to *b*), but strikingly interrupted by an octave leap *d - d'* on "erfüllt" (the promise is fulfilled: the octave is a 'perfect' interval). [151]

3) "Ein Hirt hat alles das zuvor vom Gott erfahren müssen": rising from *d* to *d'* with a melodic climax on "von Gott," which is reached through a major sixth leap (*e - c-sharp'*) on "zuvor." This phrase begins with the classic recitative formula, fourth plus third (*d - g - b*).

4) "Und nun muß auch ein Hirt die Tat": a rise from *d* to *d-sharp'*. The conclusion creates a strong tension through the augmented fourth *a - d-sharp'* on "die Tat."

5) "Was er damals versprochen hat": arch form (ascending - descending, *f-sharp - a - d-sharp*). The conclusion is also a point of tension (*d* raised to *d-sharp*) which calls for a resolution.

6) "Zuerst erfüllet wissen": descent from *c'* on "zuerst" to the final note on *e* (the resolution of the *d-sharp*) and a V-I cadence in the continuo. As the only phrase which simply descends, this line clearly rounds off the whole recitative.

15 Frohe Hirten, eilt, ach eilet

> Frohe Hirten, eilt, ach eilet,
> Eh ihr euch zu lang verweilet,
> Eilt, das holde Kind zu sehn!
> Geht, die Freude heißt zu schön,
> Sucht die Anmut zu gewinnen,
> Geht und labet Herz und Sinnen!

---

151 Cf. Steiger 2002, p. 55 (in connection with the cantata *Alles nur nach Gottes Wille*, BWV 72): "The word 'Alles' is also depicted in the octave in the continuo. The octave (Greek: *diapason*), embraces the totality of the tonal material and was in Bach's time a symbol of the totality – also called *potentia* – of God's omnipotence." Jena 1999, pp. 38-39 points out the octave on the word "Herrscher" in the introductory chorus no. 1, *Jauchzet, frohlocket!* and notes that "the octave, as the interval which contains all other intervals in it, is the symbol of dominion, which stretches out over the whole world and contains all things in it. 'Diapason' – literally 'through all (notes)' – was the name given by the ancients to this interval, which reaches the highest tone only after it has passed through all eight notes of the scale."

> Joyful shepherds, hasten, ah hasten,
> Lest you tarry too long,
> Hasten to behold the lovely babe!
> Go, the joy is all too sweet,
> Seek to acquire this grace,
> Go, and refresh both heart and mind!

In the joyful aria *Frohe Hirten, eilt, ach eilet*, an answer to the voice of God, one of the shepherds (a tenor) is speaking, urging his mates – now "joyful" rather than frightened – to hasten in search of the child (which, as noted, has not yet been named).[152] The basic affect of this aria is clearly "Freude" (the word is found in line 4). In the second aria from this cantata, *Schlafe, mein Liebster* (no. 19), this joyful theme returns: "Labe die Brust, empfinde die Lust, wo wir unser Herz erfreuen" (see no. 15: "die Freude heisst zu schön... labet Herz und Sinnen!").[153]

Frohe Hirten is a parody of the aria *Fromme Musen! Meine Glieder!* from the cantata *Tönet, ihr Pauken!*, with the same basic affect ("...Füllt mit Freude eure Brust" are the words of the fourth line in the original). The goddess Pallas Athena calls on the muses to sing a special song of joy – and not the "längst bekannte Lieder" ("long-familiar songs") – for the Polish queen.[154] As has repeatedly been emphasized, Bach took great care in creating his parodies (see the discussion of the aria *Großer Herr* in the first cantata). He changes the voice part, the instrumentation and the key: the vocal soloist has changed from alto to tenor, a traverso replaces the two oboes and the music is transposed down a fifth (from B minor to E minor, the relative minor of the central key of the second cantata).

Bach chooses a binary (A - B) rather than a ternary, da capo structure, no doubt with the intention of building up to a climax in the second part, in order to express the increasing feeling of joy: the tempo, already quick with its sixteenth notes (although with only limited melismas, in A) is driven forward by the many thirty-second notes and exuberant melismas on the words "Freude" and "labet" (in B). Thirty-second notes also appear in the ritornello in mm. 2 and 4. These rapid notes are not found in the secular cantata; in the *Christmas Oratorio*, the sense of joy is clearly that much more overwhelming. The structure of the ritornello is once again symmetrical and well-organized, with two sections of eight measures each,

---

152 Blankenburg 1999, p. 61.
153 Steiger 1981, p. 278.
154 Dürr 1999, pp. 907-908.

both divisible into four (2 + 2) plus four measures. In the first group of four measures, the third and fourth measures are sequential repetitions of the first two measures. The schematic pattern is slightly blurred by small, subtle alterations in the form of syncopations (mm. 2-3 and mm. 4-5) and upbeats (m. 10 and m. 12). Both the transparent structure and the ternary meter (3/8) suggest a dance movement. As soon as the voice takes over from the ritornello, it enters into an intriguing contrapuntal dialogue with the traverso, based on motifs taken from the ritornello. The shortened ritornello bridges the A and B sections ("Geht, die Freude heisst zu schön"). At the end of the highly virtuoso second section – note the brilliant traverso part – the movement is rounded off with a reprise of the ritornello, now condensed to eight measures.

16   *Und das habt zum Zeichen*

> Und das habt zum Zeichen: Ihr werdet finden das Kind in Windeln gewickelt und in einer Krippe liegen.

> And this shall be a sign unto you: Ye shall find the babe wrapped in swaddling clothes, lying in a manger.

The tenor, not the soprano, sings the angel's remaining words concerning the 'sign,' as recitativo secco. Bach likely found this information to be familiar enough, having been previously cited (see nos. 6 and 8), precluding the necessity to accentuate it with an accompagnato recitative. He likely also found it inappropriate to insert a fragment from the Gospel in direct speech as accompanied recitative between an aria and a chorale. And yet the message does not pass unnoticed. The recitative begins with the typical rising fourth (a - d'). Such an opening is often followed by a further rise by a third, which in this case would take it up to an *f-sharp'*. Bach, however, moves the *f-sharp* down an octave, no doubt with the intention of starting low to build up to a climax on the melodic peaks of "Windeln" (e') and – even higher – on "eine Krippe," which is reached through a saltus duriusculus, *g-sharp* - *f*. From here, the melody falls quickly to e, but then an octave lower, on "liegen" (with the typical falling fourth as a conclusion).

17 Schaut hin, dort liegt im finstern Stall

> Schaut hin, dort liegt im finstern Stall,
> Des Herrschaft gehet überall!
> Da Speise vormals sucht ein Rind,
> Da ruhet itzt der Jungfrau'n Kind.

> Behold! there in a dark stable lies
> He, who has dominion over all!
> Where once the ox sought to feed,
> There now rests the Virgin's child.

In the discussion of the general structure of the *Christmas Oratorio*, it was noted that the chorale *Schaut hin, dort liegt im finstern Stall* on the melody of *Vom Himmel hoch da komm ich her*, falls at the exact middle of the first cantata cycle (I-III). Reference was also made to the chorale's low register, in the key of C major, harmonically speaking the lowest point in the cycle: C major is the subdominant of G major (the key of the second cantata), which is in turn the subdominant of D major (the main key of the whole work). This modulation 'downwards' symbolizes the dark stable, which itself represents that world still mired in the darkness of sin. Two remarkable melodic lines in the bass, an ascent and a descent of a ninth, can be interpreted textually: the (positive) rise corresponds to "des Herrschaft gehet (überall)" and the (negative) fall to "Da Speise vormals sucht (ein Rind)". Christ humbled himself by lowering himself to the level of an animal's manger.[155]

18 So geht denn hin, ihr Hirten

> So geht denn hin, ihr Hirten geht,
> Dass ihr das Wunder seht:
> Und findet ihr des Höchsten Sohn
> In einer harten Krippe liegen,
> So singet ihm bei seiner Wiegen
> Aus einem süßen Ton
> Und mit gesamtem Chor
> Dies Lied zur Ruhe vor!

---

155 Blankenburg 1999, pp. 64-65.

> So go hence, you shepherds, go,
> That you may witness the miracle:
> And if you find the Son of God
> Lying in a manger.
> Then sing to him beside his cradle
> In a sweet voice
> And with a full choir
> This lullaby!

The second phase begins with no. 18, in which the shepherds' 'subplot' reaches its high point in their lullaby (no. 19). This leads directly and logically into the song of the heavenly host (nos. 20-21). An accompagnato recitative for bass, *So geht denn hin, ihr Hirten* provides the transition to the aria *Schlafe, mein Liebster*. The four oboes from the sinfonia establish their emphatic presence in this cantata, initially with intermittent chordal interventions, and then in continuous eighth notes starting from "so singet ihm." At this same turning point in the recitative, the continuo ceases playing the broken chords that supported the oboe accents,[156] and begins a continuous figure – significantly in quick triplets, a siciliano rhythm suggesting the rocking of the child. Once again, Bach presents a brilliant example of varying melodic lines (rising, falling, bow-form, inverted bow-form) with deviations from the normal scheme in order to make an interpretative point. The latter mostly take the form of high notes, including those on

- "ihr" (octave leap *d* - *d'*) in the phrase "das ihr das Wunder seht" (it is the shepherds who have been especially chosen to witness this miracle),
- "Höchsten Sohn" (climax after a rising line from *a* to *d'*),
- "ihm" ("so singet ihm"),
- "einem süßen (Ton)" (with a charming lowering of a *b* to a *b-flat* on "einem"),
- and at the end, both on "Lied" and on "Ruhe" (melody: *a* - *d'* - *g* - *c'* - *g*).

This brings us back from the deep regions of the previous choral to the key of G major, which holds sway for the rest of the cantata.

---

[156] Blankenburg's interpretation (1999, p. 65) of these seven broken chords in the basso continuo as a symbol of perfection (seven = perfect number) and thus of God's fulfillment, seems to me slightly far-fetched in this context (he does say "perhaps"!).

19 Schlafe, mein Liebster

> Schlafe, mein Liebster, genieße der Ruh,
> Wache nach diesem vor aller Gedeihen!
> Labe die Brust,
> empfinde die Lust,
> Wo wir unser Herz erfreuen!
>
> Sleep, my darling, enjoy Thy rest,
> Henceforth watch over the well being of all!
> Refresh the heart,
> Taste the joys
> That gladden our hearts!

A jewel in the crown of the impressive repertoire of arias composed by J.S. Bach is without a doubt the alto aria *Schlafe, mein Liebster*, a movement that at once puts to rest the persistent notion that the Thomascantor only wrote complex, inaccessible music. Indeed, the whole *Christmas Oratorio* refutes such a notion, as we have repeatedly seen (with its dance rhythms, symmetrical patterns, 'lighter' style...). Naturally (and fortunately), Bach never offers simplistic solutions, which would in any case run contrary to his conception of "well-appointed church music."[157] Even when he writes readily accessible music with tuneful melodies, it is generally supported by a contrapuntal, harmonic, rhythmic and structural finesse which gives it great profundity. An example of this is the ritornello of this aria. Unusually extensive (28 measures), the first section (a) has the character of a lullaby; the attractive melody is eminently singable, thanks to the spontaneity of its invention and its regular, four-measure phrases (4 + 4 + 4 + 4). The harmony is stable: in the first eight measures, the basso continuo constantly repeats the note g, in octave leaps, imitating the rocking of the child, a folk tradition in Germany at Christmas time (known as *Kindleinwiegen*) (see music example 8, the first vocal fragment, accompanied by the first section of the ritornello in the string part). In his *Historia der Geburt*, Heinrich Schütz adds the following words to the three 'intermedii' in which the angel speaks (to the shepherds in intermedium I, to Joseph in VII and

---

[157] In 1730 Bach produced a much-cited document, 'Kurze, iedoch höchstnöthige Entwurff einer wohlbestallten Kirchen Music' ('A short yet highly necessary outline for well-appointed church music'), his protest against the lack of resources for performing his (very demanding) music. For a translation of this interesting document, see NBR 1998, pp. 145-151.

VIII): "in which the rocking of the baby Jesus is heard" ("worunter bisweilen des Christkindlein Wiege miteingeführet wird"). The bass is characterized by an ongoing two-note figure that represents this *Kindleinwiegen*.[158]

In the b section of this ritornello, the dancing accents continue in the bass part, while the strings and oboes now develop a more complex melody with irregular syncopations, a less stable harmonic center, and a structure that no longer fits the symmetrical four-measure pattern (this second section, which starts at m. 16, is 13 measures long) (see music example 9, where the second section of the ritornello accompanies the first vocal fragment). The relatively lighthearted opening apparently did not provide Bach with enough material to flesh out an extensive aria, since he complements it with a more reserved second section – as counterbalance – which goes on to function exclusively as 'foreground'.

The A section of this da capo aria is ordered as follows:
1 Ritornello: a (mm. 1-16) - b (mm. 16-28)
2 Vokaleinbau I: on the basis of a (mm. 28-56, see music example 8)
3 Ritornello: b (mm. 56-69)
4 Vokaleinbau II: on the basis of a and b (mm. 69-96; concluding fragment in music example 9)
5 Ritornello: a (mm. 97-112).

A comparison with the original, the aria *Schlafe mein liebster* from the Hercules cantata (BWV 213), again reveals a different scoring and a new key. In the original, *Wollust* (Pleasure), in the form of a soprano (with strings), attempts to rock Hercules to sleep with her seductive song, tempting the unwitting hero down her path.[159] The key here is B-flat major. In the Christmas cantata, the mood is more introverted and sweeter, partly through its lower pitch (in G major, with alto solo) and the addition of four pastoral oboes that play together with the strings, plus a traverso whose soft timbre doubles the vocal part in the upper octave. Bach also develops several syllabic fragments in the B section into melismatic passages, to illustrate the word "erfreuen," with the longest melisma reserved for the climax at the end. The composer creates a beautiful effect by having the instruments fall silent during this final melisma, with only the voice and the traverso left over; the basso continuo reappears at the end for the cadential formula.

---

158 Bossuyt 1991, p. 143.
159 Dürr 1999, p. 902, speaks of the "enchanting character of the aria."

The entry of the voice part on the words "Schlafe mein liebster, geniesse der Ruh" is irresistible: while the instruments play the rocking first part of the ritornello, the voice descends from g' to its lowest register b on successive long notes expressive of sleep and rest. Bach employs this motif just one time, as the voice joins in with the ritornello theme when the text is repeated. Because it appears only once, the expressive power of the words is that much stronger; this detail, mainly because of its link with the accompanying ritornello melody, thus becomes a logical part of the whole and not simply a fleeting effect (music example 8).

In the B section, only the first oboe d'amore continues to play (doubling the first violin), as the other wind players fall silent. A reduction of forces was a common practice in the central section. All attention is focused on the word "erfrueuen," which is worked out melismatically (five times), ending with the above-mentioned climax. The predominantly melismatic setting of this whole movement shows how Bach is able to meaningfully integrate such detailed expression: melismas appear on the word "labe," somewhat less expansively on "erfreuet" and more discreetly still on "empfindet." The melismatic "erfreuet" is, of course, an essential element of the whole section, helping to create the appropriate atmosphere.[160]

As before, Blankenburg ascribes the words of this aria for alto voice to the Virgin, the heavenly mother (doubled by the flute, which in the sinfonia plays together with the 'heavenly' violins), as well as the 'voice of belief'. The angels (strings, flute), Mary (alto voice), and the shepherds (oboes) join together for this berceuse, which thanks to a remarkable detail, exudes a character different from that of the 'pleasure aria' as it attempts to ensnare Hercules: in the first phrase of the model, *Wollust* springs upwards on an emphatic sixth to the word "Ruh" ("rest"), while in the sacred context, the melody continues to descend stepwise to a point of rest on a *c-sharp'* (music example 8).[161]

20 *Und alsobald war da bei dem Engel*

> Und alsobald war da bei dem Engel die Menge der himmlischen Heerscharen,
> die lobten Gott und sprachen:

---

[160] Blankenburg 1999, p. 67, notes: "Although in the central section he creates a sense of relaxation through the melismas on the word 'erfreuen,' a certain restraint nonetheless defines the total character of the aria."

[161] Blankenburg 1999, p. 19.

> And suddenly there was with the angel a multitude of the heavenly host, praising God and saying:

In the recitative announcing the angels' song of praise (Luke 2:13), the vocal part fittingly remains in the highest regions: the tenor begins on an *a* with a variant of the usual fourth-plus-third formula (*a* - *c-sharp'* - *d'* - *e'* - *a'*), bringing him in quick order to the high *a'* on "da" ("in that place"). The second highest note is a *g'* on "Menge" and "Heerscharen." This recitative descends no further than its opening note of *a*. All is song and jubilation (note the major third *a* - *c-sharp* at the beginning). The Bible verse brings the story back to the Gospel story and begins phase III of the cantata, which has in fact been reduced to moments 1 (Gospel story) and 4 (concluding chorale), linked by a short recitative as transition.

21   Ehre sei Gott in der Höhe

> Ehre sei Gott in der Höhe
> Und Friede auf Erden
> Und den Menschen ein Wohlgefallen.
>
> Glory to God in the highest,
> and on earth peace,
> good will toward men!

All the performers now join forces for the angelic choir's song of praise, *Ehre sei Gott in der Höhe*, words that would later form the opening of one of the standard elements of the mass, the Gloria (Luke 2:14). This first turba chorus in the *Christmas Oratorio* is a brilliant composition in motet style, in which the vocal and instrumental ensembles unite to let God's praise resound: the four-voice choir and the instruments from the pastoral sinfonia, strings, two traversos, the four oboes and basso continuo. Bach clearly indicates the tempo (and the corresponding affect): *vivace*. In contrast to the concerted choruses, such as the opening chorus *Jauchzet, frohlocket*, the instrumental parts in a chorus in motet style are not treated independently (or in any case less so); they are not equal partners with the voices and do not play a ritornello but are generally limited to doubling the vocal parts (as in the Kyrie from the *Missa brevis* BWV 236).[162]

---

162 Bossuyt 2000, pp. 29-32.

Bach divides the text into three fragments, each of which is worked out differently, a typical procedure in a motet 'in stile antico':

A: "Ehre sei Gott in der Höhe,"
B: "Und Friede auf Erden,"
C: "Und den Menschen ein Wohlgefallen."

Common to the three fragments is the contrapuntal approach, tending to free counterpoint in B, mostly imitative in A and strictly imitative in C. After a first presentation, Bach repeats the three fragments in reduced form: A' - B' - C'.

The musical construction is highly ingenious. The basic motif of A is a rising fourth followed by stepwise motion back to the beginning note (in the soprano: *d"* - *g"* - *f-sharp"* - *e"* - *d"*). This motif is combined with a melismatic line without a strong thematic character (tenor and bass at the beginning). The choir is supported by a busy basso continuo part, which rises in an even eighth-note movement from G to g (mm. 1-5, music example 19) and then in a similar movement (with variations) continues to a concluding cadential formula in mm. 8-9. This bass line is repeated two times, each on another scale-step, starting respectively on *d* (mm. 9-16) and *e* (mm. 17-24). The strings and the winds accentuate the choir, providing an instrumental superstructure made up of two-note motifs on separate notes, played staccato. The whole musical complex consists of a layering of three elements:

(1) the bass with running eighth-note (and sometimes sixteenth-note) figures,
(2) the contrapuntal chorus,
(3) the staccato motifs (suggesting the beating of the angels' wings?).

In the short B fragment "Und Friede auf Erden," Bach creates a dynamic nuance by indicating a *piano* and marking the basso continuo *tasto solo*. The decrease in volume and the reduction of the continuo to single notes (without chords above them)[163] are suggestive of peace. The basso continuo falls silent, as it were: its contribution is now limited to three long notes. Rather than developing a clearly-defined motif, the melody of the vocal parts proceeds resolutely downwards (God's peace descending to earth). The staccato in the instruments gives way to legato.[164] The oboes play a supporting role with soft, flowing chords in gentle syncopation. All

---

163 *Tasto solo* means 'only the key': the continuo player plays only the written notes, without the usual filling out of the implied chord.
164 The interpretation of Blankenburg 1999, p. 69, that the three-note motifs in the strings and the flutes symbolize the Trinity does not seem relevant to me in this context.

elements contribute to portray the blessed rest of God's peace: dynamics (piano), phrasing (legato), continuo (long pedal notes played tasto solo), slow-motion suspensions (in the oboes).

All the more striking, as a result, is the contrast with C: the dynamics become *forte*, the bass line returns to its continuous running eighth notes, the vocal parts, in strict imitation, urge the tempo forward with long sixteenth-note melismas (on 'Wohl- gefallen'). The violins and flutes double and strengthen the voices. The oboes complete the harmony with syncopated chords. The choir parts set out from one well-defined basic theme (music example 20) which remains constantly present and is developed through the melismas.

The A-B-C structure is now repeated in shortened form (A' – B' – C'; in A' the continuo part is reduced to one presentation of the eight-measure phrase).

Each of the three sections is based on a different musical principle:

A: passacaglia,
B: organ point
C: fugue.[165]

The *passacaglia* is a form in which an instrumental bass theme, usually consisting of two, four or eight measures, is constantly repeated, while the superstructure above it changes. Bach wrote a Passacaglia for organ (BWV 582, in C minor), in which a theme of eight measures appears 21 times.[166] In B the structural basis is the long note in the bass, known as a *organ point* or *pedal point*. The omnipresent, fugally worked-out theme provides the tight structure characterizing C.

---

[165] Dürr 1999, p. 151. See also Blankenburg 1999, pp. 67-74.

[166] For the conclusion of this work, Bach provided a fugue, the theme of which is the first half of the passacaglia bass line. See Kube 1999, pp. 705-707. The passacaglia belongs to a type of composition known as '*basso ostinato* variations'. In vocal works, a stepwise figure descending (diatonically or chromatically) through a fourth often serves as the basis for such variations. This motif is usually associated with the genre of the *lamento*. Well-known examples include the lament of the dying Dido from the opera *Dido and Aeneas* by Henry Purcell and the opening chorus from Bach's cantata, *Weinen, klagen, sorgen, zagen* (BWV 12), which the composer later appropriately parodies in the 'Crucifixus' (relating Christ's death on the cross) from the Credo of the *B minor Mass*. The 'negative' descending line of this motif is the opposite of the 'positive' line in this *Christmas Oratorio* passacaglia, where it rises through a complete octave.

22 So recht, Ihr Engel

> So recht, ihr Engel, jauchzt und singet,
> Dass es uns heut so schön gelinget!
> Auf denn! wir stimmen mit euch ein,
> Uns kann es so wie euch erfreun.
>
> Then fittingly, you angels, rejoice and sing
> That this day turned out so well for us!
> Up then! We shall join your song,
> That can please us as much as you.

The autograph score of the *Christmas Oratorio* is a highly instructive document, allowing us a glimpse over Bach's shoulder during the composition process. The manuscript of the chorus *Ehre sei Gott* includes a number of corrections, suggesting almost certainly that the movement is an original composition, and not a parody (there is, in any case, no known model).[167] At first sight, the short recitative, *So recht, Ihr Engel*, linking the angels' chorus with the final chorale, would appear little more than a filler, providing the necessary transition between two stylistically completely different choral sections, which would not normally be allowed to rub shoulders. However, Bach clearly considered this to be somewhat more than a trifling moment to be dealt with summarily. His autograph score reveals the great care with which he ensured that this jewel should be given ideal form and expression. He originally conceived the movement as a recitativo accompagnato, like all the commenting recitatives. The staves for the instruments have been drawn up, the clefs and measures notated. However, he subsequently crossed out the staves and wrote a secco recitative for the bass, the voice which in this cantata is prominent as the representation of God himself. This is a radical intervention, making the instrumental accompaniment to the concluding chorale that much more striking – and consequently that much more effective. The voice part has been polished up and adapted several times. The last change was the shifting of the conclusion from its original key of E minor to the central key of the cantata, G major, which he apparently found to be more appropriate between two jubilant movements for choir in G major.[168]

---

167 Blankenburg 1999, p. 67.
168 Dürr 1967, pp. 13-14 and Blankenburg 1999, p. 74.

So recht, Ihr Engel begins with the classic recitative formula of a rising fourth plus a third (the latter here as a direct interval, *d - g - b*). A first accent follows on "jauchzt," with its high *d'*.[169] The same *d'* is repeated on "schön" and then quickly surpassed by the *e'* on the exclamation, "Auf denn!" This new verse thus begins, in function of the expression, with an inversion of the basic formula (descending interval). The continuation takes up the formula again: *e - a - b - c'* ("wir stimmen mit euch ein"). Each note, each nuance is placed to perfection.

23   Wir singen dir in deinem Heer

> Wir singen dir in deinem Heer
> Aus aller Kraft Lob, Preis und Ehr,
> Dass du, o lang gewünschter Gast,
> Dich nunmehr eingestellet hast.

> We sing to Thee amidst Thy host:
> Praise, honor and glory with all our might,
> That Thou, O long-desired guest,
> Hast now at last appeared.

The concluding chorale, *Wir singen dir in deinem Heer*, is the united confirmation of the coming of Christ to earth as the long-expected guest ("o lang gewünschter Gast"). It is the second verse of the chorale *Wir singen dir, Emmanuel* on a text by Paul Gerhardt, here sung to the melody *Vom Himmel hoch da komm ich her* (see no. 17).[170] Bach originally planned a Cantionalsatz with a 4/4 time signature, but changed this to 12/8 with its four triplets per measure.[171] In so doing, he makes a direct reference to the pastoral sinfonia, a clever turn, made even more ingenious by the addition of two independent instrumental parts that quote the two motives from the sinfonia. Between the chorale phrases, the oboes and flutes play the shepherds' motif (in the sinfonia the flutes doubled the strings in the angels' motif!). The angels' motif appears in the basso continuo as a foundation for the chorale melody, which is played by the violins. What was announced in the sinfonia, namely

---

169   The first version accentuated "Engel" on this same high note. A facsimile of this page from the autograph is found in Dürr 1967, between pp. 15 and 17 (ill. 4) and Blankenburg 1999, p. 72.
170   Dürr 1967, p. 45.
171   Dürr 1967, p. 15.

the union of God and man, has now been completed: heaven and earth are reconciled in Christ's Incarnation, and Redemption is close at hand. The (heavenly) traversos can now join freely with the (earthly) oboes.[172]

---

172 Blankenburg 1999, p. 75 formulates this as follows: "What in the beginning of Part II was at first only hinted at now appears here as fact. Thus the chorale movement can conclude with the united flutes and oboes; the heavenly and earthly sounds have now thoroughly found one another. The Christmas message cannot be presented any more clearly than this."

III Herrscher des Himmels

Introduction

The third cantata, written for the Third Christmas Day (December 27), completes the first triptych. Bach returns to the scoring of the first cantata, with strings, woodwinds (traverso and regular oboe), trumpets and timpani. The key is once again D major. The central event is the adoration of the shepherds, based on Luke 2:15-20. Bach divides the narrative over three secco recitatives:

(1) v. 15: the shepherds prepare to depart (*Und als die Engel*, no. 25), followed by the turba chorus of the shepherds (*Lasset uns nun gehen*, no. 26)

(2) vv. 16-19: the arrival at the stable and the adoration of the shepherds (*Und sie kamen eilend*, no. 30)

(3) v. 20: the shepherds return to their fields (Und die Hirten kehrten wieder um, no. 34).

With these three sections of narrative as its basis, this cantata proceeds, like the previous one, in three phases. We can again identify the four-part structure in order to gain an overview of each phase.

The cantata begins with an introductory song of praise, a chorus addressed to the "Herrscher des Himmels," in a continuation of the jubilation with which the previous cantata ends (*Herrscher des Himmels erhöre das Lallen*, no. 24).

I First phase:

1 Gospel text: the shepherds decide to set out for Bethlehem (recitative *Und als die Engel* and chorus *Lasset uns nun gehen*, nos. 25 and 26).

2 Recitativo accompagnato (*Er hat sein Volk getröst'*, no. 27): the completion of the blessed event is once again announced. The Comforter and Redeemer has come to earth and the shepherds are urged to go and behold him ("seht, Hirten ... geht, dieses trefft ihr an").

The aria, normally expected here, trades places with the chorale (3 and 4 thus reverse order).

4 The chorale verse Dies hat er alles uns getan (no. 28) fits perfectly with the preceding recitative, echoing the words of the bass soloist: "Seht, Hirten, dies hat er getan." The Incarnation, as a sign of God's love ("Sein groß Lieb zu zeigen an") is transposed to our own situation: not only the shepherds but we too, the whole of Christendom ("Des freu sich alle Christenheit"), participate in God's loving intervention.

3 The aria *Herr, dein Mitleid, dein Erbarmen* (no. 29) is a duet for soprano and bass which meditates further on God's compassion and mercy for humanity, revealing him afresh as a faithful father ("Deine wundersame Triebe machen deine Vatertreu wieder neu").

II Second phase:

1 Gospel text: the shepherds arrive at the stable and find Mary, Joseph and the child. They go forth to tell the world what they have seen, and all are amazed. Mary cherishes the miracle of Jesus' birth in her heart (*Und sie kamen eilend*, no. 30).

Once again, Bach changes the basic pattern: the recitativo accompagnato 2 is preceded by the aria 3 for alto, *Schließe, mein Herze* (no. 31), in which the miracle of the birth is held in the Christian's heart to strengthen a weak faith ("Lasse dies Wunder ... immer zur Stärke deines schwachen Glaubens sein").

2 Recitativo accompagnato (*Ja, ja, mein Herz soll es bewahren*, no. 32): a personal answer to the aria: "Yes, my heart shall guard those certain proofs."

4 Chorale *Ich will dich mit Fleiß bewahren* (no. 33): the individual's powerful affirmation. The first-person singular "ich" represents the faithful congregation which confidently takes part in this divine miracle and chooses to live ("Ich will dir Leben hier") and die ("... dort im andern Leben") with Jesus.

III Third phase:

1 Gospel narrative: verse 20 is a concluding phrase which needs little commentary: the shepherds return to their flock, praising God for what they have been shown (*Und die Hirten kehrten wieder um*, no. 34).

4 This is immediately followed by the chorale *Seid froh dieweil* (no. 35), which again expresses the joy that all Christians share with the shepherds.

As a conclusion to this festive, three-part cycle for the three days of Christmas, Bach calls for a reprise of the cantata's opening chorus (no. 24).

24   *Herrscher des Himmels*

> Herrscher des Himmels, erhöre das Lallen,
> Laß dir die matten Gesänge gefallen,
> Wenn dich dein Zion mit Psalmen erhöht!
> Höre der Herzen frohlockendes Preisen,
> Wenn wir dir itzo die Ehrfurcht erweisen,

> Weil unsre Wohlfahrt befestiget steht!
>
> Ruler of Heaven, hear our murmurings,
> Let these faint songs find favor with Thee,
> When Thy Zion exalts Thee with psalms!
> Hear our hearts' exultant praises,
> When we now render homage to Thee,
> Because our welfare is assured.

The choral introduction to this cantata, *Herrscher des Himmels*, is a parody of the concluding chorus *Blühet, ihr Linden in Sachsen* from the cantata *Tönet, ihr Pauken*, the opening chorus of which was the model for *Jauchzet, frohlocket!* Once he found a suitable text, Bach needed to make few changes. The music speaks directly in triumphant and extroverted tones, as the composer does not aim to impress us with his learned musical techniques – excepting perhaps the imitative counterpoint which was his stock in trade – and the construction is comprehensible and extremely symmetrical.

The six-line poem is divided into two times three verses: (I) "Herrscher des Himmels…" and (II) "Höre der Herzen…". Each of the halves is identically set as a concerted passage for choir: after the tenors, the sopranos and the altos have each presented a line in free imitation, the choir repeats the three verses in chordal declamation. This results in the following structure:

Section I (lines 1-3):

1 Ritornello: a sprightly, dance-like ritornello (the time signature is 3/8) of 16 measures, divided into 8 + 8 measures, each of which is divided in turn into 4 + 4 measures (mm. 1-16).

2 Vocal fragment:

- Tenor: "Herrscher des Himmels, erhöre das Lallen" (entry in m. 17)
- Soprano: "Laß dir die matten Gesänge gefallen" (entry in m. 21)
- Alto: "Wenn dich dein Zion mit Psalmen erhöht!" (entry in m. 25).

Each voice has its own theme, which is always related to the ritornello. The instruments tend to remain discreetly in the background.

3 Ritornello with Vokaleinbau: the ritornello is repeated complete and unchanged, while the choir reprises the three lines in chordal declamation (mm. 33-48).

Section II (lines 4-6):

1 Ritornello: the complete ritornello, slightly altered (mm. 49-64).

2 Vocal fragment:
- Tenor: "Höre der Herzen frohlockendes Preisen" (entry in m. 65)
- Soprano: "Wenn wir dir itzo die Ehrfurcht erweisen" (entry in m. 69)
- Alto: "Weil unsre Wohlfahrt befestiget steht" (entry in m. 73).

3 Ritornello with Vokaleinbau: see section I, with the ritornello in the slightly altered, section-II version (mm. 81-96).

25 Und da die Engel von ihnen gen Himmel fuhren

> Und da die Engel von ihnen gen Himmel fuhren, sprachen die Hirten untereinander:

> And it came to pass, as the angels were gone way from them into Heaven, the shepherds said to one another:

This short secco recitative (one half-verse from Luke) begins with an inverted version of the usual opening formula (descending fourth plus a third: *e' - b - g-sharp*), so that the first leap upwards, a seventh on the word "Himmel" (*e - d'*) is that much more striking. The two notes of the final cadential V-I formula (*e - a*) are divided between the end of the recitative and the beginning of the shepherds' chorus, which accordingly follows without interruption.

26 Lasset uns nun gehen gen Bethlehem

> Lasset uns nun gehen gen Bethlehem und die Geschichte sehen,
> die da geschehen ist, die uns der Herr kundgetan hat.

> Let us now go even to Bethlehem, and see this thing which is come to pass,
> which the Lord hath made known to us.

The words of the shepherds, urging one another to set out for Bethlehem to see what has taken place there, are presented in an enthusiastic chorus in motet style. This impetuous movement has been discussed briefly above. The contrapuntal sixteenth-note figurations in the violins and the two traversos catch the attention here, in what is likely a musical depiction (as noted above) of the shepherds' restlessness and haste (music example 2). In the process, the movement modulates from the opening key of D major to the dominant A major (and no longer to the 'negative' subdominant mood, as in the second cantata); this is thus a move 'upwards,' in a positive direction. In the second fragment "Und die Geschichte sehen ...", Bach modulates further afield to C-sharp minor, the relative minor of the secondary dominant, E major. The ensuing recitative, which follows directly out of this chorus, begins in this key of C-sharp minor (the final cadence is again divided between the end of one movement, 27, and the beginning of the next, 28).

27 Er hat sein Volk getröst'

> Er hat sein Volk getröst',
> Er hat sein Israel erlöst,
> Die Hülf aus Zion hergesendet
> Und unser Leid geendet.
> Seht, Hirten, dies hat er getan;
> Geht, dieses trefft ihr an!
>
> He has comforted his people,
> He has delivered His Israel,
> And sent help out of Zion
> And ended our suffering.
> Behold, shepherds, this He has done;
> Go, this is what you shall find!

The two traversos from the chorus no. 26 continue into this accompanied recitative for bass, which functions as something of a continuation of this voice's 'character' in the previous cantata. This 'role' is rounded off here in a final appeal to the shepherds to go and behold the Comforter and Redeemer: "Seht, Hirten, dies hat er getan, geht, dieses trefft ihr an."[173] The traversos, in the previous cantata associated with the heavenly host, strengthen the notion that these are the words of God.[174]

Beginning with the normal fourth-plus-third opening formula (g - c' - e', with the highest note on "Volk"), the vocal line undulates in intense expression, thanks partly to its large range (from B to e'). The recitative modulates back to the dominant key of A major.

---

173 Küster 1999, p. 480.
174 Blankenburg 1999, pp. 80-81.

28 Dies hat er alles uns getan

>Dies hat er alles uns getan,
>Sein groß Lieb zu zeigen an;
>Des freu sich alle Christenheit
>Und dank ihm des in Ewigkeit.
>Kyrieleis!
>
>All this He has done for us
>To proclaim His great love;
>Let all Christendom rejoice at this
>And give Him thanks eternally.
>Lord have mercy on us!

"Dies hat er getan," words from the message just delivered to the shepherds, are now brought home in the text of the chorale, the last verse of Luther's *Gelobet seist du Jesu Christ* of 1524, on which Bach also drew for no. 7 (see above).[175] He cites the same concluding verse after the introductory chorus to the cantata *Sehet, welch ein Liebe hat uns der Vater erzeiget* (BWV 64), which, like the third panel of the *Christmas Oratorio* triptych, was written for the Third Christmas Day. That cantata dates from 1723, Bach's first year in Leipzig. More than ten years later he composed a completely different harmonization in a rich Cantionalstil, as I have noted several times elsewhere. A comparison between the first phrase of the chorale from BWV 64 and no. 28 of the *Christmas Oratorio* reveals the care which Bach takes in creating his later chorale settings (music examples 21a and 21b). The bass part includes several significant features: the octave on "(groß) Lieb," the rising line from *d* to *e'* on "des freu sich alle (Christenheit)" and the melisma on "Ewigheit."

29 Herr, dein Mitleid, dein Erbarmen

>Herr, dein Mitleid, dein Erbarmen
>Tröstet uns und macht uns frei.
>Deine holde Gunst und Liebe,
>Deine wundersamen Triebe
>Machen deine Vadertreu
>Wieder neu.

---

175 Dürr 1967, p. 45.

> Lord, Thy mercy, Thy compassion
> Doth comfort us and make us free.
> Thy gracious favor and love,
> Thy wondrous affection,
> Make Thy fatherly devotion
> Ever new.

During their trek to Bethlehem, the shepherds reflect – and we with them: "tröstet *uns* und macht *uns* frei" ("doth comfort us and make us free") – on the comforting nature of God's mercy, thoughts expressed by the soprano and the bass in a duet in da capo form, *Herr, dein Mitlied, dein Erbarmen*.[176] Bach's model was once again an aria from the Hercules cantata, the love-duet between Hercules and Virtue, after the hero has chosen the right path. The text expresses the intense longing between the two characters ("Ich bin deine, du bist meine, Küsse mich, ich küsse dich" – "I am yours and you are mine; kiss me, I kiss you").[177] The violas in the original duet are replaced by two oboes d'amore, the shepherds' instruments, which also symbolize love. The movement is transposed from F major to A major and the alto and tenor are replaced by a soprano and a bass. The dancing, ternary meter remains unchanged. The choice of the soprano and bass voices, with the addition of doubled oboes d'amore, makes a link with the chorale with recitative *Er ist auf Erden kommen arm* (no. 7), which has the same vocal and instrumental scoring. In the duet *Herr, dein Mitleid, dein Erbarmen*, the idea of God's mercy is again taken up. In the chorale verse of no. 7, the text is: "Er ist auf Erden kommen arm, Dass er unser sich erbarm" ("He came to earth in poverty, to have mercy upon us"). This same chorale melody returns in no. 28 *Dies hat er alles uns getan*, right before this duet. And in the accompagnato recitative no. 27, the bass sang that "Er hat sein Volk getröst" ("He has comforted His people"). In the duet no. 29 the bass and the soprano are brought together in a duet, singing of God's love and mercy in a unison passage.[178]

The transplantation of the duet from the Hercules cantata to the *Christmas Oratorio* is a successful operation because Bach represents the affect of longing in general

---

176 Blankenburg 1999, p. 81 writes: "One can only imagine these to be the words of the shepherds, hastening to Bethlehem in happy expectation of seeing the stable," and yet "here, too, we are dealing with more than just the details of the Christmas story: the shepherds are meant as prototypes of the first believers."
177 Dürr 1999, p. 903.
178 Steiger 1981, pp. 276-277.

terms, rather than in specific expressive details. Only a few minor adaptations were necessary in the B section (the melisma on "Vatertreu"). The ritornello is yet another jewel of melodic-rhythmic invention. Particularly striking are the quick figures at the beginning of each measure (2, 4, 6, 8-15; music example 22). This short-long-short rhythm, also known as a Lombardic rhythm (for reasons unknown), appears frequently in the celebratory cantatas written by Bach in the 1730s for the Saxon royal family in Dresden, one of the centres of the new stylistic tendency of which this rhythmic formula formed a part. By making regular use of the formula, Bach was catering to the tastes of a court to which he felt increasingly drawn from 1730 onwards (cf. the commission of the Kyrie and the Gloria from the *B minor Mass*). This rhythmic motif would appear to be connected with the affect of joy, making it appropriate to the context of this duet.[179]

This ritornello is another model of regular phrase structure: sixteen measures subdivided into four times four measures. Throughout the duet, including the B section, there is constant interaction between the instrumental and the vocal parts, as ritornello motifs are constantly combined in different ways; for example, at the entry of the soprano and the bass, where the voices sing the opening motif on "Herr, dein Mitleid, dein Erbarmen," the oboes continue with the motif from the concluding measures of the ritornello. The middle section begins similarly: the bass and the soprano pick up the quick thirty-second note figure for "Deine holde Gunst" while the continuo plays the concluding motif that then remains almost constantly present in the instrumental bass part. Bach here presents a masterful and intriguing contrapuntal interplay between the soprano and the bass, the two oboes and the continuo, in which the vocal and instrumental partners sometimes come together with the same material and sometimes go their own ways. This long duet is once again a shining example of almost perfect cohesion and constructive logic, together with an irresistible charm, thanks among other things to the voice leading in thirds and sixths (as in the ritornello in mm. 3-8 and later on a regular basis between the voices), a musical depiction of God's loving mercy.[180]

---

179 Herz 1985.

180 In the duet (for alto and tenor) *Et misericordia eius* from the *Magnificat*, Bach also writes parallel thirds and sixths, a harmonious depiction of God's mercy (Steiger 1981, p. 276). Steiger 2002, p. 278, remarks on the parallels in the opening chorus of the cantata *Brich dem Hungrigen dein Brot* (BWV 39), which reflect this same affect of mercy (in this case that shown by one person for another). In connection with Bach's duets, which may often be interpreted as dialogues between the Christian soul and Christ himself, Dürr 1987 refers to the "harmonious" parallel sixths, tenths and fourteenths as "expressions of inner union" (cited in Steiger 2002, p. 168, footnote 19). Steiger

The structure is an extensive da capo form with a return to the complete ritornello between the vocal fragments in A:

A:

1 Ritornello (mm. 1-16)

2 Ritornello + Vokaleinbau 1 ("Herr, dein Mitleid," mm. 17-42)

3 Ritornello (mm. 42-58)

4 Ritornello + Vokaleinbau 2 (mm. 58-98)

5 Ritornello (mm. 98-114)

B:

1 Vocal fragment 1 ("Deine holde Gunst") with the ritornello's concluding motif in the continuo; the oboes support with modest accents (mm. 115-134)

2 Ritornello (second half, mm. 134-142)

3 Vocal fragment 2 with concluding motif in the continuo and a somewhat more substantial contribution by the oboes (mm. 142-166)

A: da capo.

The key is A major, the dominant of D major, with logical modulations to the secondary dominant in E major in the A section, and to the minor keys of B minor (relative minor of D major) and C-sharp minor (relative minor of E major) in the B section.

30 Und sie kamen eilend

> Und sie kamen eilend und funden beide, Mariam und Joseph, dazu das Kind in der Krippe liegen. Da sie es aber gesehen hatten, breiteten sie das Wort aus, welches zu ihnen von diesem Kind gesaget war. Und alle, vor die es kam, wunderten sich der Rede, die ihnen die Hirten gesaget hatten. Maria aber behielt alle diese Worte und bewegte sie in ihrem Herzen.

> And they came with haste, and found Mary and Joseph and the babe lying in a manger. And when they had seen it, they made known abroad the saying which was told them concerning the child. And all they that heard it wondered at those things which were told them by the shepherds. But Mary kept all these things, and pondered them in her heart.

2002 offers other examples of these "pleasant, sweet" harmonies, used for texts such as "durch dein angenehmes Wort" ("through your pleasing word"; and for other passages from the cantata *Jesu, der du meine Seele*, BWV 78; pp. 38, 41 and 44) and in the aria *Mein Jesus will es tun, er will dein Kreuz versüßen* (in the cantate *Alles nur nach Gottes Willen*, BWV 72; p. 77).

The second phase of this cantata starts with the four verses in which Luke tells of the arrival of the shepherds (verse 16), their broadcasting of what they have seen (verse 17), the people's amazement (verse 18) and the reaction of Mary, who "kept all these things and pondered them in her heart" (verse 20). This is an extraordinary secco recitative, mostly because of the striking presence of a descending sixteenth-note motif in the continuo which Bach uses to demarcate the caesuras. He does not, however, take the easy way out by simply separating each Bible verse with this motif; instead, it is present between verses 16 and 17 ("... in der Krippe liegen/ Da sie es aber gesehen hatten ...") and verses 17 and 18 ("... gesaget war/ Und alle für die es kam ..."), but not between 18 and 19 ("... gesaget hatten/ Maria aber ..."). In the latter place, Bach employs a strong V-I cadence. The motif does occur again in the middle of the last verse as the transition between "Maria aber behielt alle diese Worte" and "und bewegte sie in ihrem Herzen."[181] At this crucial point, the emotional high point of the recitative, the motif has less a structural than a dramatic-expressive function: the voice rises on "Ihrem" to a melodic climax on a *g-sharp'*, followed by a spectacular descent to the final fourth downwards (*b - f-sharp*) on "Herzen." This is complemented by a bass motif that is dramatically intensified by the descending chromatic eighth-note figure: *G-sharp – G – F-sharp - E-sharp*).[182]

The first three Bible verses begin with the rising fourth typical of the recitative formula ("Und sie ...", "Da sie ....", "Und alle ..."); only the exceptional verse ("Maria aber...") is treated differently, as the rising fourth comes only after a descending third (*e' - c-sharp' - f-sharp'*). Indeed, Bach deals exceptionally with this whole exceptional verse. The rising fourth accentuates the word "aber," underlining how Mary's reaction is different from that of the shepherds and the others who have heard the news. In the first two verses, the fourth is (as usual) followed by a further stepwise ascent of a third (in the first verse, to a melodic high point with the *a'* on "eilend"). In the third verse ("Und alle..."), the rising fourth of *a - d'* on "für die es kam" is, however, followed by a descending line (*a - f - a - d*), a strategic move allowing the melody room to leap up by a seventh from the low *d* to a *c'* on the word "wunderten": this striking interval clearly illustrates a sense of amazement. At exactly this point, the harmony modulates from D major to E minor (the *c'* in the vocal part is followed by the leading note *d-sharp* in the continuo). In the concluding verse ("Maria

---

181 Küster 1999, p. 480.
182 Blankenburg 1999, pp. 84-85.

aber...") the modulation continues in the direction of B minor, the relative minor of D minor and the key of the next aria (music example 23).

31   *Schließe, mein Herze, dies selige Wunder*

> Schließe, mein Herze, dies selige Wunder
> Fest in deinem Glauben ein!
> Lasse dies Wunder, die göttlichen Werke
> Immer zur Stärke
> Deines schwachen Glaubens sein!
>
> Enclose, my heart, this blessed miracle
> Fast within your faith!
> Let this miracle of divine works
> Ever strengthen
> Your feeble faith!

In the next three parts of the second phase, the idea of 'pondering all these things in one's heart' is developed and commented upon. This begins with the aria *Schließe, mein Herze, dies selige Wunder*. This movement, the only completely new aria in the *Christmas Oratorio*, has an interesting history. Bach had intended to model this aria, too, on a movement from a secular cantata; namely, *Durch die Eifer entflammeten Waffen* from *Preise dein Glücke, gesegnetes Sachsen* (BWV 215), once again a tribute to the Saxon house, performed in Leipzig on 5 October 1734 (see above). However, the composer abandoned this plan, probably because of problems with the verse structure, and he composed a new aria. The secular aria was then saved to be used as the model for no. 47 in the *Christmas Oratorio* (*Erleucht euch meine finstre Sinnen*).[183] The new aria was created in two phases, for the autograph score includes a first sketch with a 3/8 time signature – giving it a lullaby character – for alto, a string group and flute. Bach notated several measures of the instrumental parts but later crossed these out and wrote a completely new movement.[184] This movement, too, is full of corrections in the autograph score. Bach ultimately opts for a modest trio setting for alto, solo violin and continuo, in which fervent expression and

---

183   Dürr 1967, pp. 5-6.
184   Dürr 1967, pp. 14-15. Facsimile of the page from the autograph score in Blankenburg 1999, p. 87.

intimate declamation take precedence over displays of virtuosity. The alto voice may once again represent the Virgin Mary.[185]

The lullaby character that Bach intended in his first sketch (in 3/8) remains present in the 2/4 time signature used here, mostly thanks to a subtle rhythmic effect: the use of (Lombardic!) syncopation, together with regular accents in the continuo (at least in the opening measures).[186]

The various sketches, the corrections to the definitive version and the precise articulation markings in the violin part all indicate Bach's desire to produce yet another 'masterpiece'. The work is a highly concentrated da capo aria, in which the repetition of A is written out, allowing a more varied development of the material from the ritornello. The intense contrapuntal dialogue between the voice and the violin is the result of a continuous spinning out of a number of motifs, inspiring the composer to ever-new developments and melodic invention.

As so often, the ritornello is symmetrically structured (2 x 12 measures), but the division of the two sections follows a pattern that differs from that of many of the arias parodying movements from secular, 'lighter' cantatas. Bach here adopts a different structural principle: (1) motif, (2) varied motif-repetition (often with a sequence) and (3) further development to the concluding cadence, a typical characteristic for Bach and many other Baroque composers. Both twelve-measure fragments are structured as follows: mm. 1-2 is the central motif of the first phrase, mm. 3-4 the varied repetition, followed by a drive to the cadence in m. 12 (in D major) (music example 24); the second phrase proceeds identically, with a modulating return to B minor, the key of the aria. After one measure, the violin and the alto go their separate ways, although still making use of the ritornello motifs, which are then sometimes combined. According to Dürr, some of the unison passages on the words "fest in deinen Glauben ein" can be interpreted as further text expression (representing the enclosing of this miracle in the heart).[187] The complete

---

185 Blankenburg 1999, p. 88. Küster 1999, p. 480, however, writes: "The aria's position in the oratorio would seem to make it an expression of the shepherds' reaction rather than Mary's." The question of Bach's original intention remains open. All the same, the message of the aria remains clear enough.

186 Blankenburg 1999, pp. 86-88, cites (with a music example) an aria from the Christmas oratorio *Die Kindheit Jesu* (1773) by Bach's son Johann Christoph Friedrich, in which the same time signature and an identical use of syncopation is found in *Schlummre sanft in deiner Krippe*, an aria sung by Mary (with the marking *frohwehmutig* ['in joyful melancholy'] over the manger") and also given to the alto voice. On J.C.F. Bach, see Wohlfarth 1971.

187 Dürr 1999, p. 165.

ritornello is heard only at the beginning; at the other usual places (between A and B, between B and the da capo, and at the very end) it is shortened to, respectively, twelve, four and thirteen measures. Bach does not complete the da capo section as a predetermined, unbending scheme, but adapts it according to his needs.

32   *Ja, ja, mein Herz soll es bewahren*

>Ja, ja, mein Herz soll es bewahren,
>Was es an dieser holden Zeit
>Zu seiner Seligkeit
>Für sicheren Beweis erfahren.

>Yea, my heart shall guard
>Those certain proofs
>Which at this time of grace
>It experienced for its bliss.

The short recitativo accompagnato for the alto soloist with the two flutes (see no. 27) *Ja, ja, mein Herz soll es bewahren* serves as a bridge to the chorale *Ich will dich mit Fleiß bewahren*, again the words of all Christians, emphatically confirming what has gone before. In the recitative, the two traversos, the instruments linked to the powers of heaven in this cantata, are present for the last time. Bach found no place for them in the stories of the Naming (part IV) or the Wise Men (parts V and VI).

This recitative begins as usual with a rising fourth. Melodic high points occur on the words "Seligkeit" (*e"*) and "sicheren" (*d"*).

33   *Ich will dich mit Fleiß bewahren*

>Ich will dich mit Fleiß bewahren,
>Ich will dir
>Leben hier,
>Dir will ich abfahren,
>Mit dir will ich endlich schweben
>Voller Freud
>Ohne Zeit
>Dort im andern Leben.

> I shall guard Thee with fervor,
> For Thee shall I
> Live here on earth,
> For Thee shall I depart hence.
> With Thee shall I soar at last,
> Filled with joy,
> Time without end,
> There in the other life.

The harmonic progression of the chorale *Ich will dich mit Fleiß bewahren* makes of this Cantionalsatz a highly intense movement. The bass has a number of chromatic passages (*a - a-flat - g/g - g-sharp - a*). The structure of the chorale is not the usual aab form, but aa, with two identical halves that Bach gives two completely different harmonisations. The octave in the bass in the first measure between "ich will" and "dich" is no doubt intended to highlight the name of Jesus. The text is a typical 17th-century 'ich' chorale by Paul Gerhardt (verse 15 of the chorale *Frölich soll mein Herze springen*), on a melody that is an 18th-century variant of *Warum sollt' ich mich denn grämen* by Johann Georg Ebeling (1666).[188]

34 Und die Hirten kehrten wieder um

> Und die Hirten kehrten wieder um, preiseten und lobten Gott um alles, das sie gesehen und gehöret hatten, wie denn zu ihnen gesaget war.
>
> And the shepherds returned again, praising and giving thanks to God for everything that they had seen and heard, as it was told unto them.

Phase three of the third cantata is an appendix, a sort of coda by way of conclusion. The Evangelist's narration is limited to the information that the shepherds return to their flock, all the while praising God. This is immediately followed by the concluding chorale. The shepherds' return trip ("und die Hirten kehrten wieder um") is musically illustrated by an inversion of the melody in a descending direction after the typical opening fourth upwards: *b - e' - c' - a - b - f-sharp – g* (compare the

---

188 Dürr 1967, p. 88-89.

rising line on "und sie kamen eilend," no. 30). An octave leap, g - g' leads directly to the highest note on "preiseten."[189]

35 Seid froh dieweil

> Seid froh dieweil,
> Dass euer Heil
> Ist hie ein Gott und auch ein Mensch geboren,
> Der, welcher ist
> Der Herr und Christ
> In Davids Stadt, von vielen auserkoren.

> Rejoice the while
> That your Savior
> Has been born here, both God and Man,
> He, who is
> The Lord and Christ
> In David's city, chosen amongst many.

The shepherds' joy is transferred to the whole body of believers in the chorale *Seid froh dieweil*. The text is the fourth verse of the chorale *Lasst Furcht und Pein* (1653), written by Christoph Runge. The melody dates from 1592, originally linked to the text *Wir Christenleut habn jetzund Freud*.[190] Bach cites this melody in two other Christmas cantatas: *Darzu ist erschienen der Sohn Gottes* (BWV 40, 1723) and *Unser Mund sei voll Lachens* (BWV 110, 1725).[191] Bach works out this Cantionalsatz in detail and with great intensity. The upper voice stays with the existing melody but in the added parts the composer has free rein to make his expressive points. He takes full advantage of this opportunity, especially in the bass part, which as the most extreme voice in opposition to the soprano is the most clearly audible (and is also strengthened by the continuo). On the word "froh" he even writes a sixteenth-note melisma (rising, of course), while "dass eure Heil" ends, after a rising stepwise line (*g-sharp - a - b - c-sharp'*), on the highest note *c-sharp'* (like "froh") (music example

---

[189] On this passage, Blankenburg 1999, p. 91, writes: "The words 'preiseten und lobten Gott,' highlighted through the octave from g to g' illustrate in no uncertain terms the complete inner change which has overcome the shepherds, previously so frightened in their fields."
[190] Dürr 1967, p. 45 and Blankenburg 1999, pp. 90-91.
[191] Dürr 1999, pp. 128 and 138. A version for organ is included in the *Orgelbüchlein* (BWV 612).

25). The other added parts proceed almost exclusively in eighth notes, with a dramatic climax (again in the bass) on the final phrase, "Davids Stadt, von vielen auserkoren." The melody rises chromatically per quarter note from *f-sharp* to *c-sharp'* (music example 26). The conclusion is unusually intense, a tension which is released in the explosion of joy created by the reprise of the opening chorus *Herrscher des Himmels* (no. 24), a festive conclusion to this trilogy on the birth of Christ.

IV Fallt mit Danken, fallt mit Loben

Introduction

The fourth cantata comes closest to the genre of oratorio: the Evangelist's contribution is limited to just one Bible verse (no. 37, Luke 2:21), while the other six movements are newly composed texts (nos. 36 and 38-42). The central theme is the Naming, celebrated at the feast of the Circumcision, on New Year's Day, exactly one week after Christmas. The shortest cantata in the six-part cycle, concentrating completely on the name 'Jesus', it consists of one single phase, in effect a broadening of the basic four-part form: moments 2 (recitativo accompagnato) and 3 (aria) are used two times, resulting in a structure that may be expressed as 1 - 2 - 3 - 2 - 3 - 4. In the accompanied recitatives (nos. 38 and 40) Bach twice makes use of the combination technique by adding a chorale. The two arias are also exceptional in form: one is a (much celebrated) echo-aria (no. 39) and the other a four-voice, fugal aria (no.41).

The introductory chorus (*Fallt mit Danken, fallt mit Loben*, no. 36) is a song of praise and thanks to God, who has sent his son to earth as Savior and Redeemer.

1 A verse from the Gospel of Luke relates the story of the Circumcision and Naming of Jesus (*Und da acht Tage um waren*, no. 37).

2 Recitativo accompagnato *Immanuel, o süßes Wort* + chorale *Jesus, du mein liebstes Leben* (no. 38). A first contemplation on the name of Jesus. 'Immanuel' can be translated as 'God with us' and 'Jesus' means 'God helps'.[192]

3 Aria *Flößt, mein Heiland, flößt dein Namen* (no. 39). This aria, which in fact interrupts the recitative, can be interpreted as a dialogue between the Christian soul and (the child) Jesus: 'Could Thy name instil even the slightest grain of that dread fear? Shall I then be afraid to die?'

2 Recitativo accompagnato *Wohlan, dein Name soll allein* + chorale *Jesu, meine Freud und Wonne* (no. 40): further reflection on the name of Jesus, as a continuation of no. 38, in combination with the second part of the chorale melody.

3 Aria *Ich will nur dir zur Ehren leben* (no. 41). The questions asked in the preceding aria no. 39 are here answered: with God's help, a life is possible "to the

---

192 Blankenburg 1999, p. 98.

greater glory of God." This is followed by a prayer: "Give me the strength to accept your grace worthily."

4 Chorale *Jesus richte mein Beginnen* (no. 42). In this chorale verse, in which each line begins with the name 'Jesus', the congregation of the faithful reaffirms Christ as the central reference point in all aspects of their lives: desires ("die Sinnen"), thoughts ("die Gedanken") and longing ("mein Begier").

In terms of both textual and musical content, this cantata is set apart from the others in the Christmas Oratorio: as mentioned, the text includes only one Bible verse, with the rest given over to contemplative texts; the chorale melodies are probably by Bach himself (both the melody combined with the recitatives in nos. 38 and 40, and the concluding chorale no. 42); the scoring is unique (strings, two oboes and, notably, two horns); and finally the key (F major), based on the lowered third degree of the central key of D major, is the furthest removed from this home key. The new tonality of this cantata may be a reflection of the celebration of the new year. Bach's choice of the side of the harmonic spectrum characterized by flats (F major, with one flat in the key signature) may be related to the fact that for the first time the Passion is mentioned: "Der du dich vor mich gegeben, An des bittern Kreuzes Stamm!" (no. 38).[193]

36 *Fallt mit Danken, fallt mit Loben*

Fallt mit Danken, fallt mit Loben
Vor des Höchsten Gnadenthron!
Gottes Sohn
Will der Erden
Heiland und Erlöser werden,
Gottes Sohn
Dämpft der Feinde Wut und Toben.

With thanks and praise prostrate yourselves
Before the merciful throne of God on high!
The Son of God
Is willing to become the Savior

---

[193] Chafe 1991, pp. 267-270. On "bittern Kreuzes Stamm" Bach goes into C minor, even 'deeper' into the world of flats.

> And Redeemer of mankind.
> The Son of God
> Quenches the foe's furious raging.

Suitably, the feast celebrating the Naming of Jesus begins with a song of thanks and praise, worthy of a place among the opening choruses in the *Christmas Oratorio*. Of all these choruses, the symmetry is most perfectly balanced here. The A-B-A structure follows a strict mathematical scheme:

A: 80 measures
1 Ritornello (mm. 1 - 24)
2 Vokaleinbau + ritornello: "Fallt mit danken, fallt mit Loben" (mm. 25-80)
B: 80 measures
3 Ritornello (mm. 81-96, reduced to 16 measures)
4 Vokaleinbau + ritornello: "Gottes Sohn will der Erden Heiland" (mm. 97-120)
5 Ritornello (mm. 121-136, 16 measures)
6 Vokaleinbau + ritornello: "Gottes Sohn will der Erden Heiland" (mm. 137-160)
A: 80 measures
7 Vokaleinbau + ritornello: "Fallt mit Danken, fallt mit Loben" (mm. 161-224)
8 Ritornello (mm. 225-240).

The three sections are exactly equal in length, at 80 measures each. The B section, with two ritornelli and two presentations of the text, is made up of two times forty measures (each 16 + 24 measures). In the da capo, the vocal fragment and the instrumental ritornello exchange places, so that the chorus ends with the orchestral refrain. After the first presentation, the ritornello in B is reduced from 24 to 16 measures. Each fragment is a multiple of eight (often subdivided into 4 + 4). Blankenburg sees in this "wonder of Bach's sense of formal order… a mirror of the divine creation and thus the praise of the creator himself."[194] That this chorus is once again an adaptation of a movement from a secular cantata in no way negates this interpretation, since the secular and the sacred, the worldly and the divine are not strictly separated spheres, but are linked parts of a totality emanating from God – especially in light of the events of Christmas. The model is the opening chorus from the Hercules cantata *Lasst uns sorgen, lasst uns wachen*. The scoring and the

---

194 Blankenburg 1999, p. 97. The author continues: "Through its very form, this chorus is a representation of God's glorification, and would have been recognized as such in the Baroque period."

tonality are taken over intact. Thanks to the perfect fit of the new text, the changes could be kept to a minimum. The very consistently symmetrical structure, the dancing 3/8 meter and the frequently chordal declamation make of this song of praise one of the most 'modern' and *galant* works that Bach ever composed.

37 Und da acht Tage um waren

> Und da acht Tage um waren, dass das Kind beschnitten würde, da ward sein Name genennet Jesus, welcher genennet war von dem Engel, ehe denn er im Mutterleibe empfangen ward.
>
> And when eight days were accomplished for the circumcising of the child, his name was called Jesus, which was so named of the angel before he was conceived in the womb.

The recitative presenting the Gospel verse follows the typical pattern of the narrative sections: entry with a rising fourth plus a rising third (*g - c' - d' - e'*). The central place of the name of Jesus in this cantata is emphasized by the melodic high points on the words "Name" (*g'*) and "Jesus" (*c' - a'*, a leap of a major sixth).[195] On "beschnitten" the melody descends to the lowest note (*d' - b-flat - g*). The theme of the circumcision is linked to the Redemption through Christ's blood, first shed at this time. This is a foreshadowing of Jesus' sacrifice, which saved humankind from sin and eternal damnation. In the succeeding movements, the recitative no. 38 and the aria no. 39, the theme of death and its accompanying fear is alluded to: "Dein Name steht in mir geschrieben, Der hat des Todes Furcht vertrieben" (conclusion of no. 38) and "Sollt ich nun das Sterben scheuen?" (no. 39).[196]

38   *Immanuel, o süßes Wort!*

> Immanuel, o süßes Wort!
> Mein Jesus heisst mein Hort,
> Mein Jesus heisst mein Leben.
> Mein Jesus hat sich mir ergeben,
> Mein Jesus soll mir immerfort

---

195 Blankenburg 1999, p. 98.
196 Steiger 2002, pp. 181-185.

Vor meinen Augen schweben.
Mein Jesus heißet meine Lust,
Mein Jesus labet Herz und Brust.
  Jesu, du mein liebstes Leben,
  Meiner Seele Bräutigam,
Komm! Ich will dich mit Lust umfassen,
Mein Herze soll dich nimmer lassen,
  Der du dich vor mich gegeben
  An des bittern Kreuzes Stamm!
Ach! so nimm mich zu dir!
Auch in dem Sterben sollst du mir
Das Allerliebste sein;
In Not, Gefahr und Ungemach
Seh ich dir sehnlichst nach.
Was jagte mir zuletzt der Tod für Grauen ein?
Mein Jesus! Wenn ich sterbe,
So weiß ich, dass ich nicht verderbe.
Dein Name steht in mir geschrieben,
Der hat des Todes Furcht vertrieben.

Emmanuel, oh sweet word!
My Jesus is my shepherd,
My Jesus is my life,
My Jesus has given Himself to me,
My Jesus shall for evermore
Hover before my eyes.
My Jesus is my joy,
My Jesus refreshes heart and soul.
  Jesus, Thou my dearest life
  Bridegroom of my soul,
Come, I shall embrace Thee with joy,
Never more shall my heart forsake Thee.
  Thou, who gavest Thyself for me
  On the Cross, the bitter tree!
Ah, then, take me to Thee!
Even in death Thou shalt be
Dearest above all to me;
In distress, danger and discomfort
I look to Thee most longingly.
What dread did death strike into me of late?
My Jesus, when I come to die,

I know I shall not perish.
Thy name is inscribed within me
And has dispelled the fear of death.

The two accompanied recitatives *Immanuel, o süßes Wort!* and *Wohlan, dein Name soll allein* actually form one whole, a fact made clear through the scoring (soprano, bass and strings in both movements) and especially through the use of one single chorale verse divided over the two recitatives. The point of departure of the recitative text is the name "Immanuel" ("God with us"), which is further invoked by the six-fold repetition of the words "Mein Jesus," with an added reflection (Jesus is my refuge, "Mein Hort"; he is my life, "Mein Leben," etc...). Bach's setting is highly varied and full of religious conviction, albeit with a strong underlying tension. "Immanuel" begins emphatically with a high note for the bass voice (*d'*) and with each repetition of the words "Mein Jesus" on a different melody. The dynamic marking for the violins is piano.

On the exclamation "Komm! Ich will dich mit Lust empfangen" ("Come, I shalll embrace Thee with joy"), when the passionate longing for union with Christ can be held back no longer, the soprano joins the bass with a chorale melody on the words "Jesu, du mein liebstes Leben, meiner Seelen Bräutigam" (music example 27). In the first recitative and aria (nos. 3 and 4) of the first cantata, Christ has already been compared with "mein liebster Bräutigam" ("my beloved bridegroom") and in the aria no. 19 in the second cantata, the image of the beloved returns ("Schlafe, mein Liebster"). Christ is the bridegroom and the faithful soul is the bride whom Jesus takes as his own. The ultimate deed of unconditional love is the laying down of one's life. After the chorale, the recitative pursues this notion: "Even in death Thou shalt be dearest above all to me" ("Auch in dem Sterben sollst du mir das Allerliebste sein"). I have nothing to fear, for "Thy name is inscribed within me and has dispelled the fear of death" ("Dein Name steht in mir geschrieben, Der hat des Todes Furcht vertrieben"). In the recitative fragment after the chorale, Bach makes even greater use of his arsenal of rhetorical devices: the melody descends to the word "Sterben" (by way of a saltus duriusculus *g - e - c-sharp*, a diminished fifth), rises in steps to a high point on "Allerliebste" (from *c* to *b-flat*) and further to "Not" (*d'*), after which it represents "Gefahr" with a saltus duriusculus (*d' - b - g-sharp*) and "Ungemach" with a descending sixth (music example 28). The word "Tod" follows two times, each time accented by the highest note *e-flat'*. Each note, each accidental (sharpened or flattened note), each harmonic turn in the continuo (note the descending seventh *f - G-sharp* between "Gefahr" and "Ungemach," and the chromatic motion of *A-flat - A* on "Furcht" in the concluding line) has its carefully worked-out function in the context of the religious message. The combination with the chorale dramatically intensifies the recitative. Just as it enters, Bach increases the rhythmic movement in the continuo (eighth notes) and in the accompanying strings (the violin doubles the soprano part, music example 27).

The text of the chorale quotes the first verse of a poem by Johann Rist (1642).[197] Text and melody (originally by Johann Schop) were widely disseminated at the time, and well-known in Leipzig. The melody, however, was newly composed by Bach, and draws less on the traditional chorale repertoire than on the religious solo song. Such melodies were intended not so much for liturgical music, but for music-making in a domestic setting.[198] Geck cites this Bach song as a typical example of the Pietistically-inspired aria. The melodic development is more varied than in the congregational hymn, not as strictly syllabic and with a greater range of rhythms. Typical are especially the small melismatic figures of two notes and the softly rocking, flowing rhythm in a 4/4 meter.[199]

Bach's choice of a bass and a soprano as the vocal soloists leads Blankenberg to the hypothesis that the soprano stands for the bride or the Christian soul, a plausible notion, while the bass may represent the figure of Simeon, the pious elder who witnessed Christ's Presentation in the temple and the Purification of Mary in Jerusalem, an ancient tradition based on the teachings of the Old Testament. Immediately after the Naming, Luke tells the story of the Presentation in the temple (Luke 2:25-33):

> Now there was a man in Jerusalem called Simeon, who was righteous and devout. He was waiting for the consolation of Israel, and the Holy Spirit was upon him. It had been revealed to him by the Holy Spirit that he would not die before he had seen the Lord's Christ. Moved by the Spirit, he went into the temple courts. When the parents brought in the child Jesus to do for him

---

197 Cf. no. 12, *Brich an, o schönes Morgenlicht,* also a text by Rist.
198 Dürr 1967, p. 45 and Blankenburg 1999, pp. 99-102. The poet Rist described the poem *Jesu, du mein liebstes Leben* as "a song of praise for the heartfelt love and ineffable benevolence of our Lord and Savior Jesus Christ" ("Loblied von der herzlichen Liebe und den unaussprechlichen Wohltaten unseres Herrn und Heilandes Jesu Christi").
199 Geck 2000a, pp. 104-105. Steiger 2002, p. 200, compares this chorale with the melodies from the Schemelli songbook (see above).

what the custom of the Law required, Simeon took him in his arms and praised God, saying: "Sovereign Lord, as you have promised, you now dismiss your servant in peace. For my eyes have seen your salvation, which you have prepared in the sight of all people, a light for revelation to the Gentiles and for glory to your people Israel."

Simeon is thus a witness in the name of all believers: his fear of death has been overcome by Christ's Incarnation (the final line of the recitative is "Dein Name steht in mir geschrieben, der hat des Todes Furcht vertrieben").[200] The bass part can also be more generally interpreted as 'the voice of belief', which carries on a dialogue with the soprano, 'the voice of the soul': the dialogue between universal belief (the 'Credo' with a capital C) and individual belief (the 'credo' with a small c).[201]

39   Flößt, mein Heiland

>
> Flößt, mein Heiland, flößt dein Namen
> Auch den allerkleinsten Samen
> Jenes strengen Schreckens ein?
> Nein, du sagst ja selber nein. (Nein!)
> Sollt ich nun das Sterben scheuen?
> Nein, dein süßes Wort is da!
> Oder sollt ich mich erfreuen?
> Ja, du Heiland sprichst selbst ja. (Ja!)
>
> O my Savior, could Thy name
> Instil even the slightest grain
> Of that dread fear?
> No. Thou Thyself dost say no! (No!)
> Shall I then be afraid to die?
> No, The sweet word is there!
> Or should I rejoice?
> Yes, my Savior Thou dost say yes! (Yes!)

---

200 Blankenburg 1999, pp. 98-99. A number of Christmas oratorios include the story of Simeon, including *Die Geburt unseres Herrn Jesu Christi* (1602) by Rogier Michael, a composer from the Low Countries and Heinrich Schütz's predecessor at the court in Dresden; it also appears in the aforementioned work by Bach's son Johann Christoph Friedrich Bach.

201 Steiger 1981, p. 276.

In the Hercules cantata BWV 213, the classical hero resorts to the echo in the aria *Treues Echo dieses Orten* in order to resolve the dilemma of whether he should follow the path of *Wollust* or of *Tugend*. Each time, the echo confirms the correct answer he has already given: "Nein" to Pleasure and "Ja" to Virtue. Bach parodies this echo-aria in the *Christmas Oratorio* aria *Flößt, mein Heiland*, an altered scoring for two sopranos rather than two altos, with a solo for oboe instead of oboe d'amore, and transposed up a third (in C major rather than A major). The pizzicato in the stringed instrument of the continuo group is preserved.

Bach appropriately translated this echo-aria, which of itself might be considered a bit of Baroque *Spielerei*,[202] to its new function as a sacred work by recasting its specific echo character as a dialogue between the faithful soul and the Christ child. Like the echo in the Hercules aria, the second soprano here answers in the negative or the affirmative to the questions of the faithful soul: "When faced with death, does Jesus' name cause me to fear? No! Does it bring me joy? Yes!"[203] In the *Christmas Oratorio*, the aria is elevated to a higher and less specific (religious) plane. The new text is perfectly adapted to the existing music, for example with its melisma on the word "erfreuen."[204]

Through the alternation of piano and forte in the ritornello, the oboe answers its own questions. The instrument later takes part in the dialogue between the two soprano voices. In this three-sectioned, through-composed aria, the eight lines are divided into two times four ("Flößt, mein Heiland," with its concluding word "Nein", and "Sollt ich nun das Sterben scheuen," which ends with "Ja"), with a variation in the second section. The schematic structure is thus A-B-B'. Between each section, and at the end, there is a shortened variant of the opening ritornello. Through recurring motifs and through the echo effects that the singers later take up, the ritornello helps provide structural coherence.

The device of the echo plays an important role in the theological literature of Bach's time, as a reference to Christ's positive and comforting response to the questions and grievances of the Christian. In the works of the theologian Heinrich Müller, a

---

202 Blankenburg 1999, p. 103.
203 Blankenburg 1999, p. 103, formulates the hypothesis that the soprano voice represents the prophetess Anna, who accompanied Simeon in the temple (Luke 2:36-38) ("This conjecture is indeed not completely implausible, since the prophetess Anna may be numbered among the prototypes of the believing soul"). See also especially Steiger 1981, pp. 274-276.
204 In the original it is on "bahnen": the action of making a path is illustrated by the melisma.

number of which Bach possessed, the echo is explicitly interpreted as a symbol of God's merciful answer to the pleas of the individual. In a print in the theologian's *Geistlicher Danck=Altar* of 1670, a figure is portrayed at the lower left, directing the words "Erbarm dich mein" ("have mercy on me") upwards to God; the words are mirrored in turn at the upper right as an echo from God, a literal inversion of the text, "Erbarm mich dein" ("I have mercy on you"). Below the image are the words "Dulce assonat echo" ("the echo answers sweetly"). The echo is a sign of God's goodness and mercy; he is the helper (= the meaning of the name 'Jesus') who will not fail mankind. The echo poem was also a literary genre, in the tradition of the Jesuit Friedrich Spee von Langenfeld, which was thematically focused on the dialogue between the bride (from the Song of Songs) and Jesus. It is clear that Bach consciously applied this symbolism in the Christmas Oratorio and that it would have been understood by his listeners.[205]

This aria also forms part of the tradition of the 17th-century sacred dialogue, a genre that was especially popular in the Protestant motet repertoire thanks to a collection by Andreas Hammerschmidt entitled *Dialogi oder Gespräche einer glaübigen Seele mit Gott*, published in 1645.[206] The sacred dialogue is found throughout Bach's oeuvre: some cantatas are given the title 'Dialogus', such as *Selig ist der Mann* (BWV 57), with its two dialogues between 'Jesus' and the 'Soul'. In *Wachet auf, ruft uns die stimme* (BWV 140) there are two 'love duets' between Jesus (the bridegroom) and the soul (the bride).[207]

---

205 See especially Koch 1989 and Steiger 2002, pp. 177-178 (with the illustration from Müller), pp. 263-265 and pp. 308-313.
206 Whenham 2001, p. 286. Other examples are the *Geistliche Dialoge* by Johann Rudolf Ahle (1648) and the *Geistliche Harmonien* by Christoph Bernhard (1665). Ahle was the father of Johann Georg Ahle, Bach's predecessor in Mühlhausen (Bach was appointed organist of the Blasiuskirche there after the death of Johann Georg Ahle).
207 Other examples of dialogue duets can be found in the cantatas *Liebster Jesu, mein Verlangen* (BWV 32), *Ich geh und suche mit Verlangen* (BWV 49, called a 'Dialogus'), *Ach Gott, wie manches Herzeleid* (BWV 58), *O Ewigkeit du Donnerwert* (BWV 60, with dialogues between 'Furcht' [Fear] and 'Hoffnung' [Hope] and between a bass [as the 'vox Christi'] and 'Furcht' – the theme of the cantata is the resurrection of the dead). For a discussion of these works see Dürr 1999, passim. For more on the genre of the 'dialogus' see Krummacher 1991 and Märker 1995.

40   *Wohlan, dein Name soll allein*

> Wohlan! Dein Name soll allein
> In meinem Herzen sein!
> > Jesu, meine Freud und Wonne,
> > Meine Hoffnung, Schatz und Teil,
> So will ich dich entzücket nennen,
> Wenn Brust und Herz zu dir vor Liebe brennen.
> > Mein Erlösung, Schmuck und Heil,
> Doch, Liebster, sage mir:
> Wie rühm ich dich, wie dank ich dir?
> > Hirt und König, Licht und Sonne,
> > Ach! Wie soll ich würdiglich,
> > Mein Herr Jesu, preisen dich?

> So be it! Thy name alone
> Shall dwell in my heart!
> > Jesu, my joy and rapture,
> > My hope, my treasure, my portion,
> So shall I call Thee, filled with delight,
> When heart and soul burn for love of Thee.
> > My Redeemer, shelter and salvation,
> But, dearest beloved, tell me:
> How may I thank Thee and extol Thee?
> > Shepherd and king, light and sun,
> > Ah, how might I worthily
> > My Lord Jesus, praise Thee?

The recitative no. 38 resumes with the words "Wohlan, dein Name soll allein in meinem Herzen sein." From the second measure, the soprano joins the bass ("Jesu, meine Freud und Wonne"), remaining until the end: their simultaneously sung last words are "dich" and "dir," ending on an open question. An instrumental postlude of several measures prolongs the pleading doubt expressed by the *suspiratio* or 'sighing' motif (*Seufzermotiv*), a two-note musical figure comprised of a descending second in which the first note is drawn out over the succeeding beat, often creating a dissonant suspension (music example 29). This recitative is once again a veritable master-class in the use of rhetorical figures as a means of increasing the expressive power of the music. Here, several salient examples:

- "Wohlan": a rising fifth, followed by a short rest. The melody breaks off abruptly (*abruptio*) after an exclamation (*exclamatio*). The abruptio also appears after "Doch, liebster" and after "wie" ("wie dank ich dir?"), which is placed between two rests.

- the saltus duriusculus, both rising and falling, is frequently applied here with an especially strong and rather controversial expressivity, since the dissonant leap is repeatedly coupled with positive notions. This would seem once again to suggest that Bach subsumes details into the larger totality of a certain idea or affect: a word is accentuated, but in function of the whole. This recitative is chiefly characterized by a feeling of restlessness, uncertainty and inquisitiveness (the movement concludes with a question mark in both vocal parts). The resolution comes only in the ensuing aria. This mood is partly created by the ascending seventh (d - c-sharp') between "meinem" and "Herzen," a descending diminished fifth between "vor" and "Liebe" (c' - f-sharp) and even a descending seventh in the chorale melody on "Erlösung" (e-flat' - f-sharp'), a very unusual interval for a chorale melody.

41 Ich will nur dir zur Ehren leben

> Ich will nur dir zu Ehren leben,
> Mein Heiland, gib mir Kraft und Mut,
> Dass es mein Herz recht eifrig tut!
> Stärke mich,
> Deine Gnade würdiglich
> Und mit Danken zu erheben!
>
> I shall live only to honor Thee,
> My Savior, give me strength and courage,
> That my heart might do so zealously.
> Strengthen me
> That I may worthily,
> And with gratitude, extol Thy goodness!

The aria *Ich will nur dir zur Ehren leben* offers a powerful answer to the difficult questions raised in the preceding recitative. This is again a parody of an aria from the Hercules cantata: Virtue sings of her joy at Hercules' excellent choice and compares him with an eagle carried towards the stars on the wings of virtue (*Auf meine Flügeln sollst du schweben*). In the *Christmas Oratorio*, this theme is transformed: it is every Christian's duty to offer his or her life to the service of God.

This task is coupled with a request to be worthy of God's grace (grace and faith are the two basic ideas of Luther's theology). The adaptation of the text makes use of the melismatic lines on words such as "schweben" ("soar") "steigst" ("rise") and "Glanz" ("luster") which are replaced in the *Christmas Oratorio* by "leben" ("life"), "Kraft" ("strength") and "Gnade" ("goodness"); the word "erheben" ("extol") is taken over with its melisma into the new version. In order to fit into the new harmonic context the aria is transposed down a tone, from E minor to D minor (the relative minor of F major, the central key of this cantata). The scoring for the soloistic instruments, oboe and violin, is changed into the uniform setting of two violins.[208] Like the echo aria, this movement is rather exceptional: it is a combination of aria (in da capo form) and fugue, a fully worked-out imitative composition for four voices (first violin, second violin, basso continuo and tenor voice) on a strong theme that begins with a descending octave on a syncopation, followed by a sixteenth-note figure. The music exudes strength and courage ("Kraft und Mut"). The theme permeates the whole aria, including the B section, although there it is found less in the vocal part than in the instruments. Bach uses all manner of musical-technical means, including stretto-imitation, inversion and motivic isolation (whereby the prominent head motif appears separately from the rest). An analysis of the A section reveals the breadth of the thematic treatment:

- Ritornello: the theme appears successively in the second violin, first violin and continuo (the counter-subject, thanks to its many syncopations, also has a driving, forceful character) (music example 30).

- Vocal fragment 1: the fourth entry of the theme, in the tenor ("Ich wil nur"), is combined with the inversion of the head motif of the theme in the first violin.

- Ritornello + vocal fragment 2: stretto-entries in second violin, first violin and tenor voice (twice, with an inversion of the head motif in the violins towards the end).

- Ritornello: identical repetition of the opening ritornello.

For the rest, the aria proceeds according to a highly regular pattern: the ritornello is repeated unaltered and in full both between A and B and at the end.[209] The regular accents in the continuo in the first measures give this fugal aria a strong dance character (music example 30).

---

[208] Steiger 1982, p. 10, sees this change from oboe and violin to two violins as "an indication for a theological reading: the simultaneous sounding of the obligato instruments underlines the fact of two instruments in accordance with one another; that is, that the questions raised in interior conversations about life have found their answer." On this aria see also Prautzsch 1968.

[209] For a more detailed formal analysis see Dürr 1967, pp. 33-34.

Bach's choice of a concerted, fugal aria was no doubt inspired by the idea of the active engagement inherent in a life in the service of God, as well as the concept of following (the basis of a fugue, with its *imitatio*) God's will and commandments.[210] According to certain religious writings from the Baroque period, the tenor voice, here the soloist, was symbolic of the "unsträfflich Leben, da sich die Glieder alle nach Gottes Wort ergeben" (literally, "the blameless life, whereby all parts of the body direct themselves to God"). When the spirit of God is active in people, they come to life, they lead a virtuous existence and 'hold firm' to God's commandments ('hold', the German 'halten', is equivalent to the Latin 'tenere', from which the word 'tenor' is derived).[211]

42   *Jesus richte mein Beginnen*

>Jesus richte mein beginnen,
>Jesus bleibe stets bei mir,
>Jezus zäume mir die Sinnen,
>Jesus sei nur mein Begier,
>Jesus sei mir in Gedanken,
>Jesu, lasse mich nicht wanken!
>
>May Jesus guide my beginning,
>May Jesus always be at my side.
>May Jesus curb my desires,
>May Jesus be my sole longing,
>May Jesus be in my thoughts,
>O Jesus, let me never falter!

As in the accompanied recitatives, the concluding chorale is a setting of a text by Johan Rist (verse 15 of *Hilf, Herr Jesu, laß gelingen*), but on a melody by Bach himself. In the edition of the *Himmlische Lieder* by Rist, the following text appears above the poem: "Gottseliger Anfang des neuen Jahres in und mit dem allersüßesten Namen Jesu" ("Devout beginning of the New Year in and with the most sweet name of Jesus"), a fitting conclusion to a cantata for January 1.

---

210 Steiger 2002, p. 7.
211 Steiger 2002, pp. 120-123. With a quote and an illustration from the *Emblemata Sacra* by Johann Saubert, 1625. The illustration for the tenor voice includes hands and feet, as well as a heart (the 'parts of the body' or 'Glieder' which actively carry out God's will).

Once again, Bach's chorale melody is not completely characteristic of the genre; the final phrase, for instance, does not have the kind of syllabic setting expected of a chorale. However, this chorale, more than Bach's melody complementing the recitatives, does lean more towards the tradition of the congregational hymn – hardly surprising for a final hymn in Cantionalstil. The harmonic development is much less detailed than that of other chorales in the *Christmas Oratorio* (see, for example, the concluding chorale of III). As in parts I and II, however, the complete orchestra takes part in this festive finale, with independent intermezzi, the instruments even being accorded the opening and closing statements. Bach distributes the voices and the instruments over four groups in dialogue: horns, strings oboes and choir. In the chorale melody the violins and the oboes play together with the voices.[212]

---

212 See also Blankenburg 1999, pp. 106-108.

V Ehre sei dir, Gott, gesungen

Introduction

The last two cantatas concentrate on the story of the three Wise Men. In so doing, Bach does not pick up in part V the thread at the story of the flight to Egypt, the subject of the prescribed Gospel reading for the Sunday after New Year's (Matthew 2:13-23), but turns instead to the first part of the visit of the Magi: their arrival in Jerusalem after having followed the star, and Herod's reaction. The text is taken from the second chapter of Matthew, verses 1 to 6, the first half of the reading for January 6, the feast of Epiphany. The sixth cantata is then based on the second half of this Gospel reading (verses 7 to 12).

After the introductory chorus *Ehre sei dir, Gott, gesungen* (no. 43), another song of praise and glory to the creator, the six Gospel verses are distributed over three secco recitatives (nos. 44, 48 and 50), the second and third of which form a unit. The cantata can be divided into two phases, again based on variants of the pattern of four sections.

Phase I

1 Gospel: recitative (*Da Jesus geboren war*, no. 44) and chorus of the Wise Men (*Wo ist der neugeborne König der Jüden?*, no. 45). The arrival of the Three Kings in Jerusalem is announced in the secco recitative. In the turba chorus, they inquire where the new king has been born, for they have followed his star to come and worship him. Bach combines the chorus with moment 2 of the four-part phase: a recitativo accompagnato (*Sucht in meiner Brust*), that answers their question: "Where is he?" "In my heart!" After referring to the star, the second part of the recitative takes up the idea of Jesus as a light shining both for the heathen and for the community of believers (note the words "Licht," "scheinen," "Schein").

4 Instead of an aria, there follows first a chorale in which the contrasting notions of light and darkness, day and night, are juxtaposed (*Dein Glanz all Finsternis verzehrt*, no. 46).

3 This is directly followed by an aria in which these contrasts are explored and applied to the life of the Christian (*Erleucht euch meine finstre Sinnen*, no. 47): "Illumine too my dark thoughts, illumine my heart with the brightness of Thy rays!"

Phase II

1 Gospel: the story of Herod's alarm upon hearing of the birth of a king (*Da das König Herodes hörte*, no. 48), and of his enquiries concerning the child, with the answer of the chief priests and scribes (*Und ließ versammlen alle Hohepriester*, no. 50), divided over two recitatives.

Bach interrupts the story with moment 2: an accompagnato recitative as a commentary on Herod's reaction: "Why are you so afraid? Can the presence of my Jesus awake such fear in you?" (*Warum wollt ihr erschrecken?* no. 49).

3 This is followed by an aria for vocal trio, conceived as a dialogue with questions and answers (*Ach, wenn wird die Zeit erscheinen*, no. 51). The Christian still doubts the presence of the comforting Redeemer; the answer to these doubts is a resounding "Schweigt, er ist schon wirklich hier" ("Be silent, He is in truth already here").

2 In an added accompagnato recitative, the second moment returns before the final chorale. Although the trio had offered a positive answer ("er ist schon wirklich hier"), the Christian's doubts remain right to the end, in a plaintive call: "Jesu, ach, so komm zu mir." The accompanied recitative removes these last doubts, allowing the cantata to end on a brilliant note (*Mein Liebster herrschet schon*, no. 52).

4 Final chorale *Zwar ist solche Herzensstube* (no. 53). To conclude, Bach returns to the basic idea of this cantata: the contrast between light (the coming of Christ) and darkness (humanity, living in ignorance). Although the heart is but a gloomy dungeon ("ein finstre Grube") as a place for Jesus to reside, it becomes a sunny abode once God's grace shines into it ("... wird es voller Sonne dünken").

The tonality is A major, the dominant of the main key of D major and symbolic of the light that has now broken through once and for all.[213] The scoring is on the intimate side: only strings (with basso continuo) and two oboes d'amore, without horns and trumpets. It is possible that Bach's less extravagant scoring reflects this cantata's function as liturgical music for a normal Sunday service (between New Year's and Epiphany). Probably because it was a 'normal Sunday cantata', performed only in the Nikolaikirche, the passages of direct speech are not always assigned to the individuals in the story: the words of the Wise Men (*Wo ist der neugeborne König*, no. 45) are here given to a four-voice choir, and not to three soloists, and the pronouncements of the chief priests and scribes concerning the birth of Christ (*Und*

---

213 Blankenburg 1999, p. 109.

ließ versammlen alle Hohepriester, no. 50) are simply assigned to the Evangelist as part of his secco recitative (and not as a chorus). Finally, the concluding movement is a chorale in Cantionalstil, the usual scoring for a Sunday cantata, without obbligato instruments playing independent parts.[214]

43   *Ehre sei dir, Gott, gesungen*

>Ehre sei dir, Gott, gesungen,
>Dir sei Lob und Dank bereit',
>Dich erhebet alle Welt,
>Weil dir unser Wohl gefällt,
>Weil anheut
>Unser aller Wunsch gelungen,
>Weil uns dein Segen so herrlich erfreut.

>Glory be to Thee, O Lord,
>Let praise and thanksgiving be prepared for Thee.
>All the world extols Thee,
>Because our well-being pleases Thee,
>Because this day
>Our wish has been fulfilled,
>Because Thy blessing fills us so wondrously with joy.

Bach originally planned to take the concluding chorus from the Hercules cantata *Lust der Völker, Lust der Deinen* as his model for the song of praise *Ehre sei dir, Gott, gesungen*, but ultimately wrote a new composition for the introductory chorus. Although the new poem is indeed identical with the text from the Hercules cantata in terms of length and verse structure, Bach apparently found the intermezzi for bass solo, which interrupt the choral sections, not suitable for the oratorio.[215]

This introduction to the fifth cantata is an energetic chorus in the concerted style and with a da capo form: the 3/4 time signature and the 'vivace' tempo marking leave no doubt as to the character of this movement. The ritornello starts with a dialogue between oboes and strings (a) which after four measures evolves into concerted passages between the virtuoso first violins with sixteenth-note figures and

---

214   Küster 1999, pp. 481-483.
215   See Blankenburg 1999, p. 13 and especially pp. 109-110 and 112 for a more detailed comparison of the two texts.

syncopated motifs in the oboes, supported by the other strings and the continuo (b). In the opening passages of the A and B sections, both of which are rather homophonic, the dialogue motif a has the upper hand, while the concerted-syncopated fragment b tends to dominate the second, mainly imitative passage.

This opening chorus may be schematically represented as follows:
A:
1 Ritornello: a (dialogue motif) - b (concerted violins contrasted with syncopated motifs in the oboes) (mm. 1-17)
2 Vocal fragment 1, Choreinbau
- dialogue motif a: "Ehre sei dir, Gott, gesungen" (mm. 17-31)
- imitative development of a new motif (c) on "Dir sei Lob und Dank bereit"; the repetition of this line is based on the syncopated motifs of b (with concerted violins) (mm. 31-54)
3 Ritornello: dialogue motif a (mm. 54-58)
4 Vocal fragment 2: varied, more extensive repetition of fragment 1 (mm. 58-98).

B consists of one fragment (mm. 98-126), "Dich erhebet alle Welt," in which short choral sections alternate with the dialogue motif a in the instruments. The text (lines 3-7) is sung two times.

This is followed by a complete repetition of A.

The harmonic pattern follows the classic formula: the first section moves from the home key of A major to the dominant, E major, and back to A major, while the second section follows the same path in the relative minor keys: F-sharp minor - C-sharp minor - F-sharp minor. The structure is equally uncomplicated and as directly comprehensible as the text itself. The basso continuo, the 'musical foundation', plays an unbroken chain of eighth notes, except in one place, where the bass line double the words "dir sei Lob und Dank bereit" (mm. 51-53, repetition in mm. 95-97, prepared in the ritornello mm. 14-16). The melody rises with a melismatic line, in sequential repetition on a motif consisting of an eighth note and two sixteenth notes repeated through the interval of an octave ($e - e'$ in mm. 51-53, music example 31, and $A - a$ in mm. 95-97). The completed interval of an octave can in this place refer to God as the 'totality'.[216] Bach attached great importance to both the melodic and rhythmic shape of his compositions, and the harmonic

---

216 Blankenburg 1999, p. 112.

development of the basso continuo. He considered the continuo to be "the most perfect foundation of music" that should engender "a well-sounding harmony to the Glory of God and the permissible delectation of the spirit." For Bach, music rested fundamentally on the eternal laws of nature and on the sense of order inherent in God's creation.[217]

44 Da Jesus geboren war

> Da Jesus geboren war zu Bethlehem im jüdischen Lande, zur Zeit des Königes Herodis, siehe, da kamen die Weisen vom Morgenlande gen Jerusalem und sprachen:
>
> Now when Jesus was born in Bethlehem of Judaea in the days of Herod the King, behold, there came wise men from the East to Jerusalem, saying:

The recitativo secco relating the story of the arrival of the Wise Men in Jerusalem begins at the words "Da Jesus" with the characteristic rising fourth (*c-sharp'* - *f-sharp'*), but the melody immediately descends again, putting the word "Jesus" on the highest note of the first phrase. This same melody returns when the Three Kings arrive ("Da kamen die Weisen"). In this way, Bach makes the link between Christ's birth and the arrival of the Wise Men: both phrases begin with the word "da"; where one version mentions "Jesus" the other speaks of "die Weisen"; the place of Jesus' birth, "in Bethlehem," parallels the mention of "vom Morgenlande" ("from the East"), the origin of the Wise Men. Both melodic formulas follow the same course: "Da Jesus...": *c-sharp'* - *f-sharp'* - *c-sharp'* - *a* - *b* - *c-sharp'* - *f-sharp* and "Da kamen": *c-sharp'* - *f-sharp'* - *c-sharp'* - *a-sharp* - *b* - *c-sharp'* - *f-sharp*. Only the *a* is altered, to

---

[217] Cited by Blankenburg 1982, p. 311. The original text: "Der Generalbass ist das volkommenste Fundament der Musik, welcher mit beiden Händen gespielt wird, dergestalt, dass die linke Hand die vorgeschriebene Noten spielt, die rechte aber Con- und Dissonantien dazu greift, damit dieses eine wohlklingende Harmonie gebe zur Ehre Gottes und zulässiger Ergötzung des Gemüts, und soll, wie aller Musik, also auch des General-Basses Finis und Endursache anders nicht, als nur zu Gottes Ehre und Recreation des Gemütes sein". English translation: "The thorough bass is the most perfect foundation of music, being played with both hands in such manner that the left hand plays the notes written down while the right adds consonances and dissonances, in order to make a well-sounding harmony to the Glory of God and the permissible delectation of the spirit, and the aim and final reason, as of all music, so of the thorough bass should be none else but the Glory of God and the recreation of the mind" (NBR, pp. 16-17).

an *a-sharp* (the note in the bass). The highest note in the recitative is on the significant word "siehe" (g'), just before "da kamen die Weisen."

45 *Wo ist der neugeborne König*

> Wo ist der neugeborne König der Jüden?
>   Sucht ihn in meiner Brust,
>   Hier wohnt er, mir und ihm zur Lust!
> Wir haben seinen Stern gesehen im Morgenlande und sind kommen,
> Ihn anzubeten.
>   Wohl euch, die ihr dies Licht gesehen,
>   Es ist zu eurem Heil geschehen!
>   Mein Heiland, du, du bist das Licht,
>   Das auch den Heiden scheinen sollen,
>   Und sie, sie kennen dich noch nicht,
>   Als sie dich schon verehren wollen.
>   Wie hell, wie klar muß nicht dein Schein,
>   Geliebter Jesu, sein!

> Where is He that is born King of the Jews?
>   Seek him in my breast,
>   He dwells here, for my delight, and His!
> We have seen His star in the East and are come to worship Him.
>   Blessed are you, who have seen this light,
>   It is come for your salvation!
>   My Savior, Thou, Thou art the light,
>   That shall also shine on the gentiles,
>   And they, they do not yet know Thee,
>   And already want to worship Thee.
>   How bright, how clear must Thy radiance be,
>   Beloved Jesus!

The following Bible verse, with the Wise Men's question, "where is He that is born King of the Jews?" is a four-voice chorus composed according to the principles of the motet, with doubled, rather than independent, instrumental parts (two oboes d'amore and strings). The first fragment "Wo ist der neugeborne König der Jüden" is homophonic, the second "Wir haben seine Stern gesehen im Morgenlande und sind kommen ihn anzubeten" begins with imitation, but ends homophonically. The choral section is short and to the point, with particular emphasis on the interrogative exclamation "wo?", which is abruptly interrupted and repeated several times. The oboes and violins also take part in the questioning, partly by entering into a dialogue with the voices (made especially striking through the octave leaps followed by pauses). At the end of the first phrase, the word "wo?" is again repeated several times, as the question mark is musically depicted by an unresolved dissonant chord (*d-sharp - b - f-sharp - a*) (music example 32).[218]

What follows is not the second sentence of the Gospel text but an inserted accompagnato recitative for alto, with strings (the oboes take a rest), in which the question "wo?" is answered: "Sucht ihn in meiner Brust, hier wohnt er, mir, und ihm zur Lust." Jesus dwells in the heart of the true believer: an essential theme that has appeared in the previous cantatas. The third cantata includes an extensive reflection on the wonder of Christ's birth, first enfolded in the heart of the Virgin Mary, and then of all faithful Christians (cf. nos. 30-32). A further treatment of the same theme is found in no. 40 (cantata IV), when Jesus' name is taken into the heart; and finally Jesus himself is said to dwell there (in the present cantata).

The second choral phrase "Wir haben seine Stern gesehen" is also followed by a more fully work-out, accompanied recitative for alto and strings, which characterizes Jesus as the light, making a connection with the star that the Three Kings have seen and followed. Particularly striking are the many pauses, rhetorical emphases that Bach places between repeated words: "du - du bist das Licht," "und sie - sie kennen dich noch nicht." On the name "Jesus," at the end, he adds a small but emphatic melismatic figure, which has a strong effect within the otherwise completely syllabic recitative. As to the question of the speaker's identity, Blankenburg again points to the Virgin Mary, whom he has already associated with the alto part in the second and third cantatas.[219]

According to some scholars, this movement is a parody of a fragment from the now lost *St. Mark Passion* (1731),[220] but opinions differ on this subject, mainly because of the very distinctive and unique structure with the 'interrogative', unresolved cadences of the choral fragments.[221]

---

218 Blankenburg 1999, p. 113.
219 Ibid: "The words of Mary, who here again speaks for believers." Küster 1999, p. 483, has his doubts: "…it cannot be determined with certainty which 'role' is represented by these words."
220 Blankenburg 1999, pp. 13 and 113. This hypothesis was first put forward by Freiesleben 1916.
221 Küster 1999, p. 482.

46 Dein Glanz all Finsternis verzehrt

>Dein Glanz all Finsternis verzehrt,
>Die trübe Nacht in Licht verkehrt.
>Leit uns auf deinen Wegen,
>Dass dein Gesicht
>Und herrlichs Licht
>Wir ewig schauen mögen!
>
>Thy brightness doth consume all darkness,
>It turns the dismal night to day.
>Lead us on Thy pathways,
>That on Thy face
>And glorious light
>We may forever gaze!

The chorale *Dein Glanz all Finsternis verzehrt* carries further the image of the star, an image of a light that shines in the darkness and leads us on the true path to Christ, a vivid application of the Gospel message. The text is the fifth verse of the chorale for the feast of Epiphany, *Nun, liebe Seel, nun ist es Zeit* by Georg Weissel (1642), here sung on a 1581 melody (*In dich hab ich gehoffet, Herr*) which was well-known in Leipzig through the songbooks that circulated there. The text was originally linked to a melody by Johannes Eccard, a pupil of Orlandus Lassus.[222] The melody *In dich hab ich gehoffet, Herr* is found in several other works by Bach, including the early cantata *Gottes Zeit ist die allerbeste Zeit*, known as 'Actus Tragicus' (BWV 106, probably composed in 1707) and the *St. Matthew Passion* (no. 32: *Mir hat die Welt trüglich gericht*).[223]

Bach once again writes a highly detailed Cantionalsatz, with many passing notes and passages with text painting, as on "die trübe Nacht in Licht verkehrt" ("it turns the dismal night to day"), where the alto and tenor descend on "Nacht" and ascend on "Licht," and the bass line rises chromatically on "trübe" – a passus duriusculus to represent the "dismal night" – and proceeds diatonically further on the words "in Licht verkehrt" (music example 33). On the last phrase, "wir ewig schauen mögen,"

---

[222] Blankenburg 1999, p. 116.
[223] It also appears in the cantata *Falsche Welt, dir trau ich nicht* (BWV 52).

all the parts sing melismatically towards the final climax ("and glorious light we may forever gaze!")

47   Erleucht auch meine finstre Sinnen

>   Erleucht auch meine finstre Sinnen,
>   Erleuchte mein Herze
>   Durch der Strahlen klaren Schein!
>   Dein Wort soll mir die hellste Kerze
>   In allen meinen Werken sein;
>   Dies lässet die Seele nichts Böses beginnen.

>   Illumine too my dark thoughts,
>   Illumine my heart
>   With the brightness of Thy rays!
>   Thy Word shall be the brightest candle
>   To me in all my doings;
>   And shall keep my soul from wicked deeds.

Darkness and light continue as the central themes in this aria, the only parody of a movement from the cantata BWV 215, *Preise dein Glücke, gesegnetes Sachsen*. The new text *Erleucht auch meine finstre Sinnen* fits the music even better than the original *Durch die von Eifer entflammeten Waffen*, suggesting that Bach may have already played with the idea of using the aria in the *Christmas Oratorio* while he was composing the cantata (in October of 1734).[224] The scoring has been radically altered. In the cantata, the solo part is given to a soprano rather than a bass (the voice of one of the Wise Men?).[225] The oboe d'amore that doubles the soprano part appears here in a concerted role, taking the place of the two traversos in the cantata. In the oratorio an organ is indicated for the continuo but in the cantata there is no continuo, as the soprano voice is accompanied only by violins and a viola. The absence of continuo, normally the essential 'musical foundation' (see above) is likely intended here to express an unusual situation in which "evil is repaid with good" ("Bosheit mit Wohltat vergelten").[226]

---

224 Blankenburg 1999, pp. 116-117.
225 Blankenburg 1999, p. 116: "…the voice of one of the Three Wise Men, but endowed with a more timeless dimension".
226 Dürr 1999, p. 914. Another striking example of an aria without basso continuo is found in the

The original aria is transposed down an octave plus a fourth (from B minor to F-sharp minor). In the adaptation of the text, certain words, such as "Strahlen" ("brightness"), "erleuchte" ("illumine") and "allen" ("all"), have been given more emphasis by being set to melismas. A comparison between the passages "aber die Bosheit mit Wohltat vergelten, ist nur der Helden, ist Augustus' Eigenthum" ("but to repay evil with good is achieved by heroes, and Augustus alone") from the cantata and "Dein Wort soll mir die hellste Kerze in allen meinen Werken sein" ("Thy word will be the brightest candle to me in all my doings") from the oratorio clearly illustrates how Bach rewrites the original musical material in function of the content of the new text (music examples 34a and 34b).

Words such as 'Strahlen' and 'erleuchten' were common metaphors (found, for example, in Pietistic literature) for the working of God's grace in the human soul. The following quotations from devotional texts of Bach's time accord with the sentiments expressed in this aria: "You, the true light that lightens all things, lighten now my whole heart, that it not be covered in darkness" and "Shine your bright rays of light and love into my cold and dark heart." Here, again, the darkness is driven out by God's light.[227]

Bach opts for a relatively free da capo form for this aria: the text repetition of A ("Erleucht auch...") follows directly after the conclusion of B ("...nichts Böses beginnen"), without a ritornello in between and without reprising the opening theme. The whole aria thus comes across as through-composed. The musical coherence is ensured by the constant presence of motifs from the ritornello. Typical for Bach is once again the layering of melodic motifs previously introduced in sequence. This is especially clear at the beginning of the vocal part: the voice takes over the opening motif (a) from the ritornello, while the oboe d'amore plays the motif with which the second sub-section of the ritornello begins (b) (music example 35). The ritornello itself is 24 measures long, divided into 2 x 12 measures.

---

cantata *Vergnügte Ruh! beliebte Seelenlust!* (BWV 170): the aria *Wie jammern mich doch die verkehrten Herzen* speaks of "hearts that have gone astray and turned away from God." Such hearts have lost God's support, the foundation upon which every Christian life rests: the very ground under their feet disappears, as it were (Dürr 1999, p. 489).

227 "Du bist das wahrhafftige Licht, das alles erleuchtet, so erleuchte doch auch mein gantzes Hertze, dass daß nicht von der Finsternis darin beliebe" and "Scheuss in mein kalt und finster Herz Dein'n hellen Lichts- und Liebesstrahl." Langen 1968, pp. 44-45; see also pp. 127 ff.

Particularly striking within the two halves is the free spinning-out of the melodies, full of surprising turns.

In schematic terms, the aria can be represented as follows:
A:
1 Ritornello: motif a + development (mm. 1-12), motif b + development (mm. 12-24)
2 Vocal fragment + ritornello: "Erleucht euch meine finstre Sinnen." The oboe d'amore first develops motif b (music example 35) followed by motif a (mm. 24-60)
3 Ritornello: motif b + development (mm. 60-72)
B:
4 Vocal fragment + ritornello: "Dein Wort soll mir die hellste Kerze." Motif b in the oboe d'amore (mm. 72-84)
5 Short transition to the final phrase "Dies lässet die Seele" by way of motif a from the ritornello (mm. 84-92).
A:
6 Immediately follows B: vocal fragment + ritornello: "Erleucht auch meine finstre Sinnen," with motif b in the oboe d'amore (mm. 92-120)
7 Repetition of the complete ritornello in conclusion (mm. 120-144).

The modulation proceeds from F-sharp minor through C-sharp minor and B minor (in the B section) back to C-sharp minor. The continuous, non-schematic structure is also evident in the fact that the repetition of the text of A already begins in the key of B minor and that the home key of F-sharp minor is only re-established shortly before the final ritornello enters.

48   *Da das der König Herodes hörte*

> Da das der König Herodes hörte, erschrak er und mit ihm das ganze Jerusalem.
>
> When Herod the King had heard these things, he was troubled, and all Jerusalem with him.

One of the most dramatic accents in the whole work is found in this very short recitative: the leap of a sixth (*c-sharp'* - *a'*) on "erschrak er," vividly depicts the extreme, emotional reaction of the king.[228] The high *a'* lies no less than an octave plus a fourth above the opening note *e*.

49 *Warum wollt ihr erschrecken*

> Warum wollt ihr erschrecken?
> Kann meines Jesu Gegenwart euch solche Furcht erwecken?
> O! solltet ihr euch nicht
> Vielmehr darüber freuen,
> Weil er dadurch verspricht,
> Der Menschen Wohlfahrt zu verneuen.
>
> Why are you so afraid?
> Can the presence of my Jesus awake such fear in you?
> Oh, should you not rather
> Rejoice instead,
> Because by this He promises
> To save mankind once more.

An accompagnato recitative for the alto, "the prototype of belief" (the "Urbild des Glaubens"[229]), interrupts Herod's scene, in a dramatized reflection on the king's terrified reaction. This intermezzo functions as a emotion-laden intervention in the story: there is no pause provided between the secco and accompagnato recitatives, and the continuation of the Evangelist's text ("Und ließ versammlen...", no. 50) also follows the accompagnato directly. A rhythmically sharp motif in the strings, with repeated thirty-second notes (a form of tremolo) illustrates the trembling of Herod.[230] The voice part intensifies and dramatizes the previous words "erschrak er" by expanding a minor sixth into a major sixth, leading up to the question mark in "Warum wollt ihr erschrecken?' (*c-sharp' - a-sharp'*). At the end of the following question as well, "Kann meines Jesu Gegenwart euch solcher Furcht erwecken?" the melody is left hanging on an unresolved high note. Only in the next, confirming phrases does the melody come to rest after descending ("...darüber freuen" and "...Wohlfahrt zu verneuen," with the melodic high point *e"* op "Wohlfahrt"). Starting at the word "freuen" the rhythmic motif in the strings transforms melodically into a less aggressive, more lyrical movement.

---

228 Blankenburg 1999, p. 117.
229 Blankenburg 1999, p. 118.
230 Blankenburg 1999, p. 118.

50 Und ließ versammlen alle Hohepriester

> Und ließ versammlen alle Hohepriester und Schrifgelehrten unter dem Volk und erforschete von ihnen, wo Christus sollte geboren werden. Und sie sagten ihm: Zu Bethlehem im jüdischen Lande; denn also stehet geschrieben durch den Propheten: Und du Bethlehem im jüdischen Lande, bist mitnichten die kleinest unter den Fürsten Juda; denn aus dir soll mir kommen der Herzog, der über mein Volk Israel ein Herr sei.

> And he gathered all the chief priests and scribes of the people together, and demanded of them where Christ should be born. And they said unto him: in Bethlehem of Judaea; for thus it was written by the prophet: And thou Bethlehem, in the land of Juda, are not the least among the princes of Juda; for out of thee shall come a Governor, that shall rule my people Israel.

Bach turned to a secco recitative not only for the story of the assembling of the chief priests but also for their answer ("Und du Bethlehem im jüdischen Lande"), which might normally be expected to be set as a turba chorus. The direct speech does not represent the priests' own words but is a citation from an Old Testament prophecy which has now been fulfilled: "But you, Bethlehem Ephrathah, though you are small among the clans of Judah, out of you will come for me one who will be ruler over Israel."[231]

The recitative begins with a slightly altered version of the basic opening formula: a fifth (*e'-b'*, instead of a fourth), which rises to a high note (*f-sharp'*) on the first syllable of "Hohepriester" (literally, "high priests") Other melodic high points (*g-sharp'* and *a'*) are saved for the words "Christus" (leap of a seventh after "wo") and "geboren." The second phrase "Und sie sagten ihm: Zu Bethlehem" is the answer given by the chief priests and scribes, which only gains its full significance when linked to the Old Testament prophecy – a significance reflected in the tension-filled ascent on the words "denn also stehet geschrieben durch den Propheten." The melody rises from *a* to *g-sharp'* and remains suspended there. In the autograph Bach here provides the marking 'andante', a resolute, measured tempo suitable to the

---

[231] Micah 5:1. The prophet Micah (second half of the 8th century B.C.) was a younger contemporary of Isaiah. The book Micah consists of an alternation of positive and negative prophecies. Typical for the evangelist Matthew is the repeated reference to Old Testament prophets whose words have been fulfilled by the coming of Jesus. This explains the frequent formulation: "…that the word spoken by the prophet might be fulfilled."

dignified delivery of these words of God as spoken by the prophet: "Und du Bethlehem..." The character of the continuo part changes completely: the sparsely placed chords now give way to a continuous movement in eighth notes. Above this the vocal part declaims the prophecy in arioso style, with small melismatic figures (and no longer with one note per syllable, as is usual in secco recitatives). The melody is full of intense expression, thanks to the many large intervals (fourth, fifth, major sixth, octave) and an effective climax on "denn aus dir soll mir kommen der Herzog, der über mein Volk ...", which Bach carefully prepares with a rising sequence of fourths (*f-sharp - b, g-sharp - c-sharp', a-sharp - d', b - e* and further to *g'* on "mein") (music example 36).[232]

51   Ach, wenn wird die Zeit erscheinen?

>Ach, wenn wird die Zeit erscheinen?
>Ach, wenn kömmt der Trost der Seinen?
>Schweigt, er ist schon würklich hier!
>Jesu, ach so komm zu mir!
>
>Ah! When shall the time appear?
>Ah! When shall the comfort of His people appear?
>Be still, He is in truth already here!
>Jesus, ah then come to me.

The da capo aria that now follows, a trio for soprano, alto and tenor with obbligato violin, is yet another jewel in the crown of Bach's vocal art. It is not known whether it is a parody or not; in any case, no model has been found.[233] The alto takes on the role of the believer, answering the questions posed by the other two soloists. The text is distributed over the three voices as follows:

In the A section:

Question 1: soprano: "Ach, wenn wird die Zeit erscheinen?"

---

[232] For a detailed discussion, see Steiger 2002, pp. 276-278. See also p. 67: "The shift into arioso has the effect of emphasizing the quotation's dignity."

[233] On this subject Blankenburg 1999, p. 118 writes: "A model for this piece has not as yet been identified. The entry is, however, a strikingly beautiful final copy, so that here, too, we would do well to consider the possibility of a parody. And yet, one can hardly imagine this being anything but an original composition, since the trio may be numbered among the most idiosyncratic and at the same time most profound movements in the work, both in terms of its place in the train of thought of the *Christmas Oratorio* and of its musical treatment."

Question 2: tenor: "Ach, wenn kommt der Trost der Seinen?"

Answer: alto: "Schweigt, er ist schon wirklich hier!"

In the B section: the soprano and tenor together sing the plea: "Jesu, ach so komm zu mir!" The alto, not confronted with a question, falls silent.

This is followed by a varied repetition of A, as the tenor and soprano trade texts.

In four-voice counterpoint (three-voice in B), consisting of three (in B two) vocal parts plus violin, supported by continuo, there unfolds an exquisite dialogue of great profundity. The ritornello begins with the typical syncopated 'lullaby' rhythm (short-long-short), as in the aria *Schließe, mein Herze* from the third cantata (no. 31). The sixteenth-note figurations for the solo violin also recall the peaceful and hopeful atmosphere of the earlier aria, which also calls for a solo violin.[234] The key is also the same (B minor).

The figuration in the violin part functions as counterpoint to the imitatively intertwined soprano and tenor parts (the voices of the Wise Men?), which construct their questions out of the syncopated motif. After repeatedly insisting, the alto, the voice of belief (Mary?), literally intervenes with the repeated calls of "schweigt!" Soprano and tenor stop singing when the alto confirms the presence of Christ: "er ist schon wirklich hier." These words are heard during the extensive melisma on "erscheinen" (soprano) and "(Trost der) Seinen" (tenor), a concluding climax to the A section, in which the alto ultimately gets the last word, with the final repetition of the phrase "er ist schon wirklich hier." A repetition of the ritornello in the dominant key (F-sharp minor) forms the transition to the B section, in which soprano and tenor give musical expression to their plea of "komm" in sumptuous melismatic lines. The contribution of the violin remains discreet here, although the syncopated main motif does make an appearance.

Between B and the varied reprise of A, Bach inserts a shortened version of the ritornello, based on the opening motif. A brilliant touch is the unexpected, final intervention of the voices with the words "Jesu, ach, so komm zu mir" during this ritornello. On the final words, "er ist schon wirklich hier," the alto descends to the lowest note *b*. The generally descending line on these words can likely be interpreted as a symbol of the Incarnation, the descent of God to dwell among his people. Blankenburg refers to the almost identical melodic pattern on the words "Et

---

[234] Blankenburg 1999, p. 122, characterises the opening figure as an "expression of longing and hoping." On pp. 118-124 the author provides an extensive discussion of this aria.

incarnatus est" ("and was incarnate") in the Credo of the *B-minor Mass* (music examples 37a and 37b).[235]

52   *Mein Liebster herrschet schon*

> Mein Liebster herrschet schon.
> Ein Herz, das seine Herrschaft liebet
> Und sich ihm ganz zu eigen gibet,
> Ist meines Jesu Thron.

> My dearest Beloved already reigns.
> A heart which loves His dominion,
> And wholly gives himself to Him,
> Is my Jesu's throne.

Bach places a short recitativo accompagnato, *Mein Liebster herrschet schon*, before the final chorale. This recitative, again for alto, accompanied by two oboes d'amore, emphatically reconfirms that Christ, the 'dearest beloved' ("mein Liebster"), the bridegroom, has established himself in the believer's heart like a sovereign on his throne. The basic opening formula of a fourth plus a further rise of a third is intensified by being widened to a fifth plus a fourth: from the c' the alto quickly ascends to the melodic high point (c''). This recitative prepares the concluding chorale, in which the word "Herzensssstube" appears directly in the first phrase.

53   *Zwar ist solche Herzensstube*

> Zwar ist solche Herzensstube
> Wohl kein schöner Fürstensaal,
> Sondern eine finstre Grube;
> Doch sobald dein Gnadenstrahl
> In denselben nur wird blinken,
> Wird es voller Sonnen dünken.

---

235   Blankenburg 1999, p. 123. See also Blankenburg 1996, pp. 56 and 73. For more on this aria see also Steiger 2002, pp. 274-275: this author notes particularly the rising fourth on "Jesu ach komm zu mir" in "the two voices of the ensemble, soprano and tenor, which first ask and then plead."

> Although the heart's own humble dwelling
> Is no fine princely palace
> But a gloomy dungeon,
> As soon as the ray of Thy mercy
> Casts its brightness within,
> It will seem to be bathed in sun.

In the chorale *Zwar ist solche Herzensstube*, in Cantionalstil as might be heard on a normal Sunday cantata, the contrast between the brilliant light of Christ and the darkness of the all too weak human heart is eliminated through the intervention of God's grace ("dein Gnadenstrahl"), a profound message for the congregation of the faithful at the end of this cantata. The text is the ninth verse from the chorale *Ihr Gestirn, ihr hohlen Lüfte* by Johann Franck, here sung on a melody by Heinrich Albert (*Gott des Himmels und der Erden*), a nephew of Heinrich Schütz and an accomplished composer of some 170 songs (*Arien*, published in eight volumes between 1638 and 1650).[236]

---

236 Blankenburg 1999, p. 125 and Dürr 1967, p. 45.

VI Herr, wenn die stolzen Feinde schnauben

Introduction

The sixth and last cantata, for the feast of Epiphany on January 6, completes the story of the Three Kings, based on Matthew 2:7-12. The cantata is almost wholly a parody of another cantata (BWV 248/VIa), of which only a few instrumental parts now remain (violin I, violin II and continuo). The original text has not come down to us. It would appear that the original dated from shortly before the oratorio, likely the same year (1734). Both the introductory chorus (*Herr, wenn die stolzen Feinde*, no. 54) and arias (*Nur ein Wink von seinen Händen*, no. 57, and *Nun mögt ihr stolzen Feinde schrecken*, no. 62) as well as the recitatives on non-Biblical texts (*Du Falscher, suche nur den Herrn zu fällen*, no. 56, *So geht! Genug*, no. 61, and *Was will der Höllen schrecken*, no. 63) and the concluding chorale (*Nun seid ihr wohl gerochen*, no. 64) were modeled on this now lost cantata. Only the three narrative secco recitatives (*Da berief Herodes*, no. 55, *Als sie nun den König gehöret hatten*, no. 58, and *Und Gott befahl ihnen*, no. 60) and an inserted chorale (*Ich steh an deiner Krippen hier*, no. 59), were newly composed. Bach probably made major changes to the original here and there, especially in the accompagnato recitatives.[237] The pressure of completing the *Christmas Oratorio* on time may have played a role in the choice of just one model cantata, a fact also suggested by the preservation of the keys and voice types for the recitatives and arias. Moreover, only in this sixth cantata does the vocal solo part remain the same in an aria following a recitativo accompagnato (soprano in nos. 56-57, tenor in nos. 61-62).

The text deals mainly with the theme of the enemies of Christ, arising from the scene with the hypocritical Herod, who orders the Wise Men to return to him once they have found the child, ostensibly so that he too can go to worship him. The opening chorus immediately introduces the specter of the "proud enemies" ("stolzen Feinde") (*Herr, wenn die stolzen Feinde schnauben*, no. 54). Those who remain faithful to God ("im festen Glauben"), trusting in his merciful grace, will escape the enemies' sharp claws ("so können wir den scharfen Klauen des Feindes unversehrt entgehn").

The rest of the cantata may be broken down into two phases.

---

[237] Dürr 1967, p. 7, Blankenburg 1999, pp. 12 and 126, and Küster 1999, p. 483. In connection with the lost cantata, see Häfner 1977.

Phase I:

The fourth moment, the chorale, is absent here, and is transferred to the first moment of the second phase, where it functions as a commenting intervention in the Gospel story. Moments 1, 2 and 3 of this first phase are thus:

1 Gospel: secco recitative *Da berief Herodes die Weisen*, no. 55. Herod receives the Three Kings, tells them how to get to Bethlehem and instructs them to diligently seek the child and then report back to him.

2 The recitativo accompagnato comments on Herod's hypocritical behavior: *Du Falscher, suche nur den Herrn zu fällen* (no. 56). Herod is symbolic of the liar, but the Redeemer, whom no one can deceive, knows the wiles of the false heart.

3 The aria *Nur ein Wink von seinen Händen* (no. 57) speaks both of the power of God and the powerlessness of humans, who, as it were, can be obliterated in a simple wave of God's hand.

Phase II:

1 The continuation of the story of the Wise Men, *Als sie nun den König gehöret hatten* (no. 58), is interrupted by a chorale. The Kings have joyfully followed the star, found the child and offered their gifts, gold, frankincense and myrrh. The chorale relates this event to the present life of the Christian: I stand here by the manger and offer my gifts, which are nothing more or less than what I have received from Jesus himself, "my mind and spirit, heart, soul and will" (*Ich steh an deiner Krippen hier*, no. 59). The story is rounded off with the information that the Wise Men, after a dream in which God commands them not to return to Herod, return home "by another way" (*Und Gott befahl ihnen im Traum*, no. 60).

2 The extended recitativo accompagnato *So geht! Genug, mein Schatz geht nicht von hier* (no. 61) returns to the theme of Jesus as the bridegroom who remains as the eternal object of the beloved's affection: "you Wise Men, go then, my dear one shall not go from here." In this last cantata, Bach makes a cyclical return to the beginning of the *Christmas Oratorio*, where the birth of Christ, the bridegroom, is announced: the first accompagnato recitative began with the words "Nun wird mein liebster Bräutigam" (no. 3) and the following aria *Bereite dich, Zion* (no. 4) ends with the words "Eile, dein Bräutigam sehnlichst zu lieben."

3 The aria *Nun mögt ihr stolzen Feinde schrecken* (no. 62) offers a response to the longing expressed at the end of the recitative: "Herr, hilf! so laß mich Hülfe sehn." My enemies cannot frighten me, for "my treasure, my refuge" is with me: "Seht! mein Heiland wohnet hier."

Before the concluding chorale, Bach inserts a four-voice secco recitative for the four vocal soloists, with the rhetorical question: "what harm can the world and sin inflict (i.e., all that emanates from evil), since we rest in Jesus' hands?" (*Was will der Höllen Schrecken nun*, no. 63).

4 In the concluding chorale *Nun seid ihr wohl gerochen* (no. 64), the faithful congregation sings of the triumph of God over all his enemies: "Tod, Teufel, Sünd und Hölle." Evil and death have been defeated and humankind has won its everlasting place with God ("Bei Gott hat seine Stelle das menschliche Geschlecht").

The victory over death and sin: this is the ultimate meaning of Christ's coming to the world, which is greeted with so much trepidation in the first cantata. The first chorale began with the hesitating question "Wie soll ich dich empfangen?" (no. 5). In the final chorale no. 64, Bach uses the very same melody as in no. 5: the answer now resounds, confidently and definitively. The circle is now complete: Christ the bridegroom has found his sure dwelling place in the hearts of all believers, Christ the Redeemer has triumphed over death. For each individual and for all of humanity, redemption is at hand.

In this context, a return to the same scoring and key as the first cantata is highly appropriate: strings and oboes, complemented triumphantly by three trumpets and timpani, and the key of D major.

54 Herr, wenn die stolzen Feinde schnauben

Herr, wenn die stolzen Feinde schnauben,
So gib, dass wir im festen Glauben
Nach deiner Macht und Hülfe sehn!
Wir wollen dir allein vertrauen,
So können wir den scharfen Klauen
Des Feindes unversehrt entgehn.

Lord, if proud enemies rage,
Grant that we, in steadfast faith,
May look to Thy might and Thy help.
In Thee alone would we put our trust,
Thus can we escape unharmed
The enemy's sharp talons.

The contrapuntal complexity of the opening chorus of the sixth cantata sets it apart from the choruses that open the first, third and fourth cantatas. This difference is no doubt related to the movement's origin: the chorus *Herr, wenn die stolzen Feinde schnauben* is taken not from a secular but from a sacred cantata. The secular cantatas BWV 213 and 214, which served as models for parts I, III and IV of the *Christmas Oratorio*, begin or end with an extroverted welcoming or celebratory chorus, typically characterized by direct, chordal declamation with a clearly comprehensible text, rather than by 'learned' imitation techniques. This style is much less prevalent in the choral movements of liturgical church cantatas, which are structurally organized according to such principles as fugue, canon and imitative counterpoint. *Herr, wenn die stolzen Feinde schnauben* is an excellent example of this 'learned' style. At the same time, it is a brilliant example of a concerted chorus with ritornello and Choreinbau.[238] The overall form is da capo, with a varied reprisal of the A section (A-B-A'). The vocal fragments that follow after an extended ritornello of 48 measures are generally fugal in style and based thematically on the striking trumpet motif in the opening measures.

The result is a masterful construction in which chorus and instrumental ensemble are woven into a complex contrapuntal fabric. This complexity does not, however, prevent Bach from giving the whole a well-organized da capo structure, with logically built-in points of rest (cadences) and an equally logical harmonic structure (D major - A major - D major in the A and A' sections; sequences modulating to the final cadence in the relative minor key of B minor in the central B section). The thematic material is drawn from several basic motifs ('cells') which relate to one another.

Dürr and Blankenburg note the remarkable formal symmetry in this movement: the chorus's 240 measures can be divided into 2 x 120 (m. 120 is the beginning of the B section).[239] The ritornello is 48 measures long, falling into two halves of 24 measures each. 120 is a multiple of 24 (x 5). The question remains whether Bach had a particular intention with all of this. Is this perfect mathematical construction symbolic of the 'fullness of time' or the 'might of God'?[240] This intellectual approach

---

[238] A brief schematic overview of the movement may be found in Dürr 1967, pp. 37-38, and Blankenburg 1999, p. 127.

[239] Ibid.

[240] Blankenburg 1999, pp. 127-128, rightly notes that "Bach research continues to operate on shaky ground when it comes to such ... number symbolism, so that no certain statements are possible.

and any possible symbolic subtext notwithstanding, the introductory chorus, sparkling with its dancing triple meter, is highly compelling and infectious in its self-assuredness. Bach clearly took great joy in this ideal combination of a perfectly balanced structure and intense emotional expression. With this chorus, Bach also produced a brilliant and far-reaching example of the marriage of the 'old' and the 'new': the learned, contrapuntal style on the one hand and strict symmetrical structure, ushering in a new musical era (the *galant*, 'Pre-classical' style), on the other.[241]

55 Da berief Herodes die Weisen

> Da berief Herodes die Weisen heimlich und erlernet mit Fleiß von ihnen, wenn der Stern erschienen wäre? Und weiset sie gen Bethlehem und sprach:
> Ziehet hin und forschet fleißig nach dem Kindlein, und wenn ihrs findet, sagt mirs wieder, dass ich auch komme und es anbete.

> Then Herod, when he had privily called the wise men, enquired of them diligently what time the star appeared. And he sent them to Bethlehem, and said: Go and search diligently for the young child: and when you have found him, bring me word again that I may come and worship him also.

The Evangelist introduces the words of Herod, a role accorded by Bach to the bass soloist, 'the voice of the king'. The most striking interval in the Evangelist's recitative is the rising seventh on "heimlich." Herod himself repeats this expressive, tension-filled interval between "und" and "forschet," after his nervous exhortation that they seek the child (expressed by the quick notes on "ziehet hin"). The usual descending third or fourth at the end of a recitative is filled in melodically by Bach with a small melismatic figure, giving the word "anbete" ("worship") a somewhat mocking character. The conclusion is in fact rather illogical, as the final, unaccentuated syllable would normally never be accorded a melisma.

However, even in the absence of a specific symbolic order, this chorus is a magnificent composition, exuding steadfastness and confidence in faith." In connection with number symbolism, see also the commentary in footnote 121.

241 Forchert 2000, pp. 247-248.

56 Du Falscher, suche nur den Herrn

> Du Falscher, suche nur denn Herrn zu fällen,
> Nimm alle falsche List,
> Dem Heiland nachzustellen;
> Der, dessen Kraft kein Mensch ermißt,
> Bleibt doch in sichrer Hand.
> Dein Herz, dein falsches Herz ist schon,
> Nebst aller seiner List, des Höchsten Sohn,
> Den du zu stürzen suchst, sehr wohl bekannt.
>
> Deceiver, though you try to destroy the Lord,
> And use all false cunning
> To trap the Savior,
> Yet shall He, whose power no man can measure,
> Remain in safe hands.
> Your heart, your false heart
> With all its cunning, is already well-known
> To the Son of God whom you seek to overthrow.

In this recitativo accompagnato, the soprano directly addresses the false Herod, accompanied by held notes in the strings: "Du Falscher, suche nur den Herrn zu fällen." The melody is unpredictable and yet emphatic, with many rising and falling dissonant (saltus duriusculus) intervals in quick succession, as on "suche nur den Herrn (zu fällen)": e'' - a-sharp' - g'', "(kein Mensch) ermißt": g' - e-sharp", "dein falsches (Herz)": a' - g''. The lowest note (d') falls appropriately on the words "zu sturzen suchst" ("whose downfall you seek").

57 Nur ein Wink von seinen Händen

> Nur ein Wink von seinen Händen
> Stürzt ohnmächtger Menschen Macht.
> Hier wird alle Kraft verlacht!
> Spricht der Höchste nur ein Wort,
> Seiner Feinde Stolz zu enden,
> O, so müssen sich sofort
> Sterblicher Gedanken wenden.

> A mere gesture from His hands
> Topples the might of impotent man.
> Here all strength is derided!
> A single word from the Lord suffices
> To shatter His enemies' pride -
> Ah! The thoughts of mortals
> Are at once transformed.

In the dance-like (3/8) aria *Nur ein Wink von seinen Händen*, the soprano, accompanied by strings and a obbligato oboe d'amore, sings of God's power over humans. The character of this aria is perhaps slightly too carefree for its rather pedantic text.[242] Bach marks the movement 'Largo e staccato', indicating a slow tempo with no legato articulation: it is to be played sharply, but not quickly. The rhythm is capricious and unpredictable, with many syncopations and unusual accents. In contrast to this is the movement's highly-organized, once again symmetrical structure, with many instrumental ritornelli, the themes of which are repeated and developed in the solo passages, with some imitation between the voice and the instruments. The aria is through-composed, but the repetitions of successive, related ritornello sections give its melodies a continuous, typically Late-Baroque 'forward spinning' character. The ritornello consisting of 12 measures (a) is repeated with minor variations and with the Vokaleinbau of the soprano solo (on the first three lines, a'). The second ritornello is a further extension of the first (8 + 8 measures, b + c), again with somewhat strange, syncopated rhythms. The second vocal fragment, with exactly the same length as the first (12 measures), develops b from the ritornello on lines 4 to 7 ("Spricht der Höchste nur ein Wort"). A shortened ritornello interlude of four measures (the beginning of a) is then followed by a vocal reworking of fragment c on a repetition of lines 4 to 7 (again totaling exactly 12 measures). To finish, the instrumental ritornello (a b c) is heard in its entirety. This may safely be considered a singular work, as the vocal part is heard in just 36 of the 96 measures, or barely more than a third. The voice does place several striking rhetorical accents: on the word "Stolz" ("pride") with a melodic line consisting of an ascending octave leap followed by a further rise of a third; and on the word "sofort" ("at once"), which is repeated twice, each time on a higher note and separated by pauses, then followed immediately by a headlong rush downwards

---

242 Blankenburg 1999, pp. 129-130. The author remarks that "... it is difficult to reconcile the overall character of the piece with its textual content."

(falling a ninth, from *f-sharp"* to *e-sharp'*) on the word "sterblicher" ("mortal") (music example 38).

58 Als sie nun den König gehöret hatten

> Als sie nun den Konig gehöret hatten, zogen sie hin. Und siehe, der Stern, den sie im Morgenlande gesehen hatten, ging für ihnen hin, bis dass er kam und stund oben über, da das Kindlein war. Da sie den Stern sahen, wurden sie hoch erfreuet und gingen in das Haus und funden das Kindlein mit Maria, seiner Mutter, und fielen nieder und beteten es an und täten ihre Schätze auf und schenkten ihm Gold, Weihrauch und Myrrhen.

> When they had heard the king, they departed; and lo, the star, which they saw in the East, went before them, till it came and stood over where the young child was. When they saw the star, they rejoiced with exceeding great joy. And when they were come into the house, they saw the young child with Mary, His mother, and fell down and worshipped Him; and when they had opened their treasures, they presented unto him gifts: gold, and frankincense, and myrrh.

This extended recitativo secco is strongly dramatic thanks to the varied melodic turns heard at the vocal entries, the departures from the standard patterns, and the many striking intervals expressive of the text, both rising and falling. Here, a summary of the three verses, borrowed from Matthew, chapter 2:

Verse 9: "Als sie nun den König gehöret hatten." Bach begins by inverting the basic melodic formula: a rising fourth plus a third is now a falling fourth plus a third. The ascending fifth on "und siehe" (*c-sharp' - g-sharp'*) draws our attention to what follows: the star reappears (high register). The Wise Men follow the star until it stops over the place where the child is found: on "und stund oben" Bach writes a very emphatic melodic formula with a seventh followed by a third: *e - d' - f-sharp'*.

Verse 10: "Da sie die Stern sahen, wurden sie hoch erfreuet." Here Bach fills in the intervals of the basic formula, gradually rising to a melodic climax by moving stepwise from *a* to *a'*, with the melodic high point on "hoch."

Verse 11: "Und gingen in das Haus." The verse begins directly with a broken chord (compare with the opening of the recitative), a falling fourth + third, on "und gingen in das Haus": they fell to their knees (humbled themselves?) upon entering the stable (*d' - d' - a - f-sharp - a - d*). A joyful rise of melody on "und funden das Kindlein" is followed once again by the formula of a descending fourth + third on "und fielen nieder" (*b - f-sharp - d-sharp*). The final high point is saved for the opening of their gifts: "und taten ihre Schätze auf": the rising fourth starting from the *b-flat* ascends further to an *a'*, a seventh above. The enumeration of the highly prized gifts remains in this high register ("Gold, Weihrauch und Myrrhen").

All the textual nuances, so inspiring in these verses, are translated into sound by the musical orator Bach in his incomparable way; at the same time, these recitatives, full as they are of illustrative and expressive details, maintain a melodic coherence through the presence of recurring motifs (such as the descending fourth + third formula found on "Als sie nun...", "und gingen in das Haus..." and "und fielen nieder...") (music example 39).

59   Ich steh an deiner Krippen hier

>Ich steh an deiner Krippen hier,
>O Jesulein, mein Leben;
>Ich komme, bring und schenke dir,
>Was du mir hast gegeben.
>Nimm hin! Es ist mein Geist und Sinn,
>Herz, Seel und Mut, nimm alles hin,
>Und laß dirs wohlgefallen!
>
>Here I stand before Thy manger,
>O little Jesus, O my life,
>I come and bring and present to Thee
>What Thou Thyself hast given me.
>Take it, it is my mind and spirit,
>Heart, soul and will – take it all,
>And may it please Thee well!

Before the final verse of the Gospel story, Bach inserts the chorale *Ich steh an deiner Krippen hier*, on a text by Paul Gerhardt, the author of so many 'Ich-Lieder,' here sung on the melody *Nun freut euch, lieben Christen gmein*, which may possibly have been written by Luther himself.[243] As ever, the attentive listener discovers a beautifully crafted setting with many passing notes and ornaments coloring the melody.

---

243   Blankenburg 1999, p. 132, and Dürr 1967, p. 45.

60 Und Gott befahl ihnen im Traum

> Und Gott befahl ihnen im Traum, dass sie sich nicht sollten wieder zu Herodes lenken, und zogen durch einen andern Weg wieder in ihr Land.
>
> And being warned of God in a dream that they should not return to Herod, they departed into their own country another way.

In the last Bible verse, Bach highlights the illustrative detail of the Wise Men as they return home another way. The action of setting out on their way is underscored in the final measures through the accelerated movement in the continuo. As so often, melodic extremes are related to extreme contrasts in the text: the low *d-flat* on "Herodes" is miles away (an octave plus a fourth) from the high *g-sharp'* on "andern Weg."

61 So geht! Genug, mein Schatz

> So geht! Genug, mein Schatz geht nicht von hier,
> Er bleibet da bei mir,
> Ich will ihn auch nicht von mir lassen.
> Sein Arm wird mich aus Lieb
> Mit sanftmutsvollen Trieb
> Und größter Zärtlichkeit umfassen;
> Er soll mein Bräutigam verbleiben,
> Ich will ihm Brust und Herz verschreiben.
> Ich weiß gewiss, er liebet mich,
> Mein Herz liebt ihn auch inniglich
> Und wird ihn ewig ehren.
> Was könnte mich nun für ein Feind
> Bei solchem Glück versehren!
> Du, Jesu, bist und bleibst mein Freund;
> Und werd ich ängstlich zu dir flehn:
> Herr, hilf!, so laß mich Hülfe sehn!
>
> Go then, enough, my dear one shall not go from here.
> He shall stay here with me,
> Neither shall I suffer Him to leave me.
> His arm shall enfold me out of love,
> With gentle desire

And with the utmost tenderness.
He shall remain my bridegroom,
I shall dedicate to Him my heart and soul.
I know full well, He loves me,
My heart too loves Him fervently
And will always honor Him.
What enemy could hurt me
With such good fortune!
Thou, Jesus, art my friend, and ever shall be;
And should I cry in anguish to Thee:
Lord, help me! The let me find succor!

The final cadence of the secco recitative sets up a seamless connection with the recitativo accompagnato *So geht! Genug, mein Schatz* for tenor and two oboes d'amore. The V-I cadence is split between the two movements (V, C-sharp, as the last chord of no. 60; I, F-sharp, as the resolution at the opening of no. 61). The 'love oboe' once again symbolizes the intimacy and love between the bride and bridegroom, between Mary and her child, between the human heart or soul and Jesus, between the church and Christ. The tempo and dynamic markings, 'adagio' and 'piano', change several times at the alternation of verses to 'allegro' and 'forte', as the oboes and the continuo express happiness and joy in lively figures. The words "größter Zartlichkeit" are underlined by the tenor's arioso. At the last phrase, with its pleading call, "Herr, hilf! So laß mich Hülfe sehn," the continuo shifts into a continuous eighth-note movement, strengthened by the oboes, giving these words the character of a solemn and fervent prayer.[244]

62   *Nun mögt ihr stolzen Feinde schrecken*

Nun mögt ihr stolzen Feinde schrecken;
Was könnt ihr mir für Furcht erwecken?
Mein Schatz, mein Hort ist hier bei mir.
Ihr mögt euch noch so grimmig stellen,
Droht nur, mich ganz und gar zu fällen,
Doch seht! mein Heiland wohnet hier.

---

244   Blankenburg 1999, p. 133.

> Though you proud foes try to frighten me,
> What fear could you awake in me?
> My treasure, my refuge is here with me.
> Look on as grimly as you please,
> Threaten to destroy me utterly;
> But lo! Here my Savior dwells.

The response to the cry of "Herr, hilf!" comes in the following aria *Nun mögt ihr stolzen Feinde schrecken*: "Mein Schatz, mein Hort ist hier bei mir". This third, central line in the text comprises the words sung at the end of the da capo, before the concluding ritornello. The ritornello is deliberately written out, with a varied repetition of A, which has the effect of highlighting this line. The words are not only sung four times (in the first A section they are sung just twice), but the musical setting is also much more dramatic, with the four rising octave leaps (an unusual formula) and through an expressly prescribed slowing of the tempo (the allegro becomes an adagio) on the final words "ist hier bei mir" (for the voice and continuo, as the two obbligato oboes d'amore temporarily fall silent) (music example 40). It is as if we have suddenly landed in the midst of the love scene from an opera – a scene continued by the ensuing recitative for the four soloists (no. 63), the kind of ensemble piece that frequently preceded the final dénouement...

In this aria, both the tenor and the two oboes d'amore continue from the previous recitative. Remarkably, this brings the tenor to his third solo piece in a row: two recitatives (one secco, one accompagnato) and an aria. The less specific assignment of vocal 'roles' in this last cantata (there is, for example, no alto solo representing Mary, the 'voice of belief') may be an indication of a certain haste in completing the work, or at least of the almost unaltered appropriation of a complete cantata (including scoring and tonalities).[245] This is not to suggest that the result is less felicitous, for this aria is yet another brilliant example of Bach's ability to develop a few melodic-rhythmic cells through constant variation, to ensure a coherence in the dialoguing interplay between the vocal part, the two oboes d'amore and the basso continuo. As in other arias in the *Christmas Oratorio*, Bach touches on elements of the *galant* style in his dancing rhythms, emphasized by the 'vivace' tempo, and in the airy theme in parallel sixths that would not be out of place in a composition by Telemann. The more contrapuntal approach in the vocal fragments, with the

---

245 Blankenburg 1999, pp. 132-133.

concerted dialogue between the voice and the oboes, are elements that prevent Bach from yielding completely to the new inclinations of his time. The orderly structure certainly points to dance forms and to 'Pre-Classical' or, in any case, 'secular' tendencies – tendencies found throughout the *Christmas Oratorio*:

A:
16 (8 + 8) measures ritornello -
32 measures (16 + 16) vocal fragment -
repetition of ritornello.
B:
16 measures (8 + 8) vocal fragment 1 -
8 measures ritornello (second part) -
16 (8 + 8) vocal fragment 2.
A:
16 (8 + 8) ritornello -
40 measures vocal fragment (16 + 16 + 8 added measures) - repetition of ritornello.

The eight-measure phrases are further divided in to 4 + 4, as at the beginning of the ritornello, in which the four-measure theme is presented without alteration two times in succession in the first eight measures. The vocal part follows an identical pattern.

63   Was will der Höllen Schrecken nun

> Was will der Höllen Schrecken nun,
> Was will uns Welt und Sünde tun,
> Da wir in Jesu Händen ruhn?
>
> What terror now has Hell for us?
> What harm can the world and sin inflict,
> Since we rest in Jesus' hands?

A recitativo secco for four soloists is not a common occurrence. One would normally expect a recitative for such an ensemble to be accompanied.[246] The movement is full of dramatic tension, raising one last time the theme of evil's might and its

---

[246] Cf. the recitativo accompagnato for four voices *Nun is der Herr zur Ruh gebracht* (no. 67) just before the final chorus *Wir setzen uns mit Tränen nieder* (no. 68) in the *St. Matthew Passion*. Cf. Platen, 1999, pp. 210-211.

ultimate powerlessness over us, who rest in Jesus's hands ("in Jesu Händen ruhn"). Between the questions "was will der Höllen Schrecken nun?" and "Was will uns Welt und Sünde tun?", sung by the soprano, tenor and bass, the alto (the 'voice of belief'?) sings only the words "da wir in Jesu Händen ruhn." The question always begins in the same way: rising fourth - descending arpeggio - rising seventh (e.g., the soprano entry: $e"$ - $a"$ - $e"$ - $c\text{-}sharp"$ - a' - $g"$). Each time, the seventh creates a harmonic tension that is not resolved in the following chord but passes into a new tension through the next added seventh. Only at the end, after the four voices have united in a 'unanimous' quartet, homophonically declaiming the final words "da wir in Jesu Händen ruhn," comes the first – and ultimate – point of rest on the home key of D major. The succession of seventh chords that form the harmonic foundation of the whole recitative descends by fifths starting from F-sharp major in the second measure: F-sharp major - B minor - E major - A major - D major - G-major, with a final cadence on D major (the first measure sets out from the dominant, A major) (music example 41).[247] This recitative creates a strong moment of tension, which is released in the monumental concluding chorale.

64 *Nun seid ihr wohl gerochen*

>Nun seid ihr wohl gerochen
>An eurer Feinde Schar,
>Denn Christus hat zerbrochen
>Was euch zuwider war.
>Tod, Teufel, Sünd und Hölle
>Sind ganz und gar geschwächt;
>Bei Gott hat seine Stelle
>Das menschliche Geschlecht.

>Now are you truly avenged
>On your host of enemies,
>For Christ has shattered
>All who were hostile to you.
>Death devil, sin and Hell
>Are now laid low forever;
>By God's side
>Is where the human race belongs.

---

247 Dürr 1967, p. 26 and Blankenburg 1999, pp. 135-136.

'Monumental' is indeed the right word to describe the triumphant conclusion of the *Christmas Oratorio*. Bach again turns to the chorale melody he used for no. 5 (*Wie soll ich dich empfangen*), giving it a festive character with major instrumental ritornelli for the complete instrumental ensemble, complemented by trumpets and timpani (and with the added accent of a markedly soloistic first trumpet). All of this gives the final movement the allure of a concerted, opening chorus. The whole is framed by the complete ritornello (12 measures). The chorale phrases are linked by fragments from a ritornello that is designed in such a way that it can overlap with the singing of the chorale: one last example of Bach's mastery of the combination technique.

The text *Nun seid ihr wohl gerochen* is a verse from the chorale *Ihr Christen auserkoren* (1648), by Georg Werner, sung to the melody *Herzlich tut mich verlangen* by Hans Leo Hassler (see above at no. 5). Blankenburg notes the somewhat "grating, old-fashioned language" (for example, "gerochen" as the past participle of 'rächen', 'avenge', comes across as fusty).[248] However, the brilliant, concerted reworking of Hassler's well-known melody quickly eclipses the somewhat high-flown and, even for Bach's time, dated text.

---

248 Blankenburg 1999, pp. 136-137.

BIBLIOGRAPHY

Bach 1975	*Johann Sebastian Bach. Leben und Werke in Dokumenten*, ed. H.-J. Schultze, Kassel-Basel, 1975.
Bach CC	*The Cambridge Companion to Bach*, ed. J. Butt, Cambridge, 1997.
Bach H 1999	*Bach Handbuch*, ed. K. Küster, Kassel-Basel-Stuttgart-Weimar, 1999.
Bach J	*Bach Jahrbuch*, Leipzig-Berlin, 1904-.
Bach L 2000	*Das Bach-Lexikon*, ed. M. Heinemann (*Bach-Handbuch*, 6), Laaber, 2000.
Bach OCC 2000	*J.S. Bach*, ed. M. Boyd (*Oxford Composer Companions*), Oxford, 2000.
Bible	*The Holy Bible. New International Version*, International Bible Society, 1984.
Blankenburg 1982	W. Blankenburg, *Johann Sebastian Bach*, in *Orthodoxie und Pietismus* (*Gestalten der Kirchengeschichte*, 7), ed. M. Greschat, Stuttgart-Berlin-Cologne-Mainz, 1982, pp. 301-315.
Blankenburg 1996	W. Blankenburg, *Einführung in Bachs h-moll-Messe*, reprint of the 1974 edition, Kassel-Basel, 1996.
Blankenburg 1999	W. Blankenburg, *Das Weihnachts-Oratorium von Johann Sebastian Bach*, Kassel-Basel, reprint of the 1982 edition, 1999.
Bossuyt 1991	I. Bossuyt, *Heinrich Schütz (1585-1672) en de historia*, Leuven, 1991.
Bossuyt 1995	I. Bossuyt, *Georg Philipp Telemann. Johannespassie (1745)*, Leuven, 1995.
Bossuyt 1999	I. Bossuyt, *Georg Friedrich Haendel. Delirio amoroso. Italiaanse solocantaten*, Leuven, 1999.
Bossuyt 2000	I. Bossuyt, *De Missae breves (BWV 233-236) van Johann Sebastian Bach*, Peer, 2000.
Boyd 1999	M. Boyd, *Bach. Chorale Harmonization and Instrumental Counterpoint*, London, reprint of two separate parts (1967) in one volume, London, 1999.
Boyd 2000	M. Boyd, *Bach* (*The Master Musicians*), 3rd ed., Oxford, 2000.

BWV 1998	Bach-Werke-Verzeichnis. Kleine Ausgabe (BWV^{2a}), ed. A. Dürr and Y. Kobayashi, Wiesbaden-Leipzig-Paris, 1998.
Chafe 1991	'Hercules auf dem Scheidewege' and the Christmas Oratorio, in Tonal Allegory in the Vocal Music of J.S. Bach, Berkeley, 1991, pp. 255-273.
Chafe 2000	E. Chafe, Analyzing Bach Cantatas, New York-Oxford, 2000.
Comay 2001	J. Comay, Who's Who in the Old Testament, London - New York, 2001.
Dreyfus 1987	L. Dreyfus, Bach's Continuo Group. Players and Practices in his Vocal Works, Cambridge, 1987.
Dürr 1956	A. Dürr, Gedanken zu Bachs Umarbeitungen eigener Werke, in BachJ, 43, 1956, pp. 93-104.
Dürr 1967	A. Dürr, Johann Sebastian Bach. Weihnachts-Oratorium BWV 248 (Meisterwerke der Musik. Werkmonographien zur Musikgeschichte, ed. E. L. Waeltner, 8), Munich, 1967.
Dürr 1987	A. Dürr, Mystik in der Musik J.S. Bachs, in Theologische Bach-Studien, 1 (Beiträge zur theologischen Bachforschung, 4), Neuhausen-Stuttgart, 1987, pp. 47-66.
Dürr 1994	W. Dürr, Sprache und Musik. Geschichte. Gattungen. Analysemodelle, Kassel-Basel, 1994.
Dürr 1999	A. Dürr, Johann Sebastian Bach. Die Kantaten, reprint of the 6th ed. of 1995, Kassel-Basel, 1999.
Eggebrecht 1994	H.H. Eggebrecht, Bach - wer ist das? Zum Verständnis der Musik Johann Sebastian Bachs, reprint of the 1992 ed., Munich-Mainz, 1994.
Forchert 2000	A. Forchert, Johann Sebastian Bach und seine Zeit (Große Komponisten und ihre Zeit), Laaber, 2000.
Forkel 1802	J.N. Forkel, Ueber J.S. Bachs Leben, Kunst und Kunstwerke, Leipzig, 1802, reprint ed. A. Fischer, Kassel-Basel, 2000.
Francke 1969	August Hermann Francke. Werke in Auswahl, ed. E. Peschke, Berlin, 1969.
Freiesleben 1916	G. Freiesleben, Ein neuer Beitrag zur Entstehungsgeschichte von J.S. Bachs Weihnachts-Oratorium, in Neue Zeitschrift für Musik, 83, 1916, pp. 237-238.
Geck 2000a	M. Geck, "Denn alles findet bei Bach statt". Erforschtes und Erfahrenes, Stuttgart-Weimar, 2000.

Geck 2000b	M. Geck, *Bach. Leben und Werk*, Reinbek, 2000. (English edition: M. Geck, *Bach*, trans. by Anthea Bell, with an introduction by John Butt, London, 2003).
Geck 2003	M. Geck, *Bach's Art of Church Music and his Leipzig Performance Forces: Contradictions in the System*, in *Early Music*, 31, 2003, pp. 559-571.
Geller 1954	H. Geller, *'I pifferari': musizierende Hirten in Rom*, Leipzig, 1954.
Greschat 1982	M. Greschat, *Orthodoxie und Pietismus. Einleitung*, in *Orthodoxie und Pietismus* (*Gestalten der Kirchengeschichte*, 7), ed. M. Greschat, Stuttgart-Berlin-Cologne-Mainz, 1982, pp. 7-35.
Häfner 1977	K. Häfner, *Zum Problem der Entstehungsgeschichte von BWV 248a*, in *Die Musikforschung*, 30, 1977, pp. 304-308.
Häfner 1987	K. Häfner, *Aspekte des Parodieverfahrens bei Johann Sebastian Bach. Beiträge zur Wiederentdeckung verschollener Vokalwerke* (*Neue Heidelberger Studien zur Musikwissenschaft*, ed. L. Finscher and R. Hammerstein, 12), Laaber, 1987.
Herz 1985	G. Herz, *Lombard Rhythm in Bach's Vocal Music*, in *Essays on J.S. Bach* (*Studies in Musicology*, 73), Ann Arbor-London, 1985 (a collection of articles orginally written between 1935 and 1978).
Hofman 1995	K. Hofman, *"Großer Herr, o starker König". Ein Fanfarenthema bei Johann Sebastain Bach*, in *Bach J*, 81, 1995, pp. 31-46.
Jena 1999	G. Jena, *Brich an, o schönes Morgenlicht. Das Weihnachtsoratorium von Johann Sebastian Bach*, reprint of the 1997 ed., Freiburg-Basel-Vienna, 1999.
Josephson 2000	N.S. Josephson, *Formale Symmetrie und freizyklische Gesamtstruktur in einigen Vokalkompositionen Johann Sebastian Bachs*, in *Jahrbuch des Staatlichen Instituts für Musikforschung Preussischer Kulturbesitz 2000*, ed. G. Wagner, Stuttgart-Weimar, 2000, pp. 150-174.
Jung 1980	H. Jung, *Die Pastorale. Studien zur Geschichte eines musikalischen Topos* (*Neue Heidelberger Studien zur Musikwissenschaft*, ed. R. Hammerstein, 9), Bern-Munich, 1980.
Koch 1989	E. Koch, *Tröstendes Echo. Zur theologischen Deutung der Echo-Arie im IV. Teil des Weihnachts-Oratorium von Johann

	Sebastian Bach, in Bach J, 75, 1989, pp. 203-211.
Krummacher 1991	F. Krummacher, *Gespräch und Struktur: Über Bachs geistliche Dialoge*, in Beiträge zur Bachforschung, 9/10, 1991, pp. 45-59.
Kube 1999	M. Kube, *Bachs berufliche Basis. Die Orgelmusik*, in Bach H, 1999, pp. 535-712.
Küster 1995	K. Küster, *Biblischer Bericht und musikalischer Verlauf. Zu den Evangelienrezitativen in Bachs Matthäuspassion*, in Leipziger Beiträge zur Bach-Forschung, 1, 1995, pp. 47-54.
Küster 1999	K. Küster, *Nebenaufgaben des Organisten, Aktionsfeld der Director Musices. Die Vokalmusik*, in Bach H 1999, pp. 95-534.
Langen 1968	A. Langen, *Der Wortschatz des deutschen Pietismus*, 2nd ed., Tübingen, 1968.
Leaver 1983	R.A. Leaver, *Bachs theologische Bibliothek, eine kritische Bibliographie/Bach's theological library, a critical bibliography*, Neuhausen-Stuttgart, 1983.
Leaver 1985	R.A. Leaver, *J.S. Bach and Scripture: glosses from the Calov Bible Commentary*, St. Louis, 1985.
Leaver 1997a	R.A. Leaver, *Music and Lutheranism*, in Bach CC, pp. 35-45.
Leaver 1997b	R.A. Leaver, *The Mature Vocal Works and their Theological and Liturgical Context*, in Bach CC, pp. 86-122.
Lipphardt 1960	W. Lipphardt, *'Christ ist erstanden'. Zur Geschichte des Liedes*, in Jahrbuch für Liturgie und Hymnologie, 5, 1960, pp. 96-112.
Mann 1989	A. Mann, *Bach's Parody Technique and Its Frontiers*, in Bach Studies, ed. Don O. Franklin, Cambridge, 1989, pp. 115-124.
Marissen 1999	M. Marissen, *The Social and Religious Designs of J.S. Bach's Brandenburg Concertos*, Princeton, New Jersey, 1999.
Märker 1995	M. Märker, *Die protestantische Dialogkomposition in Deutschland zwischen Heinrich Schütz und Johann Sebastian Bach. Eine stilkritische Studie*, Cologne, 1995.
Marshall/Leaver 2001	R.L. Marshall and R.A. Leaver, entry on *Chorale*, in The New Grove Dictionary of Music and Musicians, ed. S. Sadie and J. Tyrrell, 2nd ed., 5, London, 2001, pp. 736-746.
Melamed 1995	D.R. Melamed, *J.S. Bach and the German motet*, Cambridge, 1995.
NBR 1998	*The New Bach Reader. A Life of Johann Sebastian Bach in Letters and Documents*, ed. H.T. David and A. Mendel (1945), revised

	and enlarged by Chr. Wolff, New York-London, 1998.
Neumann 1965	W. Neumann, *Über Ausmass und Wesen des Bachschen Parodieverfahrens*, in Bach J, 51, 1965, pp. 63-85.
Neumann 1974	W. Neumann, *Sämtliche von Johann Sebastian Bach vertonte Texte*, Leipzig, 1974.
Parrott 2001	A. Parrott, *The Essential Bach Choir*, Woodbridge, 2nd ed., 2001.
Peschke 1970	E. Peschke, *August Hermann Francke und die Bibel. Studien zur Entwicklung seiner Hermeneutik*, in Pietismus und Bibel, ed. K. Aland, Witten-Ruhr, 1970, pp. 59-88.
Platen 1999	E. Platen, *Johann Sebastian Bach. Die Matthäuspassion. Entstehung, Werkbeschreibung, Rezeption*, 3rd ed., Kassel-Basel, 1999.
Prautzsch 1968	L. Prautzsch, *Die Echo-Arie und andere symbolische und volkstümliche Züge in Bachs Weihnachtsoratorium*, in Musik und Kirche, 38, 1968, pp. 221-229.
Prautzsch 1980	L. Prautzsch, *Vor deinen Thron tret ich hiermit. Figuren und Symbole in den letzten Werken Johann Sebastian Bachs*, Neuhausen, 1980.
Prautzsch 2001	L. Prautzsch, *Bibel und Symbol in den Werken Bachs* (Thomas-Morus-Bildungswerk Schwerin Schriftenreihe, 4), n.p., 2001.
Rampe 2000	S. Rampe and D. Sackmann, *Bachs Orchestermusik. Entstehung. Klankwelt. Interpretation. Ein Handbuch*, Kassel-Basel, 2000 (articles by a variety of authors).
Rifkin 2002	J. Rifkin, *Bach's choral ideal* (Dortmunder Bach-Forschungen, V), Dortmund, 2002.
Rifkin 2003	J. Rifkin, *Bach's Chorus: Some New Parts, Some New Questions*, in Early Music, 31, 2003, pp. 573-580.
Schulze 1989	H.-J. Schulze, *The Parody Process in Bach's Music: An Old Problem Reconsidered*, in Bach. Journal of the Riemenschneider Bach Institute, 20/1, 1989, pp. 7-21.
Schulze 1997	H.-J. Schulze, *Bachs Parodieverfahren*, in Die Welt der Bach-Kantaten, ed. C. Wolff, 2. Johann Sebastian Bachs weltliche Kantaten, Stuttgart-Kassel, 1997, pp. 167-187.
Seidel 1998	E. Seidel, *Johann Sebastian Bachs Choralbearbeitungen in ihre Beziehungen zum Cantionalsatz* (Neue Studien zur Musik-

	wissenschaft, 6), Mainz, 1998.
Senden 1995	Y. Senden, *Muziek kan je vertellen. Over de aanwezigheid van retoriek in muziek*, Peer, 1995.
Smend 1966	F. Smend, *Joh. Seb. Bachs Kirchenkantaten*, 3rd ed., Berlin, 1966.
Smither 1977	H.E. Smither, *A History of the Oratorio*, vol. 2. *The Oratorio in the Baroque Era. Protestant Germany and England*, Chapell Hill, 1977.
Smithers 1987	D.L. Smithers, *Gottfried Reiches Ansehen und sein Einfluss auf die Musik Johann Sebastian Bachs*, in Bach J, 73, 1987, pp. 113-150.
Steiger 1981/1982	R. Steiger, *Die Einheit des Weihnachtsoratorium von J.S. Bach*, in *Musik und Kirche*, 51, 1981, pp. 273-280 and 52, 1982, p. 9-15.
Steiger 1993	R. Steiger, '*Fallt mit Danken, fallt mit Loben Vor des Höchsten Gnaden-Thron*'. *Zum IV. Teil des Weihnachts-Oratorium von Johann Sebastian Bach*, in Ars et musica in liturgia: celebratory volume presented to Casper Honders on the occasion of his seventieth birthday, ed. F. Brouwer and R.A. Leaver, Utrecht, 1993, pp. 198-211.
Steiger 2002	R. Steiger, *Gnadengegenwart. Johann Sebastian Bach im Kontext lutherischer Orthodoxie und Frömmigkeit* (Doctrina et Pietas. Zwischen Reformation und Aufklärung. Texte und Untersuchungen, ed. J.A. Steiger, II. Varia, 2) Stuttgart-Bad Cannstatt, 2002.
Stokes 1999	*J.S. Bach, The Complete Cantatas*, in German-English Translation by Richard Stokes, with an Introduction by Martin Neary, Lanham (Maryland), 1999.
Tatlow 1991	R. Tatlow, *Bach and the Riddle of the Number Alphabet*, Cambridge-New York, 1991.
Tromp 2000	N. Tromp, *Psalmen 1-50*, 's Hertogenbosch-Leuven, 2000.
Van Houten 1985	K. van Houten and M. Kasbergen, *Bach en het getal*, Zutphen, 1985.
von Holst 1968	O. von Holst, *Turba Chöre des Weihnachts-Oratorium und der Markuspassion*, in Musik und Kirche, 38, 1968, pp. 229-233.
Walter 1999	M. Walter, *Erschallet, ihr Lieder, erklinget, ihr Saiten. Johann*

	Sebastians Musik im Jahreskreis, Zürich-Düsseldorf, 1999.
Walther 1732	J.G. Walther, *Musicalisches Lexicon oder Musicalische Bibliotec*, Leipzig, 1732, study edition by F. Ramm, Kassel-Basel, 2001.
Whenham 2001	J. Whenham, entry on *Dialogue*, in *The New Grove Dictionary of Music and Musicians*, ed. S. Sadie and J. Tyrrell, 2nd ed., vol. 7, London, 2001, pp. 286-287.
Williams 1994	P. Williams, *Johann Sebastian Bach and the Continuo*, in *Basler Jahrbuch für historische Musikpraxis*, 18, 1994, pp. 67-86.
Wohlfarth 1970	H. Wohlfarth, *Johann Christoph Friedrich Bach. Ein Komponist im Vorfeld der Klassik*, Bern, 1971.
Wolff 1968	Chr. Wolff, *Der stile antico in der Musik Johann Sebastian Bachs. Studien zu Bach's Spätwerk*, Wiesbaden, 1968.
Wolff 1993	Chr. Wolff, *Bach. Essays on his Life and Music*, Cambridge-London, 1993.
Wolff 2000	Chr. Wolff, *Johann Sebastian Bach. The Learned Musician*, Oxford, 2000.

INDICES

Index of names

Biblical names, names from classical antiquity and names of authors ($19^{th} - 21^{st}$ c.) mentioned in the bibliography have not been included.

Ahle, Johann Rudolf (1625-1673) 133
Ahle, Johann Georg (1651-1706) 133
Albert, Heinrich (1604-1651) 155
Albinoni, Tomaso (1671-1751) 63
Bach, Anna Magdalena (1701-1760) 39
Bach, Carl Philipp Emmanuel (1714-1788) 43, 61
Bach, Johann Christoph Friedrich (1732-1795) 119, 131
Bach, Wilhelm Friedemann (1710-1784) 21
Bernhard, Christoph (1628-1692) 133
Birnbaum, Johann (1702-1748) 43
Brockes, Barthold Heinrich (1680-1747) 23
Buxtehude, Dietrich (1637?-1707) 28
Calov, Abraham (1612-1686) 30
Christian of Saxe-Weissenfels (1682-1736) 54
Corelli, Arcangelo (1653-1713) 63, 88, 89
Ebeling, Johann Georg (1637-1676) 121
Eccard, Johannes (1553-1611) 146
Erdmann, Georg (1682-1736) 20
Forkel, Johann Nikolaus (1749-1802) 61
Franck, Johann (1618-1676) 43, 155
Francke, August Hermann (1663-1727) 31, 57
Friedrich II of Prussia (1712-1786) 55
Friedrich August I of Saxony (1670-1733) 21
Friedrich August II of Saxony (1696-1763) 21, 34
Friedrich Christian of Saxony (1722-1763) 21
Gerhardt, Paul (1607-1676) 31, 43, 44, 75, 76, 106, 121, 164
Gleditsch, Johann Caspar (1684-1747) 54

Handel, Georg Friedrich (1685-1759) 23, 88, 89
Hammerschmidt, Andreas (1611/12-1675) 133
Hasse, Johann Adolf (1699-1783) 21
Hassler, Hans Leo (1562-1612) 44, 170
Haussmann, Elias Gottlob (1695-1774) 54
Heinichen, Johann David (1683-1729) 21
Henrici, Christian Friedrich (Picander) (1700-1764) 30, 70
Hunold, Christian Friedrich (Menantes) (1681-1721) 22, 23
Joseph I (1678-1711) 28
Keiser, Reinhard (1674-1739) 22, 23
Kuhnau, Johann (1660-1722) 19, 24, 25
Lassus, Orlandus (1532-1594) 146
Leopold I, Emperor (1640-1705) 28
Lully, Jean-Baptiste (1632-1687) 54
Luther, Martin (1483-1546) 26, 30, 42, 43, 76, 79, 81, 84, 113, 136, 164
Marcello, Alessandro (1669-1747) 63
Marcello, Benedetto (1686-1739) 63
Maria Josepha of Saxony (1699-1757) 21, 59, 63, 83, 95
Mattheson, Johann (1681-1764) 23, 31, 50, 52
Menantes, see Hunold
Meyer, Joachim 31
Michael, Rogier (ca. 1552-1619?) 131
Müller, Heinrich (1631-1675) 132, 133
Neumeister, Erdmann (1671-1756) 48
Palestrina, Giovanni Pierluigi da (1525/26-1594) 27
Picander, see Henrici
Pisendel, Johann Georg (1687-1755) 21
Purcell, Henry (1659-1695) 104
Quantz, Johann Joachim (1697-1773) 55
Reiche, Johann Gottfried (1667-1734) 54
Rist, Johann (1606-1667) 43, 92, 130, 137
Rosbach, C.F. 54
Runge, Christoph (1619-1681) 43, 122
Saubert, Johann (1592-1646) 137
Scheibe, Johann Adolf (1708-1776) 38
Schelle, Johann (1648-1701) 24, 25, 28

Schemelli, Georg Christian (ca. 1676-1762) 31, 130
Schop, Johann (+1667) 92, 130
Schütz, Heinrich (1585-1672) 24, 25, 67, 99, 131, 155
Spee von Langenfeld, Friedrich (1591-1635) 133
Stölzel, Gottfried Heinrich (1690-1749) 39, 66
Telemann, Georg Philipp (1681-1767) 20, 23, 29, 38, 39, 73, 167
Torelli, Giuseppe (1658-1709) 63
Vivaldi, Antonio (1678-1741) 45, 63
Walther, Johann Gottfried (1684-1748) 37
Weiss, Sylvius Leopold (1686-1750) 21
Weissel, Georg (1590-1635) 43, 146
Werner, Georg (1589-1643) 43, 170
Zelenka, Jan Dismas (1679-1745) 21
Zimmermann, Gottfried (+1741) 20

Index of works

The melodies of the one-voice chorales have not been included.

Ahle, Johann Rudolf
    Geistliche Dialoge 133
Albert, Heinrich
    Arien 155
Bach, Johann Christoph Friedrich
    Die Kindheit Jesu 119, 131
Bach, Johann Sebastian
    BWV 1 *Wie schön leuchtet der Morgenstern* 68
    BWV 4 *Christ lag in Todesbanden* 81
    BWV 11 *Himmelfahrts-Oratorium* 25
    BWV 12 *Weinen, klagen, sorgen, zagen* 104
    BWV 32 *Liebster Jesu, mein Verlangen* 133
    BWV 39 *Brich dem Hungrigen dein Brot* 115
    BWV 40 *Darzu ist erschienen der Sohn Gottes* 122
    BWV 49 *Ich geh und suche mit Verlangen* 68, 133
    BWV 52 *Falsche Welt, dir trau ich nicht* 146
    BWV 57 *Selig ist der Mann* 133
    BWV 58 *Ach Gott, wie manches Herzeleid* 133
    BWV 60 *O Ewigkeit, du Donnerwert* 133
    BWV 64 *Sehet, welch ein Liebe hat uns der Vater erzeiget* 80, 113
    BWV 72 *Alles nur nach Gottes Wille* 94, 116
    BWV 78 *Jesu, der du meine Seele* 49, 116
    BWV 85 *Ich bin ein guter Hirt* 89
    BWV 91 *Gelobest seist du Jesu Christ* 80
    BWV 92 *Ich hab in Gottes Herz und Sinn* 44
    BWV 104 *Du Hirte Israel, höre* 89
    BWV 106 *Gottes Zeit ist die allerbeste Zeit* (Actus tragicus) 146
    BWV 110 *Unser Mund sei voll Lachens* 122
    BWV 140 *Wachet auf, ruft uns die Stimme* 133
    BWV 170 *Vergnügte Ruh! beliebte Seelenlust!* 148
    BWV 172 *Erschallet, ihr Lieder, erklinget, ihr Saiten!* 61, 63, 64
    BWV 175 *Er rufet seine Schafen mit Namen* 90

BWV 184 *Erwünschtes Freudenlicht* 90
BWV 208 *Was uns behagt ist nur die muntre Jagd* 54
BWV 213 *Lasst uns sorgen, lasst uns wachen (Hercules auf dem Scheidewege)* 21, 34-36, 70-72, 100-101, 114-115, 126-127, 132, 135, 141, 172
BWV 214 *Tönet, ihr Pauken! Erschallet, Trompeten* 21, 59, 62, 63, 64, 82, 95, 110, 159
BWV 215 *Preise dein Glücke, gesegnetes Sachsen* 34, 54, 118, 147
BWV 232 *B minor Mass* 18, 21, 24, 34, 40, 56, 104, 115, 154
BWV 233-236 *Missae breves* 34, 35, 41, 45
    BWV 236 *Missa brevis* 102
BWV 243 *Magnificat* (second version) 24, 115
BWV 243a *Magnificat* (first version) 24, 84
BWV 244 *St. Matthew Passion* 15, 18, 20, 23, 30, 33, 42, 47, 48, 56, 65, 76, 80, 91, 92, 146, 168
BWV 245 *St. John Passion* 15, 23, 56
BWV 247 *St. Mark Passion* 35, 36, 145
BWV 248/VIa (cantata, text unknown) 35, 156
BWV 249 *Easter Oratorio* 25, 26
BWV 439-507 *Schemelli-Gesangbuch* 31, 130
BWV 552 *Clavier-Übung III* (prelude and fugue) 21
BWV 579 Organ fugue on a theme by Arcangelo Corelli 63
BWV 582 Passacaglia in C minor 104
BWV 599-644 *Orgelbüchlein* 58
    BWV 604 *Gelobest seist du Jesu Christ* 80
    BWV 612 *Wir Christenleut* 122
BWV 651-668 *Achtzehn Leipziger Choräle* 58
BWV 669-689 *Clavier-Übung III* (chorale arrangements) 21, 58
BWV 769 *Canonische Veränderungen über das Weihnachtslied Vom Himmel hoch* 24
BWV 802-805 *Clavier-Übung III* (four duets) 21
BWV 825-830 *Clavier-Übung I* (six partitas) 20-21
BWV 831 *Clavier-Übung II* (French overture) 21
BWV 946 Keyboard fugue on a theme by Tommaso Albinoni 63
BWV 951 Keyboard fugue on a theme by Tommaso Albinoni 63
BWV 971 *Clavier-Übung II* (Italian Concerto) 21

BWV 972-987 Sixteen arrangements for keyboard of concerti by Antonio Vivaldi and others 63

BWV 988 *Clavier-Übung IV* (Goldberg Variations) 21

BWV 1046-1051 Brandenburg Concerti 77

    BWV 1046 Brandenburg Concerto no.1 55, 83

BWV 1066 Overture in C major (Orchestral Suite no. 1) 55, 83

BWV 1068 Overture in D major (Orchestral Suite no. 3) 54

BWV 1069 Overture in D major (Orchestral Suite no. 4) 54

BWV 1079 *Musical Offering* 55

Bernhard, Christoph
    Geistliche Harmonien 133

Buxtehude, Dietrich
    Castrum Doloris 28
    Templum Honoris 28

Corelli, Arcangelo
    Concerto grosso, opus 6, no.8 88

Handel, Georg Friedrich
    Brockes-Passion 23
    Messiah 88

Hammerschmidt, Andreas
    Dialogi, oder Gespräche einer glaübigen Seele mit Gott 133

Hasse, Johann Adolf
    Cleofide 21

Hassler, Hans Leo
    Mein Gmüt ist mir verwirret 44

Keiser, Reinhard
    Der blutige und sterbende Jesu 22
    Brockes-Passion 23

Kuhnau, Johann
    Vom Himmel hoch da komm ich her 25

Mattheson, Johann
    Brockes-Passion 23

Michael, Rogier
    Die Geburt unseres Herrn Jesu Christi 131

Purcell, Henry
    Dido and Aeneas 104

Schelle, Johann
    Actus Musicus auf Weih-Nachten 24
Schütz, Heinrich
    Historia der Auferstehung 24
    Historia der Geburt 25, 99
    Passions 25
Stölzel, Gottfried Heinrich
    Bist du bei mir 39
Telemann, Georg Friedrich
    Brockes-Passion 23
    Harmonischer Gottesdienst (1725) 38
    Harmonischer Gottesdienst (1731/1732) 38
    St. John Passion (1745) 29
Vivaldi, Antonio
    L'estro armonico, opus 3 63

Drukkerij en Binderij
SCHEERDERS van KERCHOVE
9100 ST.-NIKLAAS

Example 1

Example 2

© Bärenreiter-Verlag Karl Vötterle GmbH & Co. KG, Kassel

Example 3

Example 4

Example 5

© Bärenreiter-Verlag Karl Vötterle GmbH & Co. KG, Kassel

Example 6

Example 7

Example 8

Bärenreiter-Verlag Karl Vötterle GmbH & Co. KG, Kassel

Example 9

Bärenreiter-Verlag Karl Vötterle GmbH & Co. KG, Kassel

Example 10

© Bärenreiter-Verlag Karl Vötterle GmbH & Co. KG, Kassel

Bärenreiter-Verlag Karl Vötterle GmbH & Co. KG, Kassel

Example 11

Example 12a

Example 12b

Example 13

Example 14

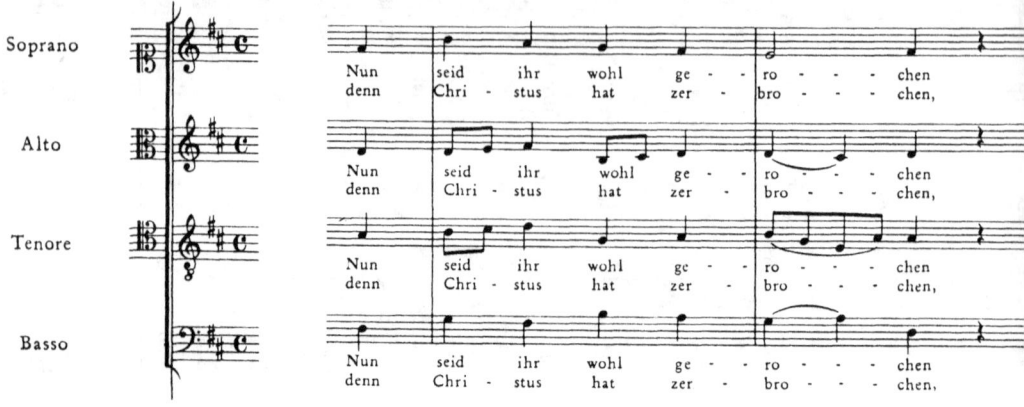

Example 15a

© Bärenreiter-Verlag Karl Vötterle GmbH & Co. KG, Kassel

Example 15b

Example 15c

Example 15d

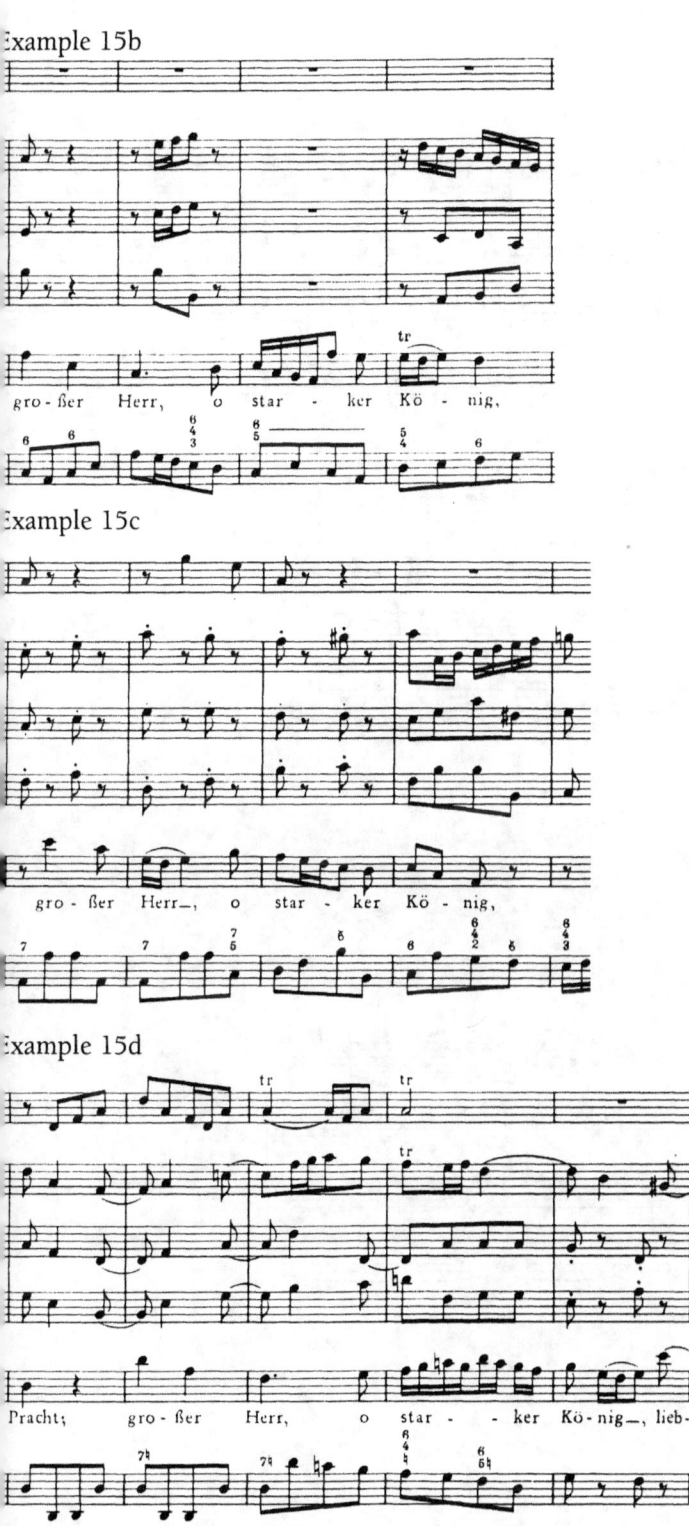

Bärenreiter-Verlag Karl Vötterle GmbH & Co. KG, Kassel

Example 16a

Example 16b

© Bärenreiter-Verlag Karl Vötterle GmbH & Co. KG, Kassel

Example 17

Example 18

xample 19

xample 20

Example 21a

Example 21b

© Bärenreiter-Verlag Karl Vötterle GmbH & Co. KG, Kassel

Example 22

Example 23

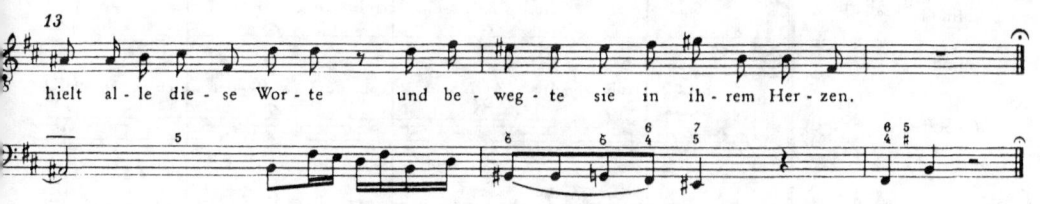

Bärenreiter-Verlag Karl Vötterle GmbH & Co. KG, Kassel

Example 24

Example 25

© Bärenreiter-Verlag Karl Vötterle GmbH & Co. KG, Kassel

Example 26

Example 27

Example 28

Example 29

© Bärenreiter-Verlag Karl Vötterle GmbH & Co. KG, Kassel

xample 30

Example 31

Example 32

Bärenreiter-Verlag Karl Vötterle GmbH & Co. KG, Kassel

Example 33

Example 34a

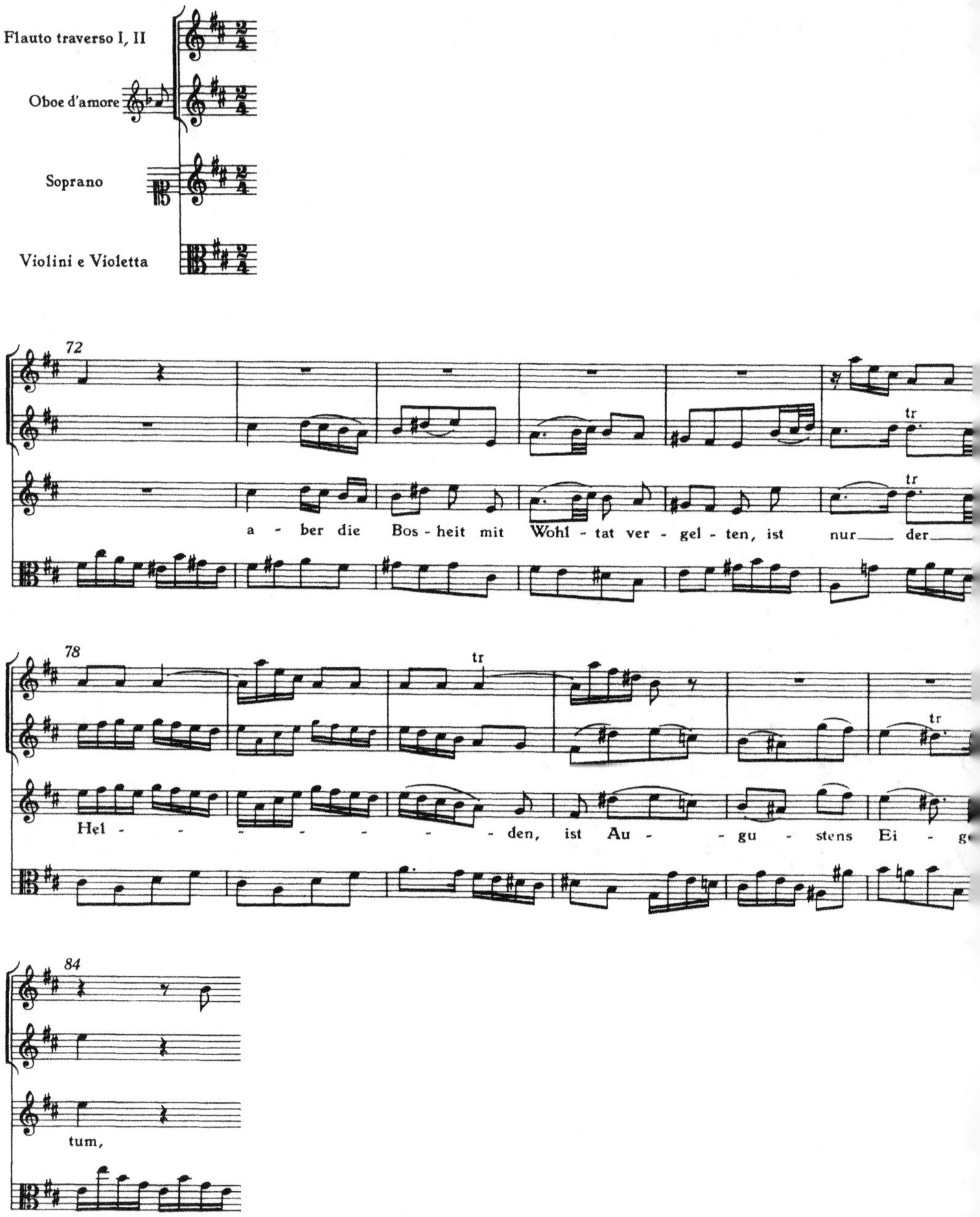
Flauto traverso I, II
Oboe d'amore
Soprano
Violini e Violetta
72
a - ber die Bos - heit mit Wohl - tat ver - gel - ten, ist nur der
78
Hel - den, ist Au - gu - stens Ei -
84
tum,

xample 34b

xample 35

Bärenreiter-Verlag Karl Vötterle GmbH & Co. KG, Kassel

Example 36

Example 37a

Example 37b

Example 38

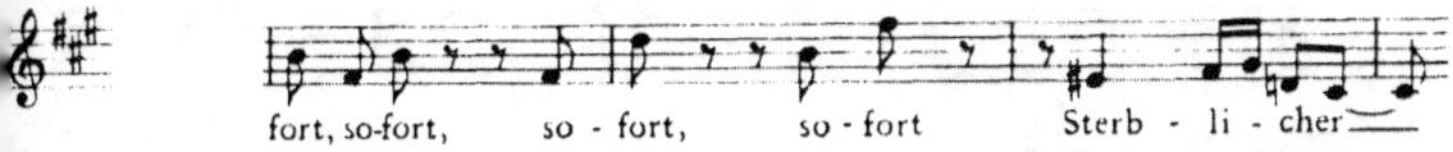

Example 39

Example 40

Example 41

Bärenreiter-Verlag Karl Vötterle GmbH & Co. KG, Kassel

www.ingramcontent.com/pod-product-compliance
Lightning Source LLC
Chambersburg PA
CBHW051057230426
43667CB00013B/2340